Praise for *A Black Hole in Economics*

"Jim Brown is one of money management's brilliant minds. His profound grasp of money creation, sound financial management and hard money policies set him above all other financial analysts. Readers of *A Black Hole in Economics* will come away with valuable insights and effective tools for protecting their wealth."

—Charles W. Peabody
Partner, Portales Partners LLC, and Wall Street Beats

"While I had some understanding of how money is created through credit by commercial banks, this book provided a wonderfully accessible explanation of how it works. And although I was aware of the dramatic increases in government spending, this book explained the terrifying magnitude of those expenditures, how they are being funded, and what the likely dire consequences will be. This book is a must-read if you want to safeguard your assets."

—Jeri Eagan
Former CFO of Shell Oil Company and
Former COO of the Ayn Rand Institute

"I loved everything about this book. It's very well organized and the concepts are concretized so the average person with no formal financial training can understand. Jim does a great job of differentiating between good money creation by privately owned banks and harmful money creation under government intervention. All of his ideas for investing under financial repression are very sound."

—Tim Blum
Managing Partner, Citadel Partners, Chicago

"In this insightful work, the author transforms complex financial subject matter into a clear, accessible narrative, making even the most technical aspects of money creation accessible to the reader.

With a masterful approach to organization, he demystifies the nature of money, ensuring that everyone can grasp his key insights."
—Mark Moses
Author of *The Municipal Financial Crisis: A Framework for Understanding and Fixing Government Budgeting*

"Jim brown has done a masterful job of turning a puzzling subject into a straightforward and enjoyable read. I keep a few important books as the cornerstone of my library on personal finance and investing. *A Black Hole in Economics* is a must have!"
—Chris Chard
General Partner and Managing Director,
Sower Farmland Fund, Omaha, Nebraska

"Not only does *A Black Hole in Economics* flip on its head what we thought we knew about money creation, it reveals the consequences of turning the modern financial system into a government planning agency. Jim Brown cuts through the complexity of money creation with remarkable clarity. He exposes the truth about the harmful effects of government involvement in money creation and arms the individual investor against its worst effects. Brilliant and vital reading."
—Richard Bardwell and Marco Ruggeri
London, UK

"If you read only Chapter One of A Black Hole in Economics, you'll want to keep turning the pages, and you'll benefit by doing so."
—Cameron Koczon
CEO, Fictive Kin

"As an entrepreneur, I lose sleep over stealthy government confiscation of my wealth through what Jim Brown aptly calls "financial repression." What I love about Jim's work is that instead of just leaving me all bummed out, he provides a recipe for understanding what the government is up to and then tells me how to protect myself against it. If you care about protecting your wealth, you should read his book."

—Tom Owen
software founder, #33 on Inc. 5000

Jim Brown's book, *A Black Hole in Economics: Money Creation and its Consequences*, serves as an informative and accessible exploration of a topic that is often overlooked by the American public. Jim clarifies, in simple language, the true source of money creation—hint: it's not fractional reserve banking—and reveals how government actions have increasingly distorted this process to finance its unsustainable obligations, leading to inflation. He compellingly argues that we are facing a long period of "financial repression" regardless of the next Administration's political affiliation. The book concludes with practical advice on safeguarding ourselves against the impacts of inflation and low economic growth. It is essential reading for anyone concerned with both our country's and their personal financial future.

—Anders Ingemarson
Author of *Think Right or Wrong, Not Left or Right: A 21st Century Citizen Guide*

"This book explodes off the page! Jim Brown tears down the impenetrable shell around banks and money creation to reveal the surprising story around money, credit and the financial institutions we unthinkingly trust. Deeply researched and passionately argued, *A Black Hole in Economics* succeeds as both a textbook and guide. The payoff is actionable ideas to thrive even amid a rocky financial future."

—Jonathan Hoenig
Fox News Contributor;
Manager, Capitalistpig Hedge Fund LLC

A BLACK HOLE
IN ECONOMICS

A Black Hole in Economics

Money Creation
and
Its Consequences

Jim Brown

Loco-Foco Press
Seneca, South Carolina

First Edition
November 12, 2024

ISBN 979-8-9914489-1-8 (Paperback)

To the men on my A-team.
You know who you are.

CONTENTS

ABOUT THE PUBLISHER
LOCO-FOCO PRESS

Loco-Foco Press is an independent publishing company founded by C. Bradley Thompson. The name "Loco-Foco" references an early 19th-century political movement in New York City, formed by working-class men and reformers who opposed slavery, government banking intervention, and monopolies. Although never a national party, Loco-Foco gained influence with the Independent Treasury Act of 1840, which separated government from banking.

Originally, "Loco-Foco" referred to a self-igniting cigar and self-striking matches. The term combines the Latin "loco," meaning "self-generated," with the Italian "fuoco," meaning "fire," symbolizing independent thought and initiative.

In the spirit of the Loco-Foco Party, Loco-Foco Press is dedicated to publishing the works of independent writers who value reason, individualism, and a free society.

ACKNOWLEDGMENTS

Many of the ideas in this book are not original to me. Numerous intellectual influences from history have shaped my thinking. This page will acknowledge just a few.

Among the Austrians, I'm indebted to Ludwig von Mises and Carl Menger for their understanding of money. In addition, special thanks go to George Reisman, the greatest living Austrian economist, who taught me most of what I know about economics in general.

I owe an equal debt to Richard Werner, the greatest living monetary scholar, whose ground-breaking work on money creation is shaking up the investment community's understanding of money and banking.

Among contemporary scholars and historians, special thanks to Russell Napier, who operates the Library of Mistakes in Edinburgh, Scotland and understands financial repression better than anyone else.

Professor Lev Menand of Columbia University generously shared his time and correspondence early in this project, providing references on the legal origins of American banking. His 2022 book *The Fed Unbound* helped me understand the historical development of American banking.

Ayn Rand, who has significantly influenced my thinking, deserves special mention for her knowledge of definitions and her insight into the connection between economic production and money.

C. Bradley Thompson, Ph.D., has my deep gratitude for advising on publication planning and for welcoming me to his publishing company, Loco-Foco Press.

Thanks to Razi Ginzberg and the staff of the Ayn Rand Centre-UK for supporting me in publicizing my work.

Thanks to all my Substack readers, whose comments and engagement are thought-provoking, challenging, and always welcome.

Thanks to Ron Pisaturo for his brilliant and thorough editing and for solving many pre-publication problems. This book could not have happened without him.

Thanks to Quent Cordair, for his creative cover art and excellent technical self-publishing advice.

Thanks to many other friends and colleagues, too numerous to mention, who made helpful suggestions along the way.

Finally, special thanks to my wife, Kathy, whose cheeky comments are always both refreshing and entertaining when the writing gets tedious.

INTRODUCTION

Pour yourself a favorite beverage and let the adventure unfold as we explore the secrets of money creation—how money is created, how governments exploit the process to siphon your wealth, and what you must do to prosper in an era of financial repression.

This book is for anyone who wants to understand money creation in the modern economy. In the following pages, I'll explain how money is created, who creates it, and the consequences of money creation, both good and bad.

Whether you're an investor navigating volatile markets, a student searching for understanding, or a conscientious voter who wants to stay well-informed, this book is for you. Get ready to have your assumptions challenged as we dive headfirst into what I call the "black hole" of economic knowledge. After reading this book, you'll emerge with insights that will transform your perspective on money, banks, and their impact on your life.

Chapter One, **Money Creation—Who Cares?** starts the journey by unraveling why modern money creation is poorly understood and why it's crucial to grasp its basic mechanics. ("Money" includes more than just paper currency and coins. Most money is in the form of bank deposits.)

In Chapter Two, **Money Creation, Then and Now**, we delve into the core principles of how banks have always wielded the miraculous power to create credit, shaping it into the medium of exchange we know as money. You'll be surprised at the unexpected similarities and critical differences between money creation under the gold standard and our contemporary "fiat-reserve" standard.

Chapter Three, **Money from Nothing**, applies the lessons of Chapter Two to understand the essential elements of modern money creation. To reinforce our new knowledge, we zoom in on concrete examples of money creation and money destruction, including a surprising revelation of where paper money comes from and why our money creation system should be called "pure credit creation."

In Chapter Four, **Good Money Creation: The Capitalist Money Factory**, we take a brief historical tour of banking in the United States to demonstrate that it was designed to promote non-inflationary money creation. We show why responsible money creation in a free-market economy is essential for growth and innovation.

But money creation in the wrong hands can cause great economic ruin. In Chapter Five, **Bad Money Creation: The Statist Wrecking Ball**, we expose the destructive power of politicians and bureaucrats who subvert the investment decisions of privately owned banks. We'll dive deep into two famous financial crises to reveal how unproductive money creation, driven by government interference in the commercial banks, causes economic destruction through price inflation, asset bubbles, wasted capital, and unjust economic inequality.

In Chapter Six, we'll focus on the most destructive consequence of the U.S. government's policy of irresponsible money creation: **Uncle Sam's Unpayable Debt**. We'll explain how irresponsible money creation encourages unsustainable government spending, leading to a mountain of sovereign debt that can never be paid with dollars of today's purchasing power.

Chapter Seven, **The Arsonist and the Fireman**, lays bare the challenges and choices posed by the United States' unpayable financial obligations. Prepare for a counter-intuitive insight: The same politicians who have misused our money creation system, burdening us with unpayable debt, will likely resort to creating even more money to alleviate that burden. Their policies will result in "financial repression"—a peculiar combination of high inflation with low "real" interest rates that makes saving for the future challenging but not impossible.

Finding ourselves in a new financial environment dominated by financial repression, we must adopt a different approach to saving and investing. In Chapter Eight, **Surviving Financial Repression**, we roll up our sleeves and delve into practical financial strategies to help you safeguard and grow your wealth in a world where interest rates will not keep up with inflation.

Although I refrain from making detailed investment recommendations, fear not! Chapter Eight recommends numerous talented investment advisors who can guide you on your specific investment program. These are the same experts I trust to help manage my family office. With the insights from this book and carefully chosen advisors, you'll be equipped to design your own saving and investment program, ensuring you're well-prepared to navigate the treacherous waters of financial repression.[1]

For serious students and enthusiasts wanting a deeper dive, I've included a bibliography of books, scholarly articles, speeches, and essays that helped sharpen my thinking for this book.

For the real strivers, there are also three Appendices to address several background issues that may be interesting to financial professionals or others who simply want to keep digging.

Appendix 1, **Defining Money**, explains why I endorse Ludwig von Mises's simple yet profound definition of money as "a commonly accepted medium of exchange." We'll also venture into the US Federal Reserve's definition of "broad money supply" and delve briefly into the controversies surrounding what the Fed classifies as "money."

In Appendix 2, **The Legal Basis of Bank Money Creation**, we'll introduce the Constitutional and legislative foundations of money creation in commercial banks.

Lastly, Appendix 3, **Paul Samuelson's Fractional Fiction**, critiques and rejects Paul Samuelson's faulty exposition of "fractional reserve banking." Based on a 2014 ground-breaking empirical experiment by Professor Richard Werner of Oxford University, the "credit creation theory" of banking is shown to be the only one consistent with actual banking practice.

That's a summary of the roadmap we'll follow on our journey to understanding money creation. However, before we dive in, let's take a few pages to explore why the topic of money creation is so significant, why you should care about it, and why you may not have previously recognized its importance. That is the subject of Chapter One.

1 MONEY CREATION—WHO CARES?

A surprising conversation; Three competing theories of banking; A psychological barrier; The need for sound money; How to become "one in a million."

A surprising conversation

A few years ago, I had an eye-opening discussion with my daughter and her husband. They had just purchased their first home, and we were chatting about their mortgage loan. At one point, I casually mentioned, "Isn't it interesting that the $300,000 you borrowed is brand new money created by the bank specifically for your mortgage? Your loan is money that didn't even exist before the banker made the loan."

My daughter, a successful lawyer, looked at me like I had gone mad. And my son-in-law, a senior tech executive, wasted no time correcting me. "No," he said, "banks lend out other people's money, the money they are not using right now."

I gently set the record straight, explaining that banks don't lend out other people's money. On the contrary, banks create new money every time they make a loan. In fact, I continued, virtually all the money that exists was created by commercial banks when they made loans or other investments, such as buying interest-bearing bonds.

My daughter, respecting my long career in finance, listened attentively. Perhaps she thought, "Maybe old dad knows a thing or two after all." Nevertheless, she was shocked by what I had said. As for my son-in-law, he remained skeptical then, and I suspect he still is today.

My daughter and her husband are both intelligent, successful professionals. They probably even took a course in money and banking in college. Yet, on the day of our conversation, they were utterly clueless about the mechanics of money creation. It got me thinking: if these two bright minds were unaware, how many others have no idea how money comes into existence?

So, I started digging deeper and soon discovered that ignorance about money creation is almost universal. Even many financial advisors and journalists recognized as experts lack the basic knowledge that banks create money through lending. For example, it's astonishing how often financial writers describe banking operations by claiming that banks "lend out their customers' deposits" or something along those lines. However, this misconception reverses cause and effect because loans are not made from prior deposits. It's lending that creates the bank deposits we know as "money."

Let's look at a typical example of this misunderstanding. Here is an excerpt from a *Bloomberg* article on Silicon Valley Bank, which failed in March 2023. To explain what went wrong there, the author, a respected columnist from Bloomberg News, starts his article by describing commercial banks as follows:

> The way a bank works is that it borrows short to lend long … a bank might get its money from demand deposits, checking and savings accounts that customers can withdraw at any time … And then it invests the money… .[1]

The author says banks invest (lend) money that they have "borrowed" from customer deposits. He thinks the bank must first get customers to deposit some money so it can "borrow" some of these deposits and then make loans or buy financial assets like bonds. Dozens of similar descriptions from many news sources appeared at the same time.

To most financial advisors, journalists, and pundits, this explanation of banking is "common knowledge"—what "everyone knows that everyone knows," that is, what nearly everyone accepts without question.[2]

But, as this book will demonstrate, the "common knowledge" about how banks work is not valid. The Bloomberg article correctly describes the workings, not of commercial banks, but of nonbank financial intermediaries. These include investment banks, mutual funds, exchange-traded funds (ETFs), money market funds, and private equity and venture capital firms.

What these nonbank entities have in common is that they invest money that already belongs to someone, money that already exists. However, "investing other people's money" is not the main activity of commercial banks. The Bloomberg article is misleading because banks don't invest customers' deposits. It's the opposite: banks *create* deposits by lending and investing, as we will show in the next chapter.

In the field of money creation, ignorance is not bliss. If you know how banks create new money, you can begin to understand how the money supply grows, its source, who benefits, and who is harmed. But if, like the Bloomberg author, you perceive commercial banks as mere financial intermediaries transferring money from a saver to a borrower, you won't understand their unique economic importance. Nor will you know how their legal privilege to create money can work for good or ill, depending on who makes the money-creation decisions.

Once you understand where our money comes from, you'll soon see how the Federal Reserve, the Treasury, and Congress have commandeered money creation decisions that should have been the prerogative of private bankers. The result has been a covert form of centralized economic planning that causes inflation, economic stagnation, cronyism, and unjust wealth distribution.

This matters to you because, as we will discover in subsequent chapters, once you grasp the concept of money creation, you can avoid falling prey to the government's monetary mischief.

How widespread is this ignorance of money creation? Journalists and pundits are not the only thought leaders who don't understand it. Even most politicians, including those who appoint and supervise our bank regulators, lack basic money and banking literacy. Professor Andrew Hook of Sussex University highlighted this fact in a 2022 paper, *Examining Modern Money Creation*:

> A study conducted by the University of Zurich in 2014 about the level of knowledge in the general population about the financial system ... found that only 13 percent knew that private commercial banks provide the majority of the money in circulation; 73 percent mistakenly believed money is created by the state or by the Swiss National Bank. This ignorance extends to politicians, with a 2014 survey by the money reform group Positive Money finding that only 15 percent of U.K. Members of Parliament (M.P.s) realized that private banks create the money supply.[3]

Three competing theories of banking

What is the cause of this widespread ignorance of banks and money creation? It's the result of a historically broken knowledge system that has never reconciled three very different and incompatible theories of banking. The result has been chaos in the information chain, up to and including the academics and theorists at the best universities. Landmark historical research by Professor Richard Werner of Oxford University helps explain this chaos.

Since the mid-19th century, writes Werner, three competing banking theories have attempted to explain the banking system and its role in creating money. These are the *credit creation theory*, the *fractional reserve theory*, and the *financial intermediation theory*. Professor Werner documented these theories and their periods of historical dominance in a 2014 paper, "Can banks individually create money out of nothing - the theories and the empirical evidence."[4] In

2016, he updated this research with another frequently cited paper, "A Lost Century in Economics."[5]

What were the fundamental tenets of each of these theories?

The *credit creation theory* holds that banks individually create money by lending or purchasing assets. As this book will demonstrate, the credit creation theory of banking is the only one that fully and adequately explains money creation. This theory was universally accepted among economists until the early 20th century.

The *fractional reserve theory*, best represented by the late Paul Samuelson's standard explanation in his best-selling textbook *Economics*, agreed with the credit creation theory that money is created in the banking system; however, it claimed that no single bank could create money and that only a system-wide interaction of many banks could create money through a "reserve multiplier" process. The fractional reserve theory gained traction through the mid-19th century, peaking in popularity in the 1960s.

(A note on terminology: Although "fractional reserve banking" is most often used to refer to Samuelson's theory, the term is sometimes applied to any explanation of how banks end up with deposits larger than their cash reserves. In this book, "fractional reserve banking" refers specifically to the money creation theory promulgated by Samuelson.)

After the 1960s, the fractional reserve theory gradually gave ground to the *financial intermediation theory*, which dominates today, according to Werner. This theory does not admit that commercial banks can create money at all; instead, it sees banks as pass-through intermediaries that borrow depositors' savings to lend to other customers. The previously cited Bloomberg article is a typical example of this view.

My observation is that the credit creation theory has regained some influence in the last ten years, mainly among a vanguard of curious professional investors striving to understand the implications of the government's meddling in the banking system. Richard Werner has been influential in spreading this understanding.

Still, confusion about money creation goes right to the top of the academic food chain. As Werner's research demonstrates, many of the world's most famous economists, including many Nobel laureates, have disagreed on how money is created. As Werner points out, very few economists today, including those who write popular textbooks, see bank credit creation as the source of new money. Nearly all undergraduate economics textbooks continue to spread other competing and contradictory explanations, year after year, decade after decade.

In his 2016 paper, Werner lamented this sad state:

> How is it possible that for the largest part of the past century, erroneous and misleading theories have dominated the discipline of economics? This is a topic for future research.... [6]

I conducted a personal experiment to test this apparent state of confusion. Based on the recommendations of a former college roommate, a veteran professor of economics at a public university, I purchased and reviewed three popular undergraduate textbooks. What I found was consistent with Werner's research: none of these books endorse the credit creation theory of banking, and their explanations are inconsistent.

The first example is *Economics,* the most famous and influential college-level economics textbook, by the late Paul Samuelson. I reviewed the original 1948 edition (the one I used in college) in which Samuelson dismissed the credit creation theory as a "false explanation." Samuelson contends that money creation must begin with a cash deposit; that part of this deposit is loaned out and then "multiplies" as it is deposited and re-loaned by different banks; that no individual bank can create new money; and that only a network of banks can create money through a series of deposits and loans. In the following chapters, both the history and the contemporary facts of modern banking will refute each of these claims.

Nevertheless, Samuelson's explanation of "fractional reserve banking" is still considered respectable by academics and other financial professionals. Post-1948 editions of *Economics* dropped all reference to the credit creation theory but retained most of Samuelson's original fractional reserve framework. The latest (2010) edition of *Economics* is still in use.

My second sample, *Money, Banking, Financial Markets and Institutions* (2017) by Michael Brandl, asserts the same fractional reserve and "reserve multiplier" descriptions of Samuelson, including the claim that only a system or network of banks can create money. Like the post-1948 editions of Samuelson's book, Brandl's popular textbook does not mention the credit creation theory at all.

The third sample, *Money, Banking, and Financial Markets* (2017) by Stephen Cecchetti and Kermit Schoenholtz, acknowledges the role of individual commercial banks in money creation; however, it repeats Samuelson's "reserve multiplier" myth, which I discuss and refute in Chapter Three. Cecchetti's book also incorrectly claims that the Federal Reserve does not create bank deposits when purchasing Treasury securities during open market operations, thereby misunderstanding the Fed's direct role in increasing the money supply. This is a common oversight, discussed in Chapters Three and Six.

Interestingly, none of these books mention the different theories of banking presented in other textbooks. Are the authors even aware of the contradictions? Also, I am unaware of any active discussion among academic economists attempting to standardize the explanation of money creation. It's as if they think contradictory theories can coexist and that all theories are acceptable, and that's just fine.

Such apathy on a crucial issue can only mean that money creation is not a topic of much interest in college economics today. Mainstream academics are simply not addressing the seminal question: Where does money come from? This lack of concern is consistent with today's dominant belief in the financial intermediation theory of banking, which does not even acknowledge the commercial banks' role in money creation.

The ignorance and confusion surrounding the three theories of banking have significant implications for those trying to understand money's origin. By failing to understand the role of banks in money creation, academic economists, journalists, and future financial advisors who attend their classes cannot identify the true source of inflation or its destructive effects on the economy. It's like trying to hit a fastball with beer goggles on: you're lucky even to tip the ball foul. However, understanding money creation clarifies inflation because, as we'll see in Chapter Five, the correct definition of inflation is *excessive money creation in the banks caused by misguided government policies and actions.*

As we proceed, I believe it will become apparent to you, as it has become to me, that in the field of money and banking, we cannot rely on most of our so-called "designated experts"—the current cadre of professors, teachers, and journalists—to provide what should be undisputed facts on money creation. Many, including most people we know as financial authorities, simply do not understand it.

I believe money creation suffers from a special kind of ignorance. The "black holes" of outer space are poorly understood because we lack the scientific knowledge to explain them. However, money creation is poorly understood because the correct credit creation theory, once widely understood, has somehow been forgotten. As financial journalist Jim Grant has observed, "Progress is cumulative in science and engineering, but cyclical in finance."

That is true in this case, although exactly *why* the knowledge was misplaced remains a puzzle. What seems clear is that money creation is a "black hole" in economics resulting from a broken knowledge system. This book aims to help fill that void in our knowledge. For us, the critical task is to re-learn the forgotten facts of money creation.

The good news is that any intellectual barriers to understanding are easy to overcome because the correct account of money creation is much simpler to grasp than the confusing and erroneous accounts that dominate today's financial literature. Learning the ABCs of money creation is as easy as understanding simple arithmetic or memorizing a poem. Any intelligent person can master the task.

A psychological barrier

However, you may encounter a different type of barrier as you read this book. I am referring to the skepticism and disbelief that strike most people when they hear that banks can create money with only a few signatures and computer keystrokes. To many, perhaps most people, this sounds like crazy talk.

The late economist John Kenneth Galbraith, who understood the credit creation theory, also understood this psychological hurdle:

> The process by which banks create money is so simple that the mind is repelled. When something so important is involved, a deeper mystery seems only decent.[7]

As the quotation implies, there is an uncomfortable disparity between the importance of modern money creation and its disarming simplicity. Something so important could not possibly be so simple!

It's not hard to see why some would react to the notion of *ex nihilo* money creation with skepticism or even moral revulsion. To most hard-working people, the money in their bank account is the frozen value of their toil, a tangible record of their financial success. Telling them that money somehow "materializes" when a bank makes a loan seems to trivialize their life savings and all the work required to accumulate it. So, it isn't surprising that the idea of "money from nothing" defies common sense. As Galbraith says, "The mind is repelled." This reaction probably explains my daughter's and her husband's skepticism when I informed them that the bank had conjured up new mortgage money just for them.

The revelation that money is "loaned into existence" strikes most people as an absurd joke, like saying storks deliver babies or Santa Claus brings toys down the chimney. In explaining his version of fractional reserve banking, Paul Samuelson expressed this exact sentiment: "As every banker well knows," wrote Samuelson, "he cannot invest money that he does not have... ."[8]

But as we'll see in Chapters Two and Three, commercial banks have *always* loaned money they do not have! Their unique ability to do so distinguishes banks from other financial institutions. The ability to create money is what makes a bank a "bank."

So, be forewarned of this psychological issue—the problem of skepticism. Learning where money comes from, some may react like the child who was raised by surrogate parents and is told only late in life that he was adopted. Some facts are hard to accept even after learning they are true, especially when conditioned by a strong prior belief or "common sense."

As you read this book, try to put aside prior bias and prejudice, such as the belief that commercial banks lend out other peoples' money. Do not allow your mind to be "repelled," as Galbraith says, merely because the correct explanation sounds simplistic or strange. Armed with facts, a few simple principles, and the lessons of history, anyone can understand money creation. A formal background in economics or finance is optional. All you need is genuine curiosity and an open mind.

The need for sound money

At this point, you may be thinking: "OK, even if it's true that confusion on the topic of money creation is pervasive, why is it my problem? It sounds like a technical problem for the academics, so let them sort it out. Why should the average person bother to understand the accurate facts of modern money creation? Why should *I* care?"

A survey of our current monetary landscape will provide the answer. Look around you. Daily commerce continues humming, but things don't seem right lately. The dollar buys thirty percent less than it did four years ago. Nagging inflation erodes everyone's wealth, but no one saw it coming or seems to have a clear idea of what to do about it. The stock market soars to new heights but enriches some and leaves others behind. House prices are out of reach for many, especially the young. Government spending is out of control, and there is no political will on either the left or the right to rein it in.

Commercial bank failures are common, requiring bailouts by the central banks to prevent widespread financial panic. The U.S. dollar is losing its reputation as the currency of choice in international trade. Almost overnight, it seems, our money has become more fragile, less stable—in a word, less "sound."

But most of us have always taken "sound money"—money that is widely accepted and retains its purchasing power over time—for granted. "Sound money" is a phrase recognized for centuries around the world. It comes from a time when everyone knew what money was (a precious metal) and where it came from (the earth). "Sound" describes the musical, metallic ring of a gold or silver coin dropped on a hard surface.

The term has its roots in Ancient Rome. As the Roman Empire expanded, the emperors needed more money to maintain their power, so they gradually debased their pure silver coins with common metals, ultimately cutting the silver content to just 5 percent of its original. It took several centuries to turn the Roman coin from sound enough to support prosperity into *unsound* enough to undermine economic progress.

Scholars have studied the disastrous economic and political consequences of Rome's currency demise, and history is full of similar currency debacles. Today, once again, our money is being debased; however, it's harder to detect because modern money is no longer rare metal but consists mainly of ledger entries in a bank account.

Currency "debasement," which means a gradual loss of purchasing power, occurs when the production of money is disconnected from the production of economic goods. This makes perfect sense if you consider that money, like all other goods used in trade, must be produced before it can be used. Someone must create it, but who should that be, and who should get the new money first? Knowing how money comes into existence is critical for judging whether our money is sound, unsound, or somewhere in between.

Let's consider the role sound money plays in everyday human affairs. Whether you spend it for personal consumption or long-term investment, sound money is essential for estimating your future income and the future prices of goods and services. How else can you know if you can afford a vacation or if you should put the money aside for a rainy day?

Sound money is essential to an economy with a highly advanced "division of labor," i.e., an economy of highly specialized production. This specialization allows each of us to concentrate on the one or two things each of us does best, selling our product or time to others for money we then use to exchange for the fruits of others' labor. As Adam Smith taught us, specialized production is the key to success in any advanced economy. However, specialized production requires detailed and accurate economic planning, which depends on sound, stable money.

Sound money allows millions of people to coordinate their specialized efforts over distance and time for mutual benefit. For example, if you buy a bicycle made in China, think of all the people you are cooperating with to get it manufactured and shipped to your home. Millions of people may collaborate in this process, each doing one specific task, but none of them need to know each other. Sound money, the profit motive, and solid contracts backed by good law are all you need to motivate these millions of people to provide that bike.

So, if sound money is required for highly specialized production, and only highly specialized production can achieve the economic prosperity everyone wants and needs, it's no exaggeration to say that sound money is in every person's self-interest and, therefore, in every country's national interest.

How to become "one in a million"

Perhaps most Americans take sound money for granted because, aside from occasional financial emergencies, our money has functioned well for decades. Sound money is not something Americans have had to worry about. And why should we have to worry? After all, we can't all be experts on every critical invention or social system. We've never had to become experts in our electric power grids, our water systems, or our cars' electronic circuitry, so why should we have to become experts on the operations of our monetary system?

It would be best if we didn't have to, but there's a problem when a critical system stops functioning correctly. Look at what's happened recently to the energy supply systems in California, Texas, the United Kingdom, and Europe. When these systems fail under the guidance of the designated "experts," it's time to get interested in how they work. Under dire circumstances, learning how your electricity is produced and distributed could become a matter of physical survival.

In the same way, as our monetary system deteriorates, we must learn about it out of self-preservation. As we will see in Chapter Eight, understanding money creation will likely be essential to your financial survival because you'll learn how to fight financial repression.

You'll also become an uncommon person because if you understand money creation, you will understand inflation. Consider this frequently quoted passage from the 20th century's most influential economist, John Maynard Keynes.

> Lenin is said to have declared that the best way to destroy the capitalist system was to debauch the currency. By a continuing process of inflation, governments can confiscate, secretly and unobserved, an important part of the wealth of their citizens. There is no subtler, no surer means of overturning the existing basis of Society than to debauch the currency. *The process engages all the hidden forces of economic law on the side of destruction, and does it in a manner which not one man in a million is able to diagnose.* [Italics added.]
>
> —John Maynard Keynes, 1924, *The Economic Consequences of the Peace.*

Keynes claimed that "not one man in a million" can diagnose inflation, but this book aims to prove him wrong. If you know how new money is created, who created it, who gets it first, and how it is spent and re-spent in the economy, you'll be able to grasp all the so-called "hidden forces of economic law" that make inflation so destructive.

This means that every reader of this book can be one of Keynes's so-called "one in a million" able to diagnose the effects of inflation. With this knowledge, you can be the rare person who can anticipate and counter the effects of inflation and financial repression, thus preserving your hard-won wealth.

And what if millions of us—not just one in a million—understood money creation and inflation well? Wouldn't we be better positioned to demand constructive change from our monetary overlords in the central banks of Washington, London, Frankfurt, and Tokyo?

If enough of us "get it," we can gradually right the listing ship that is our monetary system. And, when the time comes to take popular political action, we'll all be better equipped to choose the kinds of political representatives who will restore sound money to its rightful place in the march of human prosperity. So, read on, and let the sound money restoration project begin with you, right now.

Chapter Two tells the story of how modern banking and money creation were invented precisely in accordance with the credit creation theory.

2 MONEY CREATION, THEN AND NOW

*Money creation in banks; Money destruction by banks; The
real business of banking; Anyone can lend, but only banks
create money; Two kinds of money; Technical comments;
Modern banking benefits everyone; Is bank money creation
fraudulent? Bank reserves, then and now; Key points*

In Chapter One, we got some bad news and some good news. The
bad news was that money creation is poorly understood, even by the
economists and politicians who regulate our financial system.

The good news was that we can correct this widespread ignorance. Understanding money creation is easy once you overcome the
erroneous belief that it's complicated. To travel down the road of understanding, I aim to keep money creation simple, which means explaining the essential ideas while omitting some nonessential details.

 Our primary goal in this chapter is to understand how commercial banks create and destroy money. Many will be surprised to learn
that the banks' fundamental method is the same today as when Co-
lumbus sailed to the Western Hemisphere. In other words, the credit
creation theory accurately describes banking, then as well as now.

As we'll learn from history, commercial banks create money *ex
nihilo*, i.e., "out of nothing," by issuing promises to pay out cash
when demanded. These "promises to pay cash" are then readily accepted in commerce as if they were cash itself. The ability to "create
money" this way is fundamental to all banks and has not changed
over time. What has changed is the nature of the cash.

In this chapter, we'll explore the creation of the promise and the creation of the cash used to fulfill it.

Money creation in banks

Banks have been creating money in slightly varying forms worldwide for centuries. However, the current system can be traced to the European goldsmiths of the mid-15th century, who created an early prototype of contemporary banking built on public trust.

For thousands of years, people worldwide recognized and accepted precious metals (mainly gold and silver) as money. As culture and commerce advanced, gold gained prominence, replacing all other exchange media as the most desirable form of payment.

As the gold trade developed in Europe during the late Middle Ages (the 15th century), goldsmiths (artisans who fashioned gold into jewelry, tokens, or coins) became trusted custodians, acting as safekeepers of their customers' gold for a fee. Safekeeping was a valuable service that helped prevent theft and improved public safety.

The goldsmiths organized themselves into professional associations, known as guilds, maintaining self-imposed standards of good service and craftsmanship to discourage fraud and protect their reputation, thereby protecting the value of their industry. The goldsmith guilds earned the public's trust, gaining economic influence over time.

Modern money creation was conceived when goldsmiths began to issue paper receipts or certificates as evidence of their customers' ownership of gold. When customers returned the receipts, the goldsmith was bound to exchange them for physical gold.

Eventually, people began trading these certificates in ordinary commerce as if they were physical gold. Gold certificates became popular because of their convenience. They were lighter, easier to transport and conceal, and the gold was not subject to wear or erosion due to constant handling. The gold certificate—legal evidence of a *promise* to pay out physical gold on demand—gradually became "as good as gold" in the eyes of the public. The success of this practice depended on the public's trust in the goldsmith's honesty and integrity.

As a simple custodian and safe keeper who issued redeemable certificates, the goldsmith was not yet a money-creator. However, the goldsmiths gradually realized that most of their depositors rarely redeemed their paper receipts for physical gold. In a typical year, perhaps only one in ten redeemed his certificates.

Eventually, it dawned on the goldsmiths that they could print certificates representing more gold than they held in safekeeping. They could then lend out these extra certificates and charge interest.

Based on their trust in the goldsmiths, the public accepted these excess certificates as money in commerce, just as when the certificates matched one-for-one with the amount of physical gold available for redemption. By the mid-1600s, it was common practice for European banks to expand the money supply in this way. This simple but ingenious innovation marked the birth of modern banking and money creation.[1]

The ledger below illustrates the evolution of the goldsmith from safe keeper to banker. It captures, in accounting terms, the essential feature of modern money creation: issuing more claims for cash than the amount of cash (gold) physically deposited in the bank.

MONEY CREATION UNDER A GOLD STANDARD

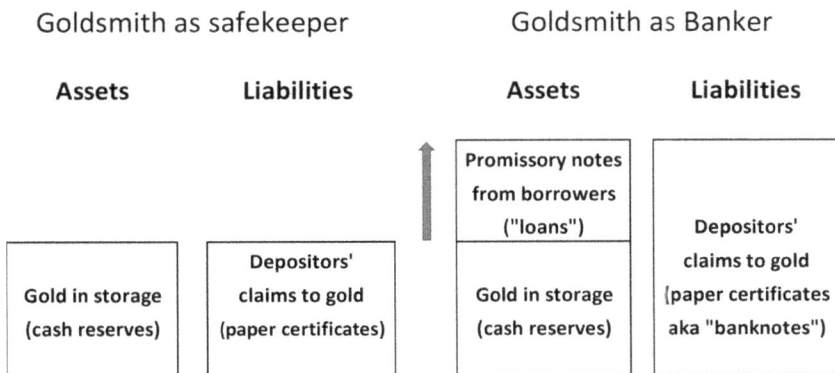

Goldsmith as safekeeper		Goldsmith as Banker	
Assets	Liabilities	Assets	Liabilities
		Promissory notes from borrowers ("loans")	
Gold in storage (cash reserves)	Depositors' claims to gold (paper certificates)	Gold in storage (cash reserves)	Depositors' claims to gold (paper certificates aka "banknotes")

On the left is the goldsmith's balance sheet when he was a safe-keeper but not yet a money creator. The goldsmith's assets (gold held in storage, called "cash reserves") consist of his customers' gold held for safekeeping, for which the goldsmith receives a fee. The goldsmith's liabilities are his obligations to return gold in exchange for the paper certificates he issued to depositors. The certificates, held by the depositors and circulated as money, are the physical evidence of this liability.

On the right is the balance sheet of the "Goldsmith Bank" after the goldsmith became an authentic banker, that is, after he started printing and lending more claims than the gold he held in his vault.

Something new and important occurred when the Goldsmith Bank started lending out excess gold certificates. By the act of lending, the Goldsmith Bank acquired a valuable financial asset from the borrower—an "IOU" or promissory note pledging to return the gold certificates, with interest, over a defined period. The banker paid for this promissory note with paper certificates that promised to pay out gold whenever anyone bearing the certificate presented it to the bank. As we've seen, these "promises to pay on demand" circulated in the economy as if they were physical gold. They were rarely redeemed for the precious metal they represented.

The banker thus loaned out additional paper claims on gold, even though no one deposited any additional gold to back the additional claims. When the borrower spent these new certificates in the marketplace, people exchanged and valued them equally with the original certificates. The old and new certificates were indistinguishable from one another. All were valued equally as money.

Over time, these gold certificates became known as "banknotes," a term I'll use from here on. A banknote is a certificate issued by a bank authorizing the bearer of the note to exchange it at the bank for gold on demand.

Notice that the Goldsmith Banker expanded his balance sheet by lending these additional banknotes. The banker has acquired an additional asset, a promissory note from the borrower. Goldsmith

Bank's assets now include the original gold in the vault *plus* the borrower's promissory note (the loan).

The bank has also taken on a new liability equal to the loan amount—the obligation to pay out gold on demand to the bearer of the new banknotes. The bank's liabilities now include the old paper claims for gold *and* the new paper claims loaned to the borrower. Since all the gold claims have equal status, the old claims are indistinguishable from the new ones.

By this elementary process of lending out an amount of banknotes greater than the amount of cash reserves in the vault, the banker has increased the economy's total money supply.

As Galbraith warned us in Chapter One, the process of money creation is so simple that your mind may be "repelled"—perhaps by the possibility that the banker can enrich himself by simply printing unlimited banknotes! However, bankers, both ancient and modern, face strict market-imposed limits on how much money they can create. Chapter Four will explore these constraints in detail.

Money destruction by banks

Money so easily created can just as easily be eradicated or destroyed when the borrower pays off the loan.

MONEY "DESTRUCTION" UNDER A GOLD STANDARD

Borrower returns the borrowed banknotes to the bank
(banknotes come out of circulation, loan is discharged)

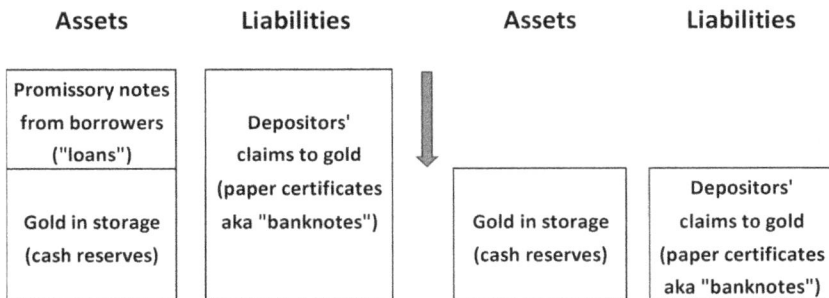

Assets	Liabilities	Assets	Liabilities
Promissory notes from borrowers ("loans")	Depositors' claims to gold (paper certificates aka "banknotes")		
Gold in storage (cash reserves)		Gold in storage (cash reserves)	Depositors' claims to gold (paper certificates aka "banknotes")

When he returns the borrowed gold certificates to the bank, the borrower has fulfilled his agreement. The bank tears up the promissory note; thus, the bank loan is no longer the bank's asset. As the banknotes now reside in the bank's vault, they are no longer anyone's claim to receive gold on demand, so they no longer count as money. (We'll have more to say about the formal definition of "money" shortly.)

In these early lending activities of the goldsmiths, we can see the basic principle of bank money creation. When a bank lends, it creates new money equal to the loan. An equal amount of money is eradicated when the loan is paid off. As one writer put it, "The bank is both the cradle and grave of money."[2]

Observe that the bank did not lend out its cash reserves. The reserves stayed in the bank when the loan was made and were still there after the loan was paid off. The bank issued new money to make the loan, and this money was eradicated when the loan was paid off. The creation and destruction of money did not change the bank's cash reserves.

In the modern economy, money is still created and destroyed in the banks similarly, except the banks have replaced paper banknotes with ledger entries called bank deposits. When a bank makes a loan, the bank records a ledger entry in the borrower's account. This ledger entry, rather than a banknote, is evidence of the bank's promise to pay out cash on demand. Replacing banknotes with bank deposits occurred gradually over several hundred years, enabled by technological improvements such as an expanding banking network and improved communication systems.

Today, people conduct most of their economic transactions by transferring ownership of bank deposits between buyers and sellers of goods. This happens when buyers instruct their bank to pay a specific sum of deposits to a seller of goods or services. We do this in several ways: write a check, wire funds, use a bank card, or dial up a smartphone application. In all these cases, the buyer is telling his bank to move some of his deposits from his bank account to the seller's bank account. (In Chapter Three, we'll discuss the mechanics of how deposits move from one party to another and from bank to bank when payments are made.)

The real business of banking

Let's pause to ensure we understand the unique business of commercial banking. In an important sense, banks do not "lend" money at all! More accurately, banks are in the business of acquiring valuable financial assets.

In everyday language, "borrowing" means accepting a loan of something that already exists. A "loan" is the temporary surrender of something valuable on the condition it is returned or repaid in the future. A loan is an extension of credit—an agreement in which the creditor (lender) supplies the debtor (borrower) with something of value to be returned, usually with interest or some other compensation for the lender.

For example, you might lend your friend $50 until payday. She agrees to pay it back promptly when she gets paid, and then the drinks are on her. You have extended credit to your friend by temporarily trusting her to use your property ($50 cash) in return for some compensation (return of the cash plus a drink). You have merely changed the form of your asset from cash to an amount due from your friend.

But when commercial banks "lend," they are not lending out the bank's or anyone else's existing property. They are purchasing an asset—the debtor's obligation to pay the bank a stream of money over time (i.e., a loan or a bond). To make this purchase, the bank is creating something new—a formal promise to pay out cash on demand. The bank's promise is first given to the borrower and then accepted as money as it is passed from one party to another in exchange for goods and services.

This explanation contradicts the typical description of bank lending, which claims that banks lend out deposits previously gathered from depositors. That description is wrong because it puts the cart of deposits before the horse of lending. As the Goldsmith Bank loan illustrates, lending creates deposits, not vice versa.

By extending credit, the bank creates money. That's why the "credit creation theory" is the correct and appropriate name for the concept of modern banking.

Anyone can lend, but only banks create money

"Nonbank" financial institutions actually do the majority of the business lending in the USA. However, there is a very big difference between lending by banks and nonbanks. Unlike commercial banks, nonbank financial institutions (also called "financial intermediaries") lend out money that is already in their possession, money that already exists, just as in our example where you loaned a friend $50 until payday.

Superficially, the differences between bank and nonbank lending are not immediately apparent. To the borrower, things look much the same. For example, I once took out a home mortgage from an insurance company. To me, the loan looked just like a mortgage from a bank, with a competitive interest rate and repayment terms.

However, from the lender's viewpoint, it was quite different. The insurance company did not create new money when it made the loan. Instead, it gathered some of its own cash and loaned it to me. This was a typical loan from a financial intermediary, but it is not what commercial banks do. Financial intermediaries invest someone's existing money, while commercial banks invest newly created money.

Here is what a loan from a *nonbank* would look like from an accounting perspective.

"Non-bank" lends $50

Before the loan		After the loan	
Assets	Liabilities	Assets	Liabilities

Assets	Liabilities	Assets	Liabilities
Cash = 100	Investors' claims = 100	Loans = 50 / Cash = 50	Investors' claims = 100

Suppose a group of friends pooled their money to form an investment company, making investments and sharing the gains or losses. On the left is the company's balance sheet before it makes any loans or other investments. On the right is the balance sheet after the group has loaned out half its assets.

This is a "true" loan in that the money already existed when the lender made the loan, i.e., the lender already had the money and temporarily gave up the use of it. The lender traded cash for a promissory note, confirmed by the fact that the balance sheet did not increase when the loan was made. Instead, one asset, cash, was replaced by another asset, the loan. The total value of assets and liabilities did not change. And when the loan from this non-bank is repaid, the balance sheet does not shrink, and money is not eradicated. An existing quantity of money is handed to the borrower when loaned and returned to the lender (with interest) when the loan is repaid.

By contrast, when the bank makes a loan, it pays for it not with cash but with a *promise* to pay cash on demand, which is accepted everywhere in commercial exchange and is, therefore, money.

The question may arise, why couldn't this group of friends simply declare their institution to be a bank and issue banknotes or deposits (money) just like a commercial bank? The answer is that this might have been possible if they were operating in the era of the Goldsmith banks. In those days, both gold and banknotes were accepted as money based on *trust*—trust in gold as the standard money, and trust in the goldsmith banker to pay gold on demand in exchange for the banknotes he issued. This trust was earned in the free market over a long period. The government was not involved except to prosecute fraud. So, if this group of friends could convince the community to accept their banknotes as money, on par with the goldsmith banks, no one would stop them.

But, of course, that is impossible today, because every government on the planet requires the banker to have a government-issued license. Today, governments, not markets, bestow the privilege of creating money by granting banking charters.

Without the understanding that banks create money, it is somewhat misleading to say commercial banks are in the business of "lending." Other, more accurate expressions, such as "banks lend money into existence," are also slightly off the mark because banks don't create money solely to "lend" it. They also create money to buy other financial assets such as sovereign bonds, local government bonds, and publicly traded bonds issued by private corporations. This is the same as "purchasing the promissory note" of a borrower, i.e., "lending" the borrower money. Both a bank loan and a bond are a type of IOU. The main difference is that a bond can be bought and sold in the marketplace, while most loans must remain the property of the issuing bank.

The point is that whether the bank is "lending" or "investing," in both cases, it is purchasing a valuable financial asset with newly created money.

Two kinds of money

I've been referring to banks "creating" money, so before we continue, let's define what money is. Ludwig von Mises, one of the great economists of the 20th century, provided a straightforward definition. Money, he said, is "a commonly used medium of exchange."[3]

Von Mises further identified two types of money falling under this definition: *standard money* and *fiduciary media*.[4]

Standard money is accepted as full and final payment and is not itself a claim to anything further. When paid, standard money is full compensation for the value received, extinguishing all previous financial claims. Standard money stands alone and does not depend on a counterparty to make full and final payment.

Under a gold standard, gold coins and bullion were the standard money. Physical gold was the full and final payment for the value received in settling payments.

Under today's money standard, paper money printed by the United States Mint, a subsidiary of the U.S. Treasury, is the standard money. Like their historic predecessor, gold, these paper bills constitute legal full and final payment.

A second kind of money, *fiduciary media*, is Mises's formal term for the kind of money created in commercial banks. Fiduciary media are transferable claims to standard money, payable by the issuer on demand and accepted in commerce as the equivalent of standard money, but for which no standard money exists. Because it is a *promise* to pay standard money, fiduciary media does not "stand alone" in fulfilling financial obligations. ("Fiduciary" comes from the Latin "fiducia," meaning trust.) As a credit instrument, fiduciary media is unique in that it is a promise to pay that is accepted as a medium of exchange in all, or nearly all, transactions.

To summarize, fiduciary media are promises to pay standard money, while standard money "stands alone," requiring no further payment action by any party.

Under a gold standard, gold owners may place their gold in a bank, and the bank can issue a paper receipt (a banknote) or record the deposit on the bank's accounting ledger. Both the banknote and the deposit are evidence of the bank's promise to redeem them for physical gold on demand. These banknotes or deposits circulate as money on a par with gold. Any additional banknotes or deposits not fully covered by the promised quantity of gold are "fiduciary media." In the goldsmith era, the "extra" paper receipts fit this description.

The critical point about the definition of money is this: Because both standard money and fiduciary media are commonly accepted as a medium of exchange, both are accurately called money. Conveniently, this comprehensive definition of money is also roughly equivalent to the U.S. Federal Reserve's definition of "broad money," known as M2.

Technical comments

At this point, a couple of technical comments are necessary. The first is the meaning of "cash." In this book, "cash" is synonymous with "standard money," meaning full and final payment. The terms cash, cash reserves, bank reserves, and vault cash are all names for standard money. Dollar bills and coins circulating in the economy (not in a bank vault) are also cash or standard money.

This use of "cash" is somewhat different from other uses of the term in everyday language. For example, a person might say she "paid cash" for her car if she wrote a check for payment rather than borrowing the money. She paid with a bank deposit, not "cash" as I use the term here.

A second technical comment on banknotes is also necessary. Under the gold standard, paper banknotes were a form of fiduciary media because they documented the bank's promise to pay gold on demand. But despite its physical resemblance to the old banknote, modern U.S. paper money is not fiduciary media, i.e., it is not a promise to pay anything further. Banknotes were a claim on physical gold, while today's paper dollars are not a claim on anything further. Today, the government's paper notes fulfill all final payment obligations by fiat. They are, therefore, standard money.

In effect, paper banknotes issued by private banks said, "IOU a specific quantity of gold." Today's paper dollars printed by the Treasury say, in effect, "IOU nothing further."

Modern banking benefits everyone

Why did modern banking, with its unique ability to create money, evolve in the first place? Social systems become popular and endure for centuries only when they receive widespread support from their public users, as the public will not long support a system that fails to provide a material benefit. Our bank-based money creation system has always been popular because it's good for everyone who uses it, including depositors, borrowers, and bankers.[5]

From the depositors' point of view, banks offer several benefits. First, they provide a secure place to store standard money, relieving the depositor of the burden of concealment or security. Of course, security was more important under a gold standard than our paper standard. But even today, banks give depositors ready access to their funds without the inconvenience of holding large amounts of paper cash.

Second, bank-issued money, whether banknotes or ledger-entry deposits, is more convenient than physical gold or silver, as it reduces reliance on couriers, armed guards, and security in transporting money. As trusted providers of payment services, banks enable smooth and reliable transactions over time and distance. Think how easy it is to use a credit or debit card to pay for the merchandise you buy online! That's all due to the banking industry's ongoing efforts to provide convenient services to depositors.

Finally, banks can provide a direct investment benefit to depositors by paying interest on deposits, even as depositors enjoy immediate use of their money.

From the borrower's or entrepreneur's perspective, banks serve as a source of new capital by offering loans for productive investments. (Productive bank lending is the subject of Chapter Four.) Furthermore, banks act as trusted intermediaries, ensuring credit reliability between transacting parties that may not even know each other. Additionally, banks establish common methods and standards of payment that are efficient for all business parties involved.

From the bankers' standpoint, creating money to acquire financial assets provides an obvious benefit: it's a profitable business when properly managed! Profitability creates competition, incentivizing banks to continually improve the services their customers want.

Is bank money creation fraudulent?

Despite the apparent benefits of modern banking, there are a few well-known economists, mainly of the Libertarian persuasion, who see money creation in the banks as a form of fraud that should be prohibited by law. They say this even though it's widely known that money creation in the banks developed organically, based on the voluntary actions of bankers, depositors, and borrowers, all of whom approved of the banks' actions through their willing participation in the business.

The late Murray Rothbard, an Austrian economist and a hero of many Libertarians, is the prime spokesman for this view. He referred to the process of issuing banknotes not fully covered by gold deposits as "... a Ponzi scheme, a fraud in which fake warehouse receipts are issued and circulate as equivalent to the cash supposedly represented by the receipts."[6]

Other economists believe that if the bank issues fiduciary media (either banknotes or bank deposits) openly—that is, if the bank discloses to the owners of bank deposits that the bank does not have sufficient standard money to back all the outstanding deposits— there is no fraud. Absent fraud, these economists say, the government has no legitimate reason to prohibit the practice of issuing "extra" money not backed by standard money.

This favorable view assumes that the owners of bank deposits should exercise "caveat emptor," buyer beware. They should realize that they are entitled to exchange all their banknotes or deposits for cash any time they want it—*unless* everyone else wants it at the same time, in which case some depositors may not get all their money when promised, and some may even lose money.

It's important to note that this feature is not unique to commercial banks: it is shared by some non-bank financial institutions. A life insurance company, for example, could not pay out all its promised benefits if too many people died simultaneously. While there's occasional fraud in the insurance industry, nobody claims the practice of selling insurance is inherently fraudulent.

Some economists who are friendly towards bank money creation think that if banks were free to issue all the fiduciary media the market could bear, the practice would be self-limiting, perhaps to the point that fiduciary media would not be issued at all. Under "free banking," virtually everyone would see the possibility of losing everything to the banks that issued fiduciary media, and therefore, virtually everyone would avoid such banks, and the issuance of fiduciary media would become practically non-existent.[7]

Ludwig von Mises expressed this point of view in *Human Action*:

> It is a mistake to associate with the notion of free banking the image of a state of affairs under which everybody is free to issue banknotes and to cheat the public *ad libitum*. … However, freedom in the issuance of banknotes would have narrowed down the use of banknotes considerably if it had not entirely suppressed it. It was this idea which [Enrico] Cernuschi advanced in the hearings of the French Banking Inquiry on October 24, 1865: "I believe that what is called freedom of banking would result in a total suppression of banknotes in France. I want to give everybody the right to issue banknotes so that nobody should take any banknotes any longer."[8]

How much fiduciary media—money in excess of cash reserves—would banks issue if regulation of cash reserves was left purely to the free market? In an environment of "free banking," if there were no government safeguards, no FDIC insurance, no ability of the government to print up new cash reserves to bail out failing banks, if gold were still the standard money, and if the public could choose to store their gold in banks that did not issue fiduciary media; if all these things were true, would the banks systematically "cheat the public"? Would banks be subject to frequent systemwide crises?

History provides an answer, as we have solid historical evidence of the efficacy of "free banking." A recent book by Professor Kevin Dowd, *The Experience of Free Banking*, defines the term as follows:

> "Free banking is a banking system in which banks issue their own notes under competitive conditions while typically operating on a commodity standard, in the absence of a central bank and in a legal environment in which the public are free to accept or reject bank currency as they choose."[9]

In an interview with the Cobden Centre, Professor Dowd elaborated:

> "Free banking is not some untested economic theory, still less one that has failed. On the contrary, free banking has been tried many times in the past, and the results have been remarkable. Because free banking systems were based on commodity standards – typically the gold standard in English-speaking countries – they delivered long-run price stability. They were also highly innovative, strongly capitalised and much more stable than contemporary banking systems. Their historical experience shows that free banking systems are much superior to modern systems of central banking.
>
> At a fundamental level, the lesson here is that historical experience shows that banking and politics make for a truly toxic mix."[10]

My view is that free banking (i.e., banking unregulated by the government) would allow commercial banks with good reputations to serve depositors with varying appetites for risk. Some depositors would seek banks that provided no more than safekeeping, others would be willing to risk exposing their deposits to a bank run in exchange for high interest, and most would fall somewhere between these extremes.

In other words, market discipline would weed out the bad actors and limit the issuance of fiduciary media, just as it did during the Scottish free banking era of the 19th century, documented in Dowd's book. We would see occasional bank failures and deposit losses but not frequent systemwide meltdowns. The historical record in *The Experience of Free Banking* supports this view.

However, free banking would require an economy where banks were regulated only by market incentives and common laws that punish fraud. This would imply an economy without FDIC insurance, a government central bank, or government-appointed rule-making agencies. Free banking would further require a culture of personal responsibility that includes choosing a sound bank without assuming the government can "protect" bank deposits by forcing taxpayers to provide universal deposit insurance. In such a culture, people's priorities would have to change. For example, the bank's depositors might find learning to read a bank's financial statements more valuable than becoming an expert player in the latest video game.

That is my view, but the reality is that "free banking" today is such a remote possibility that I do not expect to see it in my lifetime.

Bank reserves, then and now

The creation of fiduciary media (commercial bank deposits) is essentially the same today as it was hundreds of years ago. However, the production of standard money, which the banks store as cash reserves ready to redeem for deposits, is radically different.

At the risk of stating the obvious, we must remember that the widespread use of gold as money preceded the practice of bank money creation. Gold was standard money everywhere, long before modern banking, and long before there was any need to distinguish standard money from its derivative fiduciary media. That's why the system was called a gold *standard*.

A commodity such as gold is produced by a privately owned network of gold miners, refineries, and mints that turn gold ore into spendable money. Like any market in a physical commodity, supply and demand regulates the total amount of gold produced.

When gold became the banking system's cash reserves, the amount of gold deposits in the banks was determined by gold owners who chose to either deposit their gold in the bank or store it elsewhere. They could withdraw their gold if they didn't like their bank's policies, such as the interest rate paid on deposits. The need to maintain a prudent level of cash reserves made bankers responsive to their depositors' preferences.

In America, the fundamental change in bank cash reserves began when gold reserves were supplemented with fiat (paper) reserves under the Federal Reserve Act of 1913. The transition continued with the complete demise of the U.S. domestic gold standard in 1933. By outlawing gold, the government seized the power to control the amount of bank reserves away from the gold depositors and gave it to the Federal Reserve, which could easily create new cash reserves in any amount and at no cost. True, depositors could still threaten to withdraw paper money from their bank's vault, but the ability of the Fed to create unlimited cash virtually nullified the depositors' power over the banking system. The transition away from gold culminated in the U.S. banking system's complete severance from an international gold standard in 1971. Consequently, I refer to the period after 1971 as the "post-gold era."

To this day, the radical change in the nature and source of cash reserves is still not widely understood by the public. It was certainly not obvious to the average bank customer when President Franklin Roosevelt issued the executive order that outlawed private gold ownership in 1933. On the surface, banking services didn't change much. Checking accounts still worked as before, and even the paper currency looked the same. The average bank customer probably saw no reason to fear the switch from a gold standard to the new paper standard.[11]

It was as if a con man secretly replaced a diamond ring with cubic zirconium, but the owner didn't notice and moved through life believing she still had something valuable on her finger. Eventually, she might have noticed that many such rings were popping up everywhere in the market as her fake ring declined in value, but she probably never really understood what had happened to her original ring.

To understand what has happened to our money, it is crucial to understand how modern central banks create bank reserves, or "standard money."

We interrupt this chapter for a motivation alert! If you want to be one of Keynes's "one in a million" who truly understands inflation, you need to understand the procedure I am about to describe. This understanding will be fundamental when we discuss the "quantitative easing" (QE) era of 2009 to 2022. As we'll see in Chapters Three and Five, QE was the most significant monetary expansion in US history, responsible for the asset bubble in bonds, stocks, and house prices and the "unexpected" post-Covid surge in the consumer price index.

The modern process of creating cash reserves should be understood in two steps. See the diagram below. Our example uses the US Federal Reserve and a US commercial bank, but the same basic procedure applies to all modern banking jurisdictions.

In Step 1, a private investor sells a Treasury bond to a commercial bank. (The investor's balance sheet is not shown.)

The basic process of money creation in banks should now be familiar. Step 1 is identical to Goldsmith Bank's creation of money. A commercial bank purchases a Treasury bond from a private investor. By purchasing this asset, the bank enlarges its balance sheet. In doing so, the bank creates a new deposit in the investor's account, enlarging its liabilities (deposits) by an equal amount. The commercial bank has created new money for the private investor who sold the bond.

In Step 2, the commercial bank sells the Treasury bond to the US Federal Reserve (the Fed). This transaction creates new cash reserves for the commercial bank, *ex nihilo*, by simply writing the bond's purchase price into the commercial bank's account at the Fed. On the

Fed's books, this is a new liability called "cash reserves due commercial banks." By *fiat*, this new liability of the Fed becomes brand-new standard money, which can be converted to paper cash whenever the bank needs it to meet customer demand for deposit withdrawals.

"Open Market Purchase" in Two Steps

Initial Conditions

Commercial Bank Balance Sheet   **Federal Reserve Balance Sheet**

Assets	Liabilities		Assets	Liabilities
loans	deposits		non-money assets (mostly bonds)	cash reserves due banks
cash reserves				currency

Step 1: Commercial bank purchases bonds from private investor

Commercial Bank Balance Sheet   **Federal Reserve Balance Sheet**

Assets	Liabilities		Assets	Liabilities
bonds				
loans	deposits		non-money assets (mostly bonds)	cash reserves due banks
cash reserves				currency

Commercial bank balance sheet expands.   Fed balance sheet is unchanged.
Investor (bond seller) gets new deposits.

Step 2: Federal Reserve purchases bonds from commercial bank

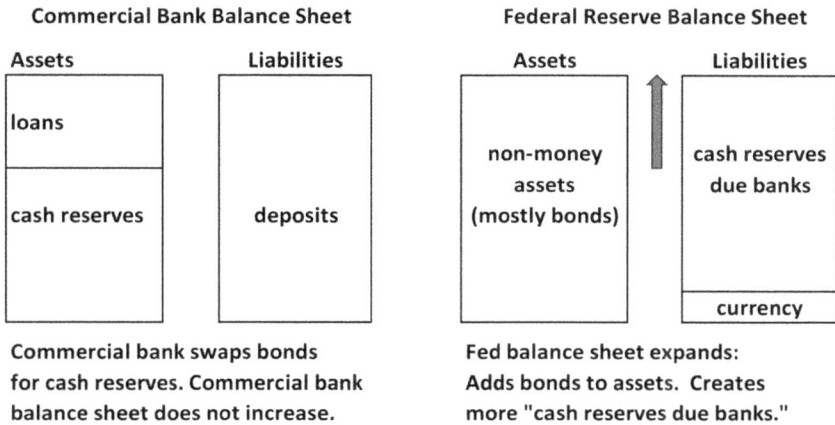

Commercial Bank Balance Sheet		Federal Reserve Balance Sheet	
Assets	**Liabilities**	**Assets**	**Liabilities**
loans			
		non-money assets (mostly bonds)	cash reserves due banks
cash reserves	deposits		
			currency

Commercial bank swaps bonds
for cash reserves. Commercial bank
balance sheet does not increase.

Fed balance sheet expands:
Adds bonds to assets. Creates
more "cash reserves due banks."

Note that the Fed creates these cash reserves like the bank creates deposits: with a few computer keystrokes and, perhaps, a signature.

The critical difference between these two transactions is that the commercial bank creates fiduciary media (a *promise* to pay standard money). In contrast, the Fed creates standard money (cash reserves that, when withdrawn from the bank, can be used to make full and final legal payment).

Step One puts the Treasury bond on the commercial bank's balance sheet so it can become the "raw material" for creating standard money. Step Two illustrates the most important operation of modern central banks: the creation of standard money, which commercial banks hold as cash reserves.

Sometimes, as shown in this example, these transactions are done separately. For example, the bank might first have bought the Treasury bond as an investment, creating new money. Later, if the Fed needs to inject new cash reserves to fortify the commercial banks, it purchases the bond. When both transactions have been completed, the result is 1) new money available to spend in the economy and 2) new cash reserves injected into the commercial bank.

Most often, these two transactions are performed simultaneously, at the direction of the Fed, in an "open market purchase." Since its inception, the Fed has used "open market operations"—the purchase and sale of government bonds in the public bond market—to adjust bank reserves, make minor changes to the money supply, and nudge short-term interest rates up or down. Perhaps this is why most explanations of open market operations focus on cash reserve creation and fail to mention deposit creation. However, as we'll soon see, ignoring the deposit-creation side of this transaction is a significant oversight.

Here's an official explanation of an open market purchase from a 1981 Federal Reserve publication.

> "When the Federal Reserve wants to increase bank reserves, for example, it contacts dealers or financial institutions that are willing to sell their government securities. In exchange for the securities, the Federal Reserve credits the financial institution's commercial bank with additional bank reserves equal to the value of the securities. The commercial bank, in turn, credits the institution's account. *The net result is that the Federal Reserve has more government securities, the commercial bank has larger reserves, and the dealer has larger deposits with the commercial bank. Both bank reserves and the money stock have increased.*" [Italics added.][12]

Here is a more recent explanation of the same operation.

> For example, when the Federal Reserve permanently purchases a security, the Desk buys eligible securities from primary dealers at prices determined in a competitive auction. The Federal Reserve pays for those securities by crediting the reserve accounts of the correspondent banks of the primary dealers. (The correspondent banks, in turn, *credit the dealers' bank accounts*.) In this way, the open market purchase leads to an increase in reserve balances. [Italics added.][13]

I leave it to the reader to speculate why the modern Fed explanation of open market operations barely mentions deposit creation, granting it a mere parenthetical remark.

Under traditional open market operations (OMO), creating cash reserves was the main objective: the amount of new spendable money (new bank deposits) created by the Fed's action was considered a by-product of the creation of cash reserves. Significant changes in the money supply were the responsibility of the commercial banks through their routine lending and investing programs.

However, the Fed eventually learned to use OMO to remove commercial bankers from money-creating decisions. As we'll see in Chapter Five, the Fed employed this exact procedure over many years on a colossal scale to massively increase the money supply during the years of "quantitative easing" (QE) from 2009 to 2022.

Key points

Commercial banks have been creating and destroying money in the same way for hundreds of years. Banks make loans or acquire other financial assets, paying for them with a promise to pay out cash, or "standard money," on demand. These promises—formerly bank-notes and now bank deposits—circulate in the economy as equivalents to paper currency or cash.

The money banks lend out, or use to make other investments, does not come from customer deposits or the bank's horde of cash reserves. Bank lending and asset purchases create deposits, not the other way around.

This money creation system—the essence of modern banking—became popular because it benefits everyone who uses it. Although some economists have alleged that bank money creation is systematic fraud, the history of free banking and banking's enduring popularity indicate otherwise.

On the surface, that is, at the level of interaction with the customer, banking has not changed much for centuries. However, in the post-gold era, the nature and source of cash reserves held by commercial banks are radically different. Under a free market, when gold was standard money, cash reserves were a precious physical commodity that had to be produced through considerable effort. Moreover, the depositors decided whether or not to entrust it to a commercial bank. By contrast, under today's fiat reserve standard, the quantity of cash reserves is determined solely by the wisdom (or whim) of Ph.Ds who can conjure any amount with a mere mouse click.

Understanding how modern central banks can simultaneously create both new cash reserves and new deposits in commercial banks is key to understanding our recent inflation.

In Chapter Three, we'll concretize these money-creation concepts with examples of everyday bank transactions and explain the origin of paper money in today's economy.

3 MONEY FROM NOTHING

Understanding modern banking; How banks change the money supply; How central banks determine the quantity of cash reserves; Erroneous beliefs about quantitative easing; Our "fiat reserve" monetary system

Understanding modern banking

Chapter Two taught us that modern banking developed when gold was the universal form of "standard" money. Banks became a unique industry by storing their customers' gold, printing more paper claims to gold than the actual gold held in their vaults, and then lending out these additional claims, which circulated as money. We also learned that modern banks continued to create money the same way long after the gold standard was abandoned.

The final abandonment of gold was not a clean break; it occurred over decades between 1933, when the domestic gold standard ended, and 1971, when the international gold standard ended. At that point, the link between the dollar and gold was entirely severed. Henceforth, as mentioned, we'll refer to post-1971 banking operations as the post-gold era.

To fully understand the post-gold system, let's expand on what we've already learned by delving deeper into the mechanics of modern money creation. This chapter will address three topics crucial to comprehending the process.

First, through realistic examples of everyday banking transactions, we will illustrate how banks influence the money supply, reinforcing our understanding of money creation basics from Chapter

Two. This demonstration will also reveal how paper money, known as Federal Reserve Notes, is created in the modern banking system.

Next, in plain language, we will explain how modern central banks determine the quantity of standard money, or cash reserves, to provide to the banking system. How it really works is likely different from what you were taught if you ever took a college course in money and banking.

Lastly, we will identify the radical transformation of central banks in the aftermath of the Great Financial Crash (GFC) of 2008–9. In the pre-crisis era, central banks mainly supplied bank reserves to support money creation in commercial banks. However, in the post-GFC years, central banks became aggressive money creators under a program called "quantitative easing" (QE). In this chapter, we'll review the mechanics of QE (introduced in Chapter Two) in preparation for a detailed discussion in Chapter Five.

Some of the examples presented in this chapter are slightly technical but easy enough, so stick with it! Going through each one will solidify your knowledge of money mechanics, and this knowledge will be beneficial when we discuss the positive and negative effects of money creation in later chapters.

How banks change the money supply

> The money supply is the total amount of money—cash,
> coins, and balances in bank accounts—in circulation.[1]

As discussed in Chapter Two, as defined by von Mises, money comprises both standard money, which conveys full and final payment, and fiduciary media, which are commercial banks' promises to pay standard money. In the post-gold banking system, fiduciary media refers to bank deposits, while standard money includes circulating currency and coins plus the cash reserves held by commercial banks. The commercial banks' cash reserves are excluded from the money supply because they can only be exchanged for goods and services after they are withdrawn from the bank. So, while a bank's cash reserves can be instantly converted to money upon withdrawal, they do not function as a medium of exchange while held within the bank. They are not, per the Fed's definition, "in circulation."

Approximately 88 to 90% of the dollar's money supply is in bank deposits, the most widely used form of payment. Second is "currency-in-circulation," the physical currency consisting of Federal Reserve Notes and coins, circulating independently of the banking system. Therefore, the money supply of an economy consists of all paper currency and coins outside the banking system plus the total deposits within commercial banks. As of July 2024, the broad money supply of the USA, as reported by the U.S. Federal Reserve, was approximately $21.0 trillion.[2]

The money supply is a snapshot taken at an instant in time. It is always changing because commercial banks constantly create and destroy money through their lending and investing operations. To get a realistic idea of how and why the money supply changes, let's look at a series of true-to-life bank transactions by an average person to see how they affect the quantity and composition of the money supply.

Suppose Andy, a middle-class consumer with a good job, wants to take a vacation but needs more money. He is willing to borrow a small amount because he will get a quarterly bonus in a few months to pay off the loan promptly. Let's see how Andy's transactions affect the money supply as he borrows and spends money for his vacation.

Most readers will find following the transactions on the ledger below helpful. Reading from left to right, Column 1 lists the name of the transaction; Column 2 records changes in Andy's Bank; Column 3 records changes in Other Banks, i.e., banks other than Andy's; Column 4 records changes in All Banks, which is the sum of Andy's Bank plus all other banks; and Column 5 records changes in the total money supply caused by Andy's transactions.

Andy's transactions are as follows:
1. Andy borrows $2000 from his bank to pay for his vacation.
2. Andy buys a plane ticket costing $1000.
3. Andy withdraws $500 cash for general vacation spending.

4. Andy receives his quarterly bonus of $3000 after returning from vacation.
5. Andy pays back the loan.

Col 1	Col 2		+	Col 3		=	Col 4		Col 5	
Andy's Transactions	Andy's Bank			Other Banks			All Banks		Change in money Supply	
	Assets	Liabilities		Assets	Liabilities		Assets	Liabilities	(bank deposits+currency in circ)	
1. Borrows $2000	2000 loan	2000 deposit					2000 loan	2000 deposit	2000	new money is created
2. Buys airline ticket	-1000 cash reserves	-1000 deposits		1000 cash reserves	1000 deposits					
3. Withdraws from ATM	-500 cash reserves	-500 deposits					-500 cash reserves	-500 deposits	500 / -500	currency in circulation / bank deposits
4. Deposits bonus check	3000 cash reserves	3000 deposits		-3000 cash reserves	-3000 deposits					
5. Repays $2000	-2000 loan	-2000 deposits					-2000 cash reserves	-2000 deposits	-2000	money is extinguished
									0	net change in money supply

Transaction One: Andy borrows $2000 from his bank. Start at the upper left of the illustration. Andy gets a loan and signs a promissory note to pay the bank $2000 within the following year. (For simplicity, we will ignore interest payments.) The bank records the loan as a new asset on its balance sheet. The bank creates a new deposit in Andy's account to purchase Andy's promissory note. This deposit is evidence of a promise to pay cash on demand that Andy can spend just like cash. The bank records this deposit as a new liability. Under Column 3, "Other Banks" are unaffected by this loan. Under Column 4, all banks in aggregate have acquired new money because of the money created in Andy's bank. Thus, the money supply increases, as recorded in Column 5.

Andy's bank did not need a prior deposit to make this loan, nor did it lend out any cash reserves. Andy's bank, all by itself, created the money for this loan and added it to the money supply.

Transaction Two: Andy buys an airline ticket for $1000. Suppose Andy writes a $1000 check to the airline company for his roundtrip ticket. Andy's check is a document that directs his bank to "pay $1000 to the order of" the Airline Company. By signing this check, Andy gives the airline company the right to demand $1000 in cash from Andy's bank.

The airline company could take the check to Andy's bank and demand cash, but this would be impractical because payments through bank accounts are more convenient and secure than exchanging physical cash.

If Andy and the airline use the same bank, the airline will deposit Andy's check. The bank will record a $1000 increase in the Airline's account and a $1000 decrease in Andy's account. But let's assume the airline does not have an account at Andy's bank. In that case, the airline company deposits Andy's check with its bank. Next, the airline's bank presents Andy's check to Andy's bank for payment. Andy's bank then pays the airline's bank by sending cash reserves. The result is that $1000 in deposits and $1000 in cash reserves have moved from Andy's Bank to Other Banks.

Andy, the airline, and their banks could also have done this transaction with a bank card or a mobile application like Venmo or Zelle instead of writing and clearing paper checks. Any of these methods would also move deposits and cash reserves between the two banks but at lightning speed.

Transaction Two illustrates how cash reserves moved from Andy's Bank to the airline's bank ("all other banks") to satisfy the airline's claim to receive cash from Andy's Bank. In the real banking world, hundreds of millions of payments between deposit owners at different banks are settled and clear daily. Rather than settle payments individually, as in our example, banks net out their transactions and pay what they owe each other by moving cash reserves at the end of each day. Because banks are constantly processing payments, withdrawals, and deposits, the level of cash reserves in any individual bank changes very little on a typical day. This netting and clearing system allows the banking network to function like the One Big Bank we assumed in Chapter Two.

Looking at Column 5, Andy's payment to the airline company does not affect the money supply. Some money supply has moved

from Andy's bank to "Other Banks," but the total money supply remains unchanged. So far, the only change in the total money supply
is due to Andy's bank making a loan.

Transaction Three: Andy withdraws $500 from an ATM. Having
bought his airline ticket, Andy has $1000 left to spend from his $2000
loan. To have some cash to spend on his vacation, he heads to the
nearby ATM operated by his bank. Using a debit card, he instructs
his bank to give him $500 in cash. Out pops $500 in paper cash, a
form of "standard money." Andy's bank has kept its promise to pay
out standard money on demand. Andy's withdrawal reduces the
bank's deposit liabilities (its "promises to pay") by $500 and its cash
reserves by $500.

At the very moment this paper money drops into Andy's hands,
it becomes what economists call "currency-in-circulation," or paper
money exchanged between transacting parties independent of the
banking system. When Andy withdrew this money, bank deposits
decreased, and currency-in-circulation increased by an equal
amount, resulting in no change in the total money supply. You can
see this in column 5.

So far, the total money supply has increased solely because of the
$2000 loan; however, the composition of the money supply has also
changed because $500 of the $2000 addition to the money supply is
now in the form of currency-in-circulation rather than bank deposits.

Andy's cash withdrawal illustrates how paper bills become
money. Note that a bank's cash reserves, whether held as a book entry
in its account at the Fed or sitting in the bank as vault cash, are not
part of the money supply because cash reserves are not available for
spending. Remember our definition of money: "a commonly accepted medium of exchange." A bank's cash reserves, bottled up in
the bank, are available for exchange only after withdrawal from the
bank, at which point the reserves become money. This makes sense
because a thing is money only if it can be exchanged for goods. Currency can be used in exchange only after it leaves the bank's vault.

This is why "currency in circulation" is the only form of standard money counted in the money supply. The other form of standard money, the bank's cash reserves, is not counted in the money supply.

The paper cash Andy withdrew from his bank can now be physically exchanged outside the banking system. There is a lot of currency in circulation—typically ten to twelve percent of the total U.S. money supply.

Andy's withdrawal illustrates the fact that *all paper money comes originally from a bank deposit*. Notice that Andy's paper money could only have gotten into the money supply if there first was money in the form of a bank deposit to draw against. We reach the surprising conclusion that the entire money supply, including all deposits and all currency-in-circulation (except for new bills and coins exchanged for the old, worn-out ones), starts as a bank deposit![3]

Now, let's return to Andy's vacation.

Transaction Four: Vacation is over, Andy has returned to work, and he receives his quarterly bonus check of $3000. We'll assume the check came from his employer's account at some "Other Bank." Andy deposits his bonus check into his bank account. $3,000 of deposits and cash reserves are transferred from "Other Banks" to Andy's bank. Here is another example of a transfer of existing money from one bank account to another. No new money is created; it simply moves from one bank account to another. The money supply remains the same.

Transaction Five: Andy directs his bank to pay off the loan. The bank makes the necessary entries in its records: it deletes $2000 from Andy's deposits and simultaneously deletes the $2000 loan asset, equivalent to tearing up the promissory note. No other banks are involved in this transaction. Looking at column 5, the economy's money supply has declined by $2000.

We can draw several conclusions from this simple illustration. First, the money supply increased because the bank loaned Andy $2000. Second, it decreased by $2000 because Andy paid off the loan. Third, the money supply changed in composition (but not quantity) when Andy withdrew money from his bank account. $500 of his deposit money disappeared from the banking system, offset by an increase of $500 in currency-in-circulation.

Let's review some additional bank transactions to ensure we understand money creation and destruction. In each situation, decide if the transaction adds to, subtracts from, changes in composition, or does not affect the money supply.

Example One: You pay for groceries using a paper check, a debit card, or a payment app like Venmo or Zelle.

When you pay your grocer with a check or payment app, deposits are transferred from your bank account to the grocer's bank account, just like Transaction Two above. No new money is created, so the money supply is unchanged.

Example Two: You pay for groceries using a credit card.

When you use a "credit" card, a bank lends you money. Therefore, when you pay for anything using a credit card, new money is created, adding to the money supply.

When you pay off your credit card, your bank deposits decline and your credit card loan balance declines by the same amount, decreasing the money supply.

Example Three: You deposit paper currency into your bank account.

No new money is created. When you deposit currency, currency-in-circulation declines, but bank deposits increase. Bank cash reserves also increase because the paper currency you deposit is added to the bank's vault cash. Money supply is unchanged, but its composition has changed, as the form of your money has changed from currency-in-circulation to a bank deposit.

Example Four: You get a cash advance from a local finance company to tide you over until payday.

No new money is created. Why? Because "payday lenders," like pawn shops, are not commercial banks. Most of the money loaned in the payday loan industry comes from investors who profit from the high interest rates charged on payday loans. Most payday loans are "true loans" in that they temporarily transfer possession of existing money from the lender to the borrower, causing no change in the money supply.

Example Five: You take out a mortgage (i.e., borrow money to buy a house).

This one is easy. If you borrow money from a commercial bank, money is created, and the money supply increases.

Example Six: A bank buys a corporate bond from a private investor.

A new deposit is created in the bond seller's bank account, increasing the money supply. The general rule is that when a commercial bank purchases an asset, it creates new money. When a commercial bank sells an investment, it extinguishes money.

Example Seven: A bank sells a bond to a private investor.

Money is extinguished. The investor writes a check to the bank that is selling the bond. The selling bank presents the check to the investor's bank, which reduces the investor's deposit balance and sends cash reserves to the selling bank. The selling bank's total assets are unchanged, as it has simply swapped the bond for cash ("cash reserves"). The investor's bank reduces both deposits and reserves. Due to the reduction in deposits, the money supply decreases.

Example Eight: A commercial bank sells a bond to another commercial bank.

The selling bank receives cash reserves from the buying bank. The buying bank gets a bond from the selling bank. The banks have merely swapped one asset (bonds) for another (cash reserves). No new money is created, so the money supply is unchanged.

Example Nine: You send money to the US Treasury to pay taxes or to buy a Treasury bond directly from the Treasury.

Officially, the money supply decreases when you send money to the US Treasury for any reason. This is because the US Treasury does not keep its money in commercial bank accounts but in an account at the Federal Reserve called the Treasury General Account (TGA). After receiving your check, the Treasury deposits it with the Fed in the TGA. The Fed then presents your check to your bank for payment. Your bank pays the Fed in cash reserves, which are transferred from the bank's reserve account at the Fed into the Treasury's TGA. Consequently, commercial bank deposits decline, and bank reserves move from your bank to the TGA. The TGA is "out" of the banking system, so the Fed's economists do not consider the Treasury's cash balances part of the money supply.

However, some non-Fed economists (including me) think this classification is dubious. After all, when a taxpayer sends money to the Treasury, this money is still available for the Treasury to spend at any time, so it meets our definition of money ("a commonly accepted medium of exchange") even though it is not in a commercial bank account. When the Treasury pays the government's bills (defense, entitlements, etc.), money from the TGA goes right back into the bank deposits of the payees, increasing the "official" money supply once again. Because it never loses its status as spendable money, I believe the TGA should be included in the broad money supply.[4]

All the previous examples involved transactions involving commercial banks and their customers. Next, let's examine how central bank transactions affect the money supply. We'll use the U.S. Federal Reserve to illustrate the principles, with the understanding that all central banks operate similarly.

How central banks determine the quantity of cash reserves

Every commercial bank needs an adequate quantity of cash reserves to meet depositors' cash withdrawals and to settle payment imbalances among different banks. Cash reserves provide credibility to the bank's deposit-creating operations. Banks as we know them could not exist without cash reserves, so it's critical to understand how central banks decide how many reserves are needed in the banking system.

In our post-gold banking industry, the standard money used as cash reserves by banks is no longer gold or any commodity. Instead, standard money consists of the paper Federal Reserve notes residing in the banks' vaults, plus the banks' digital cash reserve accounts at the Federal Reserve Bank. Although the customer-facing "front office" of commercial banks hasn't changed much, the "back office" that manages the creation of cash reserves is profoundly different from that of the gold standard. The most fundamental difference is that in the post-gold era, all standard money that the banks use as cash reserves is created *ex nihilo* by central banks. (*Ex nihilo* means "from nothing" in Latin; hence the title of this chapter.)

Chapter Two illustrated how the Fed creates cash reserves by purchasing assets from commercial banks. The Fed pays the bank by simply making a ledger entry and creating new cash reserves in the bank's account at the Fed. Like money creation at the commercial bank level, it's another *ex nihilo* moment. With only a few computer keystrokes, the Fed performs a feat of alchemy, creating new standard money that is a fiat imitation of gold.

Under a gold standard, there are both market and natural limitations on the amount of physical gold banks can access. However, in the post-gold era, what constraints (if any) affect the Ph.D.'s working at the Federal Reserve's computer terminals? Without the inherent market discipline provided by the gold standard, how do central bankers determine the appropriate level of cash reserves in the banking system? We will explore two explanations: the academic perspective and the more accurate one.

Some academic economists believe that central banks can control the money supply (expand or limit deposit creation) based on the amount of cash reserves they supply to banks. This theory is known as the "deposit multiplier" theory.

Under this theory, the central bank establishes a minimum "reserve requirement ratio" to determine the quantity of deposits the banks can create. For example, the Fed might set the reserve requirement ratio at 20%, which means the banks would be allowed to create deposits equal to five times their cash reserves, five being the "money multiplier." This theory assumes commercial banks will always want to lend right up to the point where they reach this regulatory limit.[5]

The Fed can then allegedly control the growth rate of the money supply by gradually growing cash reserves and occasionally adjusting short-term interest rates to stimulate or slow down bank lending. If the central bank wants to increase the money supply, it can buy bonds to provide more cash reserves to the commercial banks, and the banks will respond by lending more money to stay fully loaned up. If the Fed wants to decrease the money supply or slow its growth rate, it can sell bonds or slow down its bond purchases, thus reducing bank reserves, which will cause the banks to decrease their lending.

Or so the theory goes. These doctrines were assumed to be true in Samuelson's 1948 textbook and are still taught in college textbooks today.[6]

But there's a problem. The "deposit multiplier" theory does not describe how central banks really operate. In the post-gold era, central banks have always created enough cash reserves to keep pace with the commercial banks' creation of bank deposits. In reality, commercial banks first create deposits by lending and investing. The central bank then follows up by purchasing enough commercial bank assets to provide the banks with a comfortable level of cash reserves. In normal (non-crisis) economic times, commercial banks have been the leaders in money creation, while the central banks were the banks' supportive followers.

In contrast to the academics, central bankers have known for many years that the "money multiplier" theory is flawed. We know this because most central banks have either abolished minimum cash reserve requirements or set their reserve requirement ratio so low that it is effectively zero. The Fed finally eliminated all minimum reserve requirements for commercial banks in March 2020. However, this was only after years of setting reserve requirements so low that the reserve requirement ratio was never a constraint on bank lending. The Bank of England, the Bank of Canada, and the Bank of Australia had abandoned reserve requirements years earlier.[7]

Here is a realistic explanation from the Bank of England of how all modern central banks determine cash reserve levels in the post-gold era.

> In reality, neither are reserves a binding constraint on lending, nor does the central bank fix the amount of available reserves. As with the relationship between deposits and loans, the relationship between reserves and loans typically operates in the reverse way to that described in some economics textbooks. Banks first decide how much to lend depending on the profitable lending opportunities available to them — which will, crucially, depend on the interest rate set by the Bank of England. These lending decisions determine how many bank deposits are created by the banking system. The amount of bank deposits in turn influences how much central bank money [i.e., cash reserves] banks want to hold in reserve (to meet withdrawals by the public, make payments to other banks, or meet regulatory liquidity requirements), which is then, in normal times, supplied on demand by the Bank of England. [Brackets added.][8]

To put it another way, commercial banks' loan and bond portfolios lead the way, and central banks then create enough cash reserves to back them up. Most central bankers believe a lack of cash reserves should not constrain loan growth. So, they accommodate loan growth by purchasing enough assets (mostly sovereign bonds) from commercial banks to keep the reserve pile growing. Unlike under a gold standard, the depositors are not the final regulators of cash reserves. Instead, commercial bankers are in the driver's seat—or at least they were until the QE period, which we will discuss shortly.

In the post-gold era, bank reserves are not a significant constraint on lending, but this does not mean that bank lending has no limits. Commercial bankers face numerous market constraints, such as loan demand, interest rates, a limited pool of creditworthy borrowers, and the expenses associated with lending operations. As commercial entities, banks aim to generate profits for their shareholders while avoiding insolvency. Straying beyond these market limitations can result in low profitability and potential bankruptcy. Chapter Four will delve more deeply into the market constraints on bank lending.

The critical point is that the limited opportunity for profitable investments, not the level of cash reserves, constrains money creation at the commercial bank level. In practice, central banks always create enough reserves to accommodate the level of investment already made by their commercial banks. This accommodating policy encourages the gradual expansion of the money supply because commercial banks can always count on the central bank to create ample cash reserves.

In our post-gold era, central bankers can create both cash reserves and bank deposits. As we saw in Chapter Two, when the central bank makes an open-market purchase from a private investor (a nonbank), both bank reserves and new money are created *ex nihilo* in equal quantities.

Let's use a concrete example to illustrate how open-market purchases affect both cash reserves and the money supply. This example will be repetitive from Chapter Two; however, the transaction is presented in a different format to show the balance sheet effect on the private sector. The process is worth reviewing again as it is crucial to understanding modern money creation.

Let's say the Fed (or any central bank) wants to increase the money supply, perhaps because it believes the banks are not lending enough. It contacts a private, nonbank investor—an insurance company, pension fund, hedge fund, etc.—and asks if it wants to sell some of its Treasury bonds. If the investor agrees, the Fed must arrange payment. Private investors do not have accounts at central banks, so the Fed uses the investor's commercial bank as an intermediary. The Fed directs the investor's bank to create a deposit in the company's account; simultaneously, the Fed gives the bank new cash reserves to offset its new deposit liability.

Here is what the transaction looks like, recorded as simultaneous changes on the balance sheets of all three parties.

Open Market Purchase of $1000

Central Bank buys asset from private investor

Central Bank			Commercial Bank		
Assets	**Liabilities**		**Assets**	**Liabilities**	
+1000 Sovereign bond	+1000 cash reserves due banks		+1000 Cash reserves	+1000 Bank deposits *(investor's new money)*	

Private Investor	
Assets	**Liabilities**
-1000 Sovereign Bonds	
+1000 Bank deposits	

The investor gets new money in its bank account in exchange for its Treasury bond. The commercial bank gets new cash reserves to offset its new deposit liability owed to the investor. The central bank receives a new asset (the Treasury bond) and assumes a new liability in the cash reserves it owes to the commercial bank.

For most of the post-gold era, the Fed used this "open market purchase" mechanism to supply cash reserves to commercial banks to accommodate a growing banking industry. However, in the aftermath of the 2008–9 crisis, the Fed found that commercial banks were shrinking, not increasing, their loan books in response to widespread economic stress. As borrowers paid off their existing loans and banks reduced their new lending, bank deposits shrunk. Money was being extinguished faster than it was being created.

With the money supply shrinking, central bankers were deathly afraid of a 1930s-style deflationary spiral. In response, they adopted a radical new strategy of money creation. In 2009, Fed Chair Ben Bernanke began deploying the traditional tool of open market purchases on an unprecedented scale, a policy called "quantitative easing," or QE.[9]

QE was an unprecedented development in the post-gold banking era. From 2009 to 2022, QE Policy defined a new era of radical central bank activity.

The purpose of QE was to avoid a deflationary meltdown by creating money that the banks were unwilling to create. After the Great Financial Crisis of 2009, the Fed implemented this transaction on a massive scale, adding trillions of dollars in new deposits in the bank accounts of bond sellers, i.e., professional investors. In Chapter Five, we will examine the effects of this massive money-creation exercise in depth. For now, it is essential to understand that QE was simply the Fed engaging in open market purchases on a grand scale and over a long period.

In normal times, the main objective of open market purchases was to provide banks with cash reserves; money creation (new deposits) was a by-product. Under QE, these objectives were reversed: money creation became the central bank's primary objective, while cash reserves were the by-product.

The Bank of England spelled out the purpose of Quantitative Easing in a 2014 paper:

> … QE is intended to boost the amount of money in the economy directly by purchasing assets, mainly from non-bank financial companies. QE initially increases the amount of bank deposits those companies hold (in place of the assets they sell). Those companies will then wish to rebalance their portfolios of assets by buying higher-yielding assets, raising the price of those assets, and stimulating spending in the economy.
>
> As a by-product of QE, new central bank reserves are created. But these are not an important part of the transmission mechanism. This article explains how, just as in normal times, these reserves cannot be multiplied into more loans and deposits and how these reserves do not represent "free money" for banks.[10]

Erroneous beliefs about quantitative easing

Unfortunately, the purpose and methods of QE are often misunderstood. For example, a common error among "experts" who write about QE is that only bank reserves are increased when the Fed buys a bond in the open market, leaving the broad money supply (bank deposits) unaffected.

Here's an example of this error from a 2013 CNBC article written by a veteran currency trader who claimed the Fed does *not* create new money when it purchases bonds.

> So we can see that while the central bank's balance sheet does expand, the only impact in the private sector is to change the composition of the banks' balance sheets, exchanging bonds for reserves. The total assets of the private sector don't change. Hence, no money is being created any more than, say, if someone sold their stocks and put the money into bonds.[11]

The article claims that quantitative easing creates new bank reserves but does not create new money to spend in the economy. In other words, the author writes as if the banks are merely swapping Treasury bonds for new cash reserves, with no increase in commercial bank deposits. The author provides an accounting ledger purporting to show that when the Fed engages in QE, it buys bonds only from commercial banks. If that were true, the author would be correct because when central banks buy bonds from commercial banks, they pay in new cash reserves, which do not add to the money supply.

But that is not how QE works. Apparently, the author is (or was) unaware that under QE, the Fed buys nearly all its bonds from private investors using commercial banks as intermediaries, immediately increasing the money supply, as shown in the "T-account" table above. He also seems unaware that central banks' traditional "open market" purchases were *always* designed to create both new cash reserves *and* new bank deposits, even though creating deposits was not the primary objective.

To put it bluntly, QE was nothing more than traditional open-market bond purchases "on steroids," where money creation rather than reserve creation became the main event. Many financial experts missed this point.

Simple ignorance partially explains this widespread error, but there are possibly other reasons. For example, some analysts are obsessed with interest rates as the central bank's primary policy tool. By focusing solely on rates, they ignore the money-creation elephant in the room.

Another source of error could stem from a mistaken view of how banks create money. Under the traditional (Paul Samuelson) version of fractional reserve banking, bank deposits are "multiplied up" by repeatedly depositing and lending out cash. This error encourages an erroneous conclusion that QE was designed to stimulate lending by first flooding the commercial banks with reserves, after which the banks would "multiply" these reserves through increased lending to reverse the falling money supply. This was and still is a common belief of many economists and bankers, some recognized as experts or industry leaders. Under this view, QE failed because it did not induce the banks to increase their lending, even after the Fed stuffed them full of new cash reserves.

However, these spurious explanations are based on the erroneous belief that if banks get more reserves, they will automatically lend more because they will have "more reserves to lend out" or that banks somehow "multiply" their deposits by lending and re-lending the same cash.[12]

The confusion persists today, even among professional economists. For example, the influential Khan Academy, which relies on expert academic economists for its online curriculum, describes money creation this way: "When a bank makes loans out of excess reserves, the money supply increases. We can predict the maximum change in the money supply with the money multiplier."[13]

But banks do not "loan out excess reserves." Unless commercial banks are severely deficient in reserves in the first place, increasing their reserves will not encourage them to lend any more than pushing on a string will move an object it is tied to. Furthermore, the "money multiplier"—the ratio of bank deposits to cash reserves—is not a cause of money creation; it is mainly an artifact of bank lending activity.

The purpose of QE was straightforward. It was designed to create money the banks had refused to create. Here's the final word on QE from the eminent scholar, investor, and monetary analyst Russell Napier:

> The whole point of QE, at least initially in 2009, was to make sure that the contraction in bank credit that was destroying money was offset by a central bank creating money. The Fed created money by buying assets from financial institutions, primarily Treasury securities, and with little delay those financial institutions used their growing liquid funds to buy assets. The downward spiral in asset prices was prevented, and, with a lag, bank credit stabilized and slowly began to grow again as the U.S. private sector began to increase their borrowing.[14]

Under QE, the additional bank deposits, not the extra cash reserves, counted the most. QE did increase the banks' cash reserves, but this was incidental and not important as a source of "stimulus" to the economy. This makes sense when you realize that "stimulus" means more spending in the economy. But bank reserves cannot be spent, while bank deposits can.

As we'll see in later chapters, central banks eventually employed QE in the extreme, turning it into a weapon that radicalized monetary policy everywhere.

Our "fiat reserve" monetary system

As we have seen, in the post-gold era, the entire money supply, including currency-in-circulation, originates in the commercial banks, either because of the commercial bankers' investment decisions or the central bankers' policy decisions.

Although money is always created *in* commercial banks, it is not always created *by* commercial bankers. Until the Great Financial Crisis, commercial bankers made most of the investment decisions that grew the money supply. However, with the advent of QE, central bankers made decisions that vastly inflated the money supply.

How should we describe the money produced by this banking system? Some call it "fiat currency," but that is not entirely accurate. The modern banking system was designed to allow commercial bankers to make voluntary, market-based money-creation decisions, while the central bankers provided the cash reserves by fiat. For this reason, I believe our money creation system should be called a "fiat reserve" system instead of a pure "fiat money" system.

In the QE era, central banks radically expanded their influence by seizing much of the power to create money from the commercial banks. As I'll discuss in forthcoming chapters, we may be entering yet another new era in which politicians push central bankers aside to become more influential in money-creation decisions, ushering in more monetary mischief and moving us closer to full fiat money.

However, as of this writing, our banking system is bent but not entirely broken. In Chapter Four, we will concentrate on the positive side of money creation to see how lending by privately owned commercial banks can be productive, non-inflationary, and beneficial to everyone.

4 GOOD MONEY CREATION: THE CAPITALIST MONEY FACTORY

Money must be produced; the American Monetary Settlement; productive money creation; the Cantillon Effect; how markets regulate money production; how to know when money creation is legitimate

Money must be produced

In Ayn Rand's novel *Atlas Shrugged*, the great industrialist Francisco d'Anconia rightly proclaims that productive effort is a prerequisite for sound money.

> "So you think that money is the root of all evil?" said Francisco d'Anconia. "Have you ever asked what is the root of money? Money is a tool of exchange, which can't exist unless there are goods produced and men able to produce them. Money is the material shape of the principle that men who wish to deal with one another must deal by trade and give value for value. Money is not the tool of the moochers, who claim your product by tears, or of the looters, who take it from you by force. Money is made possible only by the men who produce. Is this what you consider evil?"
>
> —Francisco d'Anconia, the "Money Speech," *Atlas Shrugged*.

The connection between productivity and sound money goes both ways. Just as being productive is essential for creating a reliable currency, stable money is vital for a productive economy. This makes sense, considering that money needs to be produced just like other economic goods.

It's helpful to think of a commercial bank as a "capitalist money factory," as did the British monetary theorist Henry A. MacLeod, who wrote in 1894:

> A bank is therefore not an office for 'borrowing' or
> 'lending' money, but it is a Manufactory of Credit.[1]

In Chapter Three, we delved into money supply mechanics, revealing a curious truth: every dollar circulating in our economy owes its existence to a commercial bank deposit. Despite all dollars having the same purchasing power once in circulation, not all money is created equal. Sometimes, money creation plays a constructive role, fueling productivity and progress, while at other times, it can be downright harmful. The difference between the two can be understood by comparing money production to the production of physical goods.

Picture a bustling free-market factory churning out sought-after smartphones, delighting consumers and enriching livelihoods. This factory embodies productivity, converting labor and resources into products that enhance lives and drive profits.

Now consider a darker scenario: an authoritarian regime that forces the factory to produce goods that benefit the government and its cronies but that consumers would never buy voluntarily.

There are historical examples of precisely this. Several decades ago, in the Soviet Union, factories produced goods based on quotas assigned by a state central planning committee. To meet its production quota, a factory might produce vast quantities of ball bearings that no one needed, while ordinary consumer items, like toasters, were unavailable to the average person because the state planners had used up the factory's capacity. Millions of useless ball bearings might get the factory manager a pat on the head from the Central Planning

Committee, but not from the consumers unable to heat a slice of bread for breakfast.

Money creation in the money factories known as commercial banks mirrors this narrative. When aligned with market forces, money creation fosters prosperity. Conversely, government-directed money creation often creates economic discord with adverse consequences.

This chapter focuses on "good money creation" in the context of the American banking system, which I view as generally sound but imperfect. It explores how sound money emerges from the voluntary actions of bankers and borrowers within a free-market framework driven by profit incentives. This chapter aims to demonstrate that even an imperfect but mostly free banking system can produce *sound* money—money that is widely accepted and holds its value over time.

To understand money creation in America, we'll cover four key points.

First, we'll survey the historical roots of the American banking system, which, despite its imperfections, has served our economy well for many decades.

Second, we'll see why privately owned, profit-seeking banks tend to make productive, non-inflationary loans. In explaining productive lending, we'll introduce an important concept called the Cantillon Effect, which is associated with all money creation, both good and bad.

Next, we'll describe how a system of privately owned, profit-seeking banks limits and regulates money creation, preventing it from expanding out of control.

Finally, we'll engage in a practical exercise to help judge when modern money creation is legitimate or illegitimate.

The American monetary settlement

Based on new and vital work from monetary scholar Kevin Dowd, we now have a solid historical record of free banking systems worldwide. In his 2023 book, *The Experience of Free Banking*, Professor

Dowd provides numerous case studies demonstrating that unregulated banking systems with no government central bank produced
non-inflationary growth in the economies they served.[2]

Unfortunately, fully free banking was never a reality in America.
Aside from a few temporary regional experiments, banking in the
United States has always been semi-free. We live in a mixed economy
that relies on a partly free, partly regulated banking system to create
its money supply. To understand money creation in the contemporary world, we must understand its banking system, including its free
and un-free characteristics. To that end, a basic knowledge of U.S.
banking history is critical to understanding today's money creation
system.

The American banking system of the 19th century had two key
characteristics that allowed it to create productive, non-inflationary
money that was sound enough to power a dynamic, growing American economy through the 19th century and well into the 20th.

The first important feature was using gold, sometimes supplemented by silver, as standard money or legal tender, constituting full
and final payment. In a new nation founded on freedom and individual rights, gold and silver were unanimously accepted as money
without government coercion. By contrast, an early attempt at issuing fiat currency, the "Continentals" of 1795, proved so disastrous it
would be many decades before the national government attempted
such a thing again.

The second crucial historical feature was the private ownership of
commercial banks, which means a system of profit-motivated bankers lending to profit-motivated borrowers and depositors.

With some interruptions, notably the issuance of fiat "green-
backs" to fund Civil War debts, the USA adhered to the first half of
this successful formula (a gold standard) until the Federal Reserve
Act of 1913. As previously mentioned, from 1913 through 1971, the
US Federal Reserve employed a mix of gold and fiat money as bank
reserves to control the dollar's value. Then, in 1971, under Richard

Nixon's executive order, the USA fully abrogated all remnants of the gold standard and entered the post-gold banking era.

The first half of the American banking formula, the gold standard, had been selected on a free market premise. But now, in the post-gold era, our "standard money," the money commercial banks use as cash reserves, is created solely on the authority of the US Federal Reserve, on the autocratic premise that only government central planning can generate enough cash reserves to smooth out the booms and busts in a cyclical economy.

On the other hand, the second component of the American formula—the private ownership of the commercial bank "money factories"—has survived to this day. It's true that government regulators and legislators increasingly influence money creation decisions; however, except for extraordinary episodes like Quantitative Easing, most of the money used in the economy is still created by the investment decisions of profit-seeking lending officers working for privately owned banks.

I rely on Professor Lev Menand, a legal and monetary scholar at Columbia University, for a history of US banking. Menand's 2022 book, *The Fed Unbound*, explains the evolution of the US Federal Reserve Bank from its historical origins until its formal inauguration in 1913, then on to its expanding mission in the mid 20th century, culminating in its unprecedented and radical expansion of power following the Great Financial Crisis of 2009.

In Chapter Two, "Money and Banking in America," Menand summarizes Congress's thinking as it developed and refined the US banking system during the 19th-century formative years of American economic expansion.

> … A defining feature of the American economy, from the turn of the nineteenth century to the present day, is that it relies on investor-owned banks to create the vast majority of the money that people use. For the government to delegate this sort of power to private shareholders is no small matter, and for most of American

history it was a source of continuous political controversy. …

Proponents of investor-owned banks argued that the
profit motive was indispensable: if the government issued the whole money supply, politicians would inevitably fall prey to the temptation to create too much
money and the country's economy would eventually
stagnate.[3]

Like many legal and economic customs, the American practice of
using private banks to expand the money supply came from England.
During the 1690s, Parliament, the Crown, and London's top busi-
nessmen devised a kind of public-private partnership agreement on
money and banking. Parliament agreed to fix the amount of gold and
silver bullion in the national currency and promised it would not issue pounds without backing them with gold or silver. To expand the
money supply when needed, Parliament chartered a private, investor-owned corporation, the Bank of England, which it empowered to
issue banknotes (paper promises to redeem gold on demand) and to
maintain account entries known as deposits (ledger promises to redeem gold on demand). The Bank of England was set up as a privately owned bank, but it also functioned as a central bank, providing
settlement services for other smaller banks.

While quite successful, the English banking system was not applied directly in America because America lacked the political unity
required to impose a uniform banking system. The decades before
the Civil War witnessed bitter political disputes over the structure of
the banking industry. Some leaders, like Alexander Hamilton,
wanted a federal banking system with centralized regulation. Others,
like Andrew Jackson, favored decentralized and competing banks.
Despite the controversy, the American banking sector expanded
during the 19th century, successfully supporting the nation's economic growth.

Between about 1840 and 1880, through a series of legislative efforts at both the state and federal level, a system that Menand calls

"the American Monetary Settlement" took shape. The state legislators who initially developed its key features agreed with some of America's founders that granting politicians the power to expand the money supply would lead to a debased currency, corruption, and stagnation. This power, they believed, should be left in private hands.[4]

But they were also afraid that completely unregulated banking would allow influential politicians to concentrate financial power in the hands of a few unelected private banking executives. They feared that wealth concentrated in the financial centers, like New York and Boston, would dominate the country and impose undesirable political consequences. To counteract this danger, they attempted to spread the banks' money-creating power across different entities and a vast geography.

In 1864, Congress passed the National Bank Act, creating an office in the Treasury Department with the power to charter "national banks." National banks, which remain the backbone of our monetary system even today, had the exclusive power to expand the money supply based on the lending decisions of privately owned banks. Moreover, owning a bank was not overtly political—if you could comply with certain terms and conditions, you could apply for a banking license, which was permission to create money.

To avoid conflicts of interest, these bank charters prohibited banks from engaging in non-banking commercial activities; in other words, banks could not compete with the customers they loaned to. Bank charters were widely distributed geographically to avoid concentration in money centers and the influence of local partisan politics. The government also established broad supervisory oversight to ensure banks operated in the public interest. And of course, these banks held their cash reserves in the form of gold, or notes and bonds convertible to gold, because gold was universally recognized as standard money, the only form of full and final payment.

My interpretation is that during the evolution of this so-called "American Monetary Settlement," the better freedom-minded politicians implicitly recognized the essential difference between political power and economic power. They understood that political power derives from *force* while economic power comes from *choice*.

> In a free economy, where no man or group of men can use physical coercion against anyone, economic power can be achieved only by voluntary means: by the voluntary choice and agreement of all those who participate in the process of production and trade.[5]

Pure economic power relies on voluntary trade between parties acting in their own interest. It does not involve force; it can only be earned in the marketplace. But economic power contaminated by political power ceases to be true economic power. The result is a mix of freedom and control that inevitably moves towards less freedom and more control.

Few people today distinguish between economic and political power, but apparently, some of our influential 19th-century politicians got it. Grasping the difference allowed them to understand that money creation should not fall into the hands of the government.

America's economic success over the last 200 years is evidence that Menand's "American Monetary Settlement" empowered a viable if imperfect money-creation industry to nourish the American economy through many decades of impressive economic growth. The 19th-century American politicians who crafted this monetary settlement deserve credit for preserving a free-market orientation to money creation.

By contrast, an oppressive, government-controlled fiat currency system would undoubtedly have inhibited economic progress. We have numerous examples of currency blowups and hyperinflation in the fiat-currency countries of Latin America. The disastrous financial records of Argentina, Venezuela, Bolivia, and other countries are well known.

For our purposes, the main inference from America's banking history is that the mostly free banking system provided new money where and when needed to feed America's entrepreneurial business culture. Although many banks experienced trouble, American banks as a whole successfully accommodated a growing, westward-pushing economy. Even after the Federal Reserve Act of 1913, the harms done by the U.S. central bank could not prevent another century of positive economic growth. And even after the US went off the gold standard, Americans retained confidence in the US dollar. This could only have happened with a generally sound banking system.

Productive money creation

To illustrate how semi-free banks can still create sound money, let's "follow the money" from a hypothetical bank business loan. We have already seen how lending adds to the money supply. This exercise will demonstrate the positive role money creation can play in the economy.

Imagine a businessman, we'll call him Mr. Chow, who wants to start a new restaurant. Mr. Chow goes to Advance Bank to borrow the money he needs. From Chapters Two and Three, we already know how the loan works: Chow presents his business plan; Advance Bank agrees to the loan; Chow signs a promissory note; and Advance Bank purchases the promissory note by creating a new deposit in Chow's account, which Chow is free to spend on his new business.

From the bank's point of view, this loan will be successful only if it is profitable, i.e., if Mr. Chow pays back all the borrowed money on time, with interest. From Mr. Chow's point of view, the loan will be successful only if he can invest the borrowed money into a business that will generate enough revenue to repay the loan, plus earn a profit for Chow (and his shareholders, if he has any).

In other words, the bank's success depends on Chow's venture being profitable. How will Mr. Chow deploy his new money to make a profit? He applies his energy and intelligence to create a restaurant offering that will bring in new business, that is, a revenue stream. Chow buys or rents real estate. He hires workers. He invests in equipment. Chow buys all these things with new purchasing power that came into being only when the loan was made.

The Cantillon Effect

The loan gives him a temporary advantage over his competitors in that he can use it to out-bid them for the factors of production (rent, labor, and machinery) needed to build his new restaurant. After all, Chow has *new* money, and his competitors don't. Therefore, to some degree, Chow can buy labor and goods his competitors cannot afford.

Chow's temporary pricing advantage from the new money is called the "Cantillon Effect," named after the early 18th-century Irish-French economist Richard Cantillon. In his *"Essay on The Nature Of Trade In General,"* Cantillon pointed out that new money raises prices unevenly by awarding a competitive advantage to the first person who receives it.[6]

Let's pause our story to consider the Cantillon Effect. We need this concept now to grasp how Mr. Chow creates value in the economy, and we'll need it again in Chapter Five to explain both asset price bubbles and rapid increases in consumer prices.

Cantillon's essay's main point was that new money injected into the economy does not reach everyone simultaneously. New money increases the purchasing power of those who receive it first, enabling them to bid resources away from those who receive it later, after prices have risen.

Before Cantillon's essay, economists had some understanding of the Quantity Theory of Money, which states that prices rise when the quantity of money in the economy increases. The primitive quantity theory goes back to the Renaissance mathematician Nicolaus Copernicus in 1517 and has been cited by philosophers and economists ever since.[7]

The naïve or "mechanical" version of the quantity theory holds that the general price level is proportional to the quantity of money circulating: if the quantity of money doubles, the "mechanical" version predicts that all prices will double.

But this strictly proportional relationship between money and prices is purely imaginary. No one has ever observed that commodity prices fluctuate proportionally with the money supply because it never happens that way. We know the mechanical, or strictly proportional, quantity theory of money is nonsense.

But that doesn't mean the quantity theory is utterly devoid of insight. All else being equal, an increase in the quantity of money available for spending generally causes spending to increase somewhere, to some extent. As the biographer of John Law (the 18th century financier and grandmaster of asset bubbles) put it, "The new money needs something to buy."[8]

More specifically, the prices of the goods the new money is spent on will rise to a level higher than they would have without the injection of new money.

Cantillon's important contribution to the quantity theory of money was the understanding that an increase in money's quantity does raise prices, but not all prices at the same time or to the same extent. He expressed this principle with an interesting analogy:

> *The river, which runs and winds about in its bed, will not flow with double the speed when the amount of water is doubled.*[9]

Cantillon's unique insight was that market prices are derived by comparing the supply of the specific goods offered for sale to the demand for those goods—demand being the total quantity of money offered to buy these specific goods. It is not true, as the mechanical interpretation of the quantity theory implies, that all the goods in the economy are for sale against all the money in the economy all the time. The *particular goods* offered for sale and the quantity of money offered for them determine the prices of these (and only these) goods.

Cantillon pointed out that the first recipients of new money will benefit the most from it because, having more money, they will be able to spend money on the goods *they* want before their prices increase. In doing so, the new money recipients will increase demand

and thus bid up the prices of these goods at the expense of those who do not have the new money.

We can understand the Cantillon Effect intuitively by considering how prices might react near a gold mine that has made a new discovery. With abundant new gold circulating in the local trading area, the price of a single egg might rise to a dollar near the mining camp, while hundreds of miles away, the price is unchanged. This is because new money is spent first by the first recipients with specific spending preferences. The new money is then passed on to other new parties, each with a unique spending preference. As in Cantillon's river analogy, the new money raises the prices of various goods unevenly via successive transactions over distance and time, as its pricing effects change along the way.

As a result, relative prices will change, resources will be reallocated, and income will be redistributed during the interval between money creation and its complete diffusion into the economy. Cantillon pointed out, for example, that the original recipients of new money often enjoy higher living standards at the expense of later recipients, which sounds a lot like what happened to the professional investment community during Quantitative Easing.

Economists sometimes cite the Cantillon Effect as "inflationary," but it is important to note that the phenomenon is associated with all new money creation, both good and bad. The Cantillon Effect is the natural consequence of introducing new money into an economy, just as the changing flowing water pattern is a natural consequence of adding more water to a river. It is a feature, not a bug, of money creation. It is neither good nor bad; it just describes how people will likely behave when they get new money.

Furthermore, in typical, competitive lending, the Cantillon effect from any one loan is small, perhaps even unnoticeable, when the quantity of new money issued is small relative to the total spending in a large industry or an economy.

Back to our entrepreneurial hero, Mr. Chow. According to the Cantillon Effect, Chow's new money gives him a slight temporary advantage in acquiring scarce factors of production. But he also has a big challenge. Chow has to generate a new income stream to pay for his expensive real estate, equipment, and labor purchases, pay his bills, feed his family, and make enough profit to repay the loan. To do this, he must compete for his customers' money by offering a product they want more than the goods they already spend their money on. After all, the customers have only so much money to spend, so buying Chow's product means *not* spending money on something else. This means Chow must make a *better* product— cheaper, faster, friendlier, more delicious, whatever combination of values his customers will pay for. To repay the loan, Chow must create these kinds of improvements when he invests the new money.

Note that Mr. Chow is not just competing against other restaurants but ultimately against all his customers' economic preferences. For example, if his product is good enough, some people might even choose to save or invest less money so that they can eat more meals at his establishment. Chow's product might be so good that he expands the entire restaurant market, causing people to eat less at home and more in restaurants. This was the true story of McDonald's, which accounts for over 25% of the worldwide fast-food market today.[10]

The question might arise: Does Advance Bank's creation of new money confer an unfair advantage on Mr. Chow? Some economists criticize bank money creation, pointing out that Chow did not receive the real accumulated savings of voluntary lenders. Instead, he received new claims on wealth—new purchasing power, created out of thin air. Thus, they claim that Chow received "something for nothing," making the creation of bank money illegitimate.

However, the bank's new money grant to Mr. Chow was not an arbitrary gift. To get the loan, Chow had to earn the bank's trust and compete against other borrowers, and now he must earn revenue from the public to make a profit. So yes, Mr. Chow has a temporary advantage in purchasing power, but he earned this advantage.

Accordingly, Chow did not get "something for nothing" when the bank created new money. As we'll see in a moment, bank loans are a limited resource, just like all other factors of production, due to built-in feedback mechanisms in the loan market. Chow had to compete hard against all other potential borrowers to get this resource, so there is nothing "unfair" about what has happened.

Moreover, if the loan is successful, Mr. Chow will pay it back in total, extinguishing the money created for him by the bank. Over the full life of the loan, from the time it is granted until it is paid off, no net new money will be created; however, the new or improved products Chow created will still be there as an addition to the economy's reservoir of real wealth.

Chow's success improves his entire industry. If customers choose Chow's new restaurant, they may spend less on older restaurants, thus requiring the old establishments to improve if they want to stay in business. Because of Chow's success, the entire industry is held to a new, higher standard of excellence.

Chow's success also improves the overall economy by putting other less desirable restaurants out of business. Less efficient companies that can no longer satisfy consumer demand will be unable to generate enough revenue to pay their costs and earn a sustainable profit. As the marginal players exit the industry, their labor, plant, and equipment can be redeployed to projects the market deems more important.

What's happening here is the process Joseph Schumpeter called "creative destruction," in which companies that can no longer satisfy the changing desires of consumers are liquidated, freeing up their economic resources to be put to better use. The story of Mr. Chow shows how bank lending helps to facilitate creative destruction, an essential process in any advancing economy.

Here is Schumpeter on how money creation gives the creative entrepreneur access to factors of production:

> [C]redit is essentially the creation of purchasing power
> for the purpose of transferring it to the entrepreneur,

but not simply the transfer of existing purchasing power. … By credit, entrepreneurs are given access to the social stream of goods before they have acquired the normal claim to it. And this function constitutes the keystone of the modern credit structure.[11]

Richard Werner makes a related point, emphasizing why new money need not cause inflation:

When bank credit is used for productive investments, such as the implementation of new technologies, measures to increase productivity, or the creation of new goods and services (whose value is higher than the mere sum of their inputs, thus adding value), then such new money creation—which always happens when banks grant credit—will not result in any form of over-all inflation—neither consumer price inflation nor asset price inflation. This is because the new purchasing power created is used to produce higher value-added output and hence the extra demand due to the money creation is met with a higher supply.[12]

Mr. Chow's restaurant project is a clear example of "good" money creation, that is, money creation that results in productive, non-inflationary growth. However, good loans are not restricted to entrepreneurial startups like Chow's. Banks lend successfully against prospective future cash flows from many different sources. These include short-term business loans, mortgage loans, automobile loans, and even direct-to-consumer loans, like Andy's in Chapter Two. The proceeds from these loans are not always invested in a project that will create a new income stream but are often paid back with funds from an existing income stream that both the lender and borrower believe will be sustained long enough to pay off the loan.

Looking back on Chapter Two, was Andy's loan productive? After all, Andy is spending new, borrowed money on airline tickets and hotels. The Cantillon Effect says this spending will raise the price of the goods he purchases. Isn't this loan inflationary, and how can anyone say it is "productive"?

Andy borrowed money today to take a vacation, knowing he would receive a bonus shortly, allowing him to pay off the loan. The loan allowed Andy to bring his vacation from the future to the present. He, therefore, was able to match his reward with his successful work production. Loans like Andy's are undoubtedly productive in the eyes of the borrower in that they enhance the borrower's quality of life. A better quality of life might very well incentivize the borrower to be even more productive by working harder and earning more money in the future. So overall, we have to conclude that even consumer lending, as long as it is profitable and sustainable, supports production and may lead to future productivity improvements.

How markets regulate money creation

The architects of the American Monetary Settlement understood that a privately owned, profit-driven banking system cannot create unlimited quantities of money. Unlike state-sponsored central banks, commercial banks must react to market forces when they originate money. Even in the post-gold era, commercial banks operate in a lending market that places inherent limitations on money creation. Let's delve into these limitations further.

Firstly, the limited availability of profitable lending opportunities constrains bank credit expansion. Worthy producers like Mr. Chow are scarce. In an economy where banks are incentivized to lend profitably, their capacity to extend credit is limited by their borrowers' real economic potential. Initially, banks channel new funds to the most creditworthy applicants, gradually followed by less-qualified ones. As the volume of loans increases, the creditworthiness of the remaining borrowers diminishes, establishing a natural limit on further credit creation.

Secondly, lending limitations arise from depositors' inclination (households and businesses) to retain cash, often called their "demand" for money. As described by George Reisman, "demand for money" characterizes the extent to which individuals wish to maintain cash balances relative to their incoming revenue and expenses. The greater the demand for money, the greater the cash balance they want to hold relative to their revenues and expenses, and vice versa. Anything that induces individuals to hold more money will cause them to spend less out of income, and vice versa. If depositors want to increase their cash holdings, they might be willing to borrow at higher interest rates to acquire more cash, potentially boosting borrowing and expediting new money creation. On the other hand, they might be in a "pay-off" mode, which means they want to pay down their debt, and not take on new debt. In that case, the creation of new money would slow down.[13]

Furthermore, there is a limit on the demand for loans based on the market's capacity to repay them. Repayment of loans requires a stable income source. Therefore, the total income flow within the economy (typically represented by national income or Gross Domestic Product or GDP) imposes a cap on the cumulative debt that can be extended against it.

Finally, despite central bank bailouts and guarantees, depositor behavior still plays a role in constraining credit creation within banks. Depositors can transfer their funds from banks deemed as high-risk. This shift can occur through cash withdrawals or investing in Treasury bills, both of which reduce aggregate bank deposits. Individual banks are bound by the necessity to hold prudent cash reserves; however, reserves move when deposits move. When deposits leave a bank, reserves diminish accordingly, curbing the banks' capacity for loan expansion. To attract fresh deposits and thereby gain new cash reserves, banks may be compelled to offer higher interest rates to depositors. This heightens banking costs, subsequently requiring higher interest rates on loans, which exert a restrictive influence on lending activities at the margin.

Private ownership generally incentivizes banks to make good loans with a carrot and a stick. The "carrot" is the incentive to earn profits, the same as any privately owned business. The bank's shareholders want a steady income stream from their invested capital, so they will try to steer a prudent course of good lending to maintain that earnings stream. The "stick," on the other hand, is the specter of bankruptcy that would inevitably follow excessive loan losses. Bankruptcy consequences include financial loss for shareholders, damage to the institution's reputation, and potential legal repercussions, all serving as a strong deterrent against taking on undue risks.

The inherent market discipline in the lending sector means it is possible to have sound money even under a system that supplies fiat cash reserves, as long as there is some reasonable restriction on the cash reserves provided. Most of the economic history of the United States in the post-gold era validates this view. For the most part, economic growth and prosperity have prevailed in the fiat reserve era. This could not have happened under a fundamentally unsound money production system. Sustained unsound money production would have led us down the path of catastrophic inflation, monetary crises, economic stagnation, and mass poverty—in other words, the financial path of Venezuela, Argentina, Bolivia, Cuba, Zimbabwe, Hungary, and other countries with fully fiat currencies.

Understanding government power and human behavior reveals the inherent vulnerabilities of our fiat reserve system. Unlike commercial banks, the Fed has the legal power to create unproductive money without facing repercussions from the market. Only Fed officials' good sense and wisdom can control bureaucratic money-creation impulses. But isn't it unrealistic to depend on a permanent succession of "wise rulers" who will let the market do its job? When government officials are granted nearly unlimited power, we should expect them to use it.

When some economically significant company comes on hard times and can no longer get the loans necessary to stay afloat, the bureaucrat wants to ride to the rescue. He thinks the market is failing and feels compelled to provide credit. To an interventionist, there is no "creative" destruction. Seeing only destruction, he wants to stop it. He thinks he can save uncompetitive, dying industries from their natural demise. This is something like trying to save the rotting flesh of a patient with gangrene. At some point, the market must excise the putrid tissue or the disease will continue to fester.

In recent decades, especially since the introduction of Quantitative Easing in 2009, the Fed has been increasingly willing to prop up failing businesses by creating new, cheap money. But this policy only prolongs the problem and makes it worse. The market is fully capable of self-correction. If the Fed did not step in with unlimited new cash every time a bank went under, wouldn't people learn to read a bank balance sheet and think carefully before they trusted the bank with their deposits?

Of course, they would, and they used to do this. There is good historical evidence that the banking industry, indeed the entire economy, can recover from its periodic troubles without central bank intervention.

Several American examples from the early 20th century point in this direction. One prominent example is the banking panic of 1907, characterized by falling asset prices, bank runs, and widespread bankruptcies of companies needing credit. How was this debacle resolved without a central bank? We can thank financier J. Pierpont Morgan, who organized his fellow New York bankers to provide liquidity to troubled but deserving banks.[14]

Another example is the severe post-war depression of 1920–21. In that crisis, U.S. GDP declined by 24 percent (nine percent real), stock prices fell 46%, wholesale prices dropped 37%, and unemployment soared to 15%. The Fed had existed since 1913 but was not yet organized to take decisive action. Still, the economy healed itself, as it always does. After a sharp 18-month depression, stocks, consumer prices, and employment bounced back as economic growth resumed. For details, see *The Forgotten Depression*, by James Grant, who writes that "constructive federal inaction" was key to a happy crisis resolution.[15]

Practical exercises in judging money creation

This chapter opened with a quotation from a fictional hero who reminded us that money is a noble tool that enables productive trade. However, trade is only possible for those who can produce something valuable, such as labor, commodities, property, or a means of production. Economic trade is the domain of producers. That is what Francisco D'Anconia meant when he said money is made possible only by those who produce.

When the government causes banks to make unproductive loans, thus bestowing purchasing power on the undeserving, it is counting on the production of others to confer value on its fraudulent money. The government gets away with selective instances of unproductive money creation only to the extent that real, legitimate production is going on somewhere else. After all, the plunderer needs something or someone to plunder.

However, because all modern money creation occurs in commercial banks, all money creation looks the same on the surface. The government can camouflage unproductive money creation under the veil of public investment that appears legitimate. This is why you need to look beneath the treetops, down deeper into the forest, to judge whether any individual act of money creation is productive and non-inflationary, i.e., legitimate.

Here are three simple questions to help decide if any particular bank loan or investment—that is, any act of money creation—is legitimate.
1. Who decided to create the new money?
2. Who benefits from the new money?
3. Was force or fraud employed in creating the new money?

Example One: Let's consider Mr. Chow's loan situation. Answering our three questions reveals that his loan was indeed legitimate. The loan agreement between Advance Bank and Mr. Chow was a sound business decision. The loan proved beneficial for all involved parties, including Mr. Chow, his customers, the bank, and even the broader economy—a classic "win-win" scenario. And clearly, no force or fraud was involved in the transaction.

Example Two: Let's re-consider Andy's consumer loan from Chapter Three. He borrowed $2000 for a vacation and promptly re-paid it upon receiving his bonus. The bank's decision to approve the loan benefitted the bank, Andy, and the businesses where Andy spent the funds. There were no signs of fraud or coercion. This loan, too, passes the smell test for legitimacy.

Example Three: Consider a scenario where Advance Bank purchases a Treasury bond from a private investor for investment purposes. The goal is to acquire a profitable income-generating asset. This transaction leads to the infusion of new funds into the bond seller's bank account. The bank and the bond seller engage in this transaction for their own benefit, believing it advantageous. Unless the government mandated the purchase, there are no indications of coercion or fraud. Despite my wariness toward banks creating money to buy government bonds, in this instance, I believe this transaction is legitimate because neither the buyer nor the seller of the bond were subject to force or fraud.

In some banana republics, like Argentina in the early 2000s, the monetary authority (the finance ministry or central bank) *requires* commercial banks to purchase government bonds and "monetize" sovereign debt to fund government spending. ("Monetizing debt" occurs when governments require their country's banks to create new money to buy the government's bonds.) As of this writing, U.S. commercial banks are not forced to buy government bonds to fund the government. However, as we will see in Chapter Seven, they are increasingly being nudged or "encouraged" to do so. We cannot rule out the possibility that the U.S. Treasury will someday *require* commercial banks to finance government deficits by purchasing government bonds. Such a requirement would be illegitimate due to its coercive nature.

Example Four: Next, let's explore a scenario in which the Federal Reserve Bank of New York instructs Advance Bank to execute an open-market purchase as part of a Quantitative Easing program.

First, let's review once again how this works. The Fed offers to buy a Treasury bond from a private investor, say a pension fund, which agrees to the transaction. To complete the transaction, the Fed directs Advance Bank, where the pension fund already has an account, to create a deposit in the pension fund's account. (This is the exact point where new money is created.) Simultaneously, the Fed gives new cash reserves to Advance Bank. The pension fund has swapped its bond for a bank deposit, which it will spend to buy a new investment. The Fed has added an asset, the bond, and a liability called "reserves due to Advance Bank." Advance Bank has added an asset, cash reserves, and this asset is offset by a new liability to the pension fund—a deposit, which is, of course, new money for the pension fund.

Who decided to do this transaction? The Fed made the "offer," and the pension fund accepted. The commercial bank had no choice — it was *directed* by its regulator, the Fed, to participate in this transaction. Who benefits? The Fed benefits because it achieves its policy objective. The government benefits because the Fed has monetized some of its debt, opening the window to issuing even more debt. The pension fund benefits because it now has new money for further investment. Advance Bank perhaps receives some benefit because it earns a small fee or markup on the transaction, and it now has more cash reserves, even though it may soon lose them if the new deposit leaves the bank.

Was force involved? The Fed directed Advance Bank to participate, so at least "soft" coercion was involved. How about fraud? The Fed caused the pension fund to get new money, increasing the total amount of money sloshing around in the investment universe. Moreover, this transaction was but one small transaction in a program designed to create hundreds of billions in new money. Through no merit or effort of its own, the pension fund received an advantage in purchasing new investments via the Cantillon Effect. Upon getting the new money, the pension fund can outbid other investors for valuable financial assets simply because it was invited to the QE party while other investors (like you and me) were not. Unlike a productive loan or bond purchase, QE creates new money to subsidize the professional investment community. Because it is done in great size, QE causes asset prices to rise, transferring more purchasing power to all asset owners. The transaction also puts downward pressure on bond yields because as bond prices rise, bond yields (interest rates) must decline, making it harder for the average person to accumulate savings.

The bottom line is that this transaction was part of a massive program that benefited not only the pension fund but all asset owners at the expense of those who did not receive the subsidy. QE is specifically designed to raise prices, not to award credit to productive enterprises.

The central bank instigated this act of money creation. But central banks do not produce anything. They pay for assets by invoking their legal privilege to conjure new money. However, unlike commercial banks, there are no market-based limits on how much money they create. Is this a form of theft? Is it fraudulent? Is it deceptive if most people don't understand it? I know where I stand on these questions. What do you think?

Example Five: Consider the hypothetical scenario, which, though fictional, is plausible. In response to recent legislative changes introduced by Congress, the Federal Reserve enforces new lending criteria applicable to all U.S. commercial banks. The new legislation restricts lending to fossil fuel enterprises and promotes lending to environmentally friendly, or "green," energy firms by providing tax breaks and loan guarantees paid for by taxpayers. Enticed by these incentives, Advance Bank extends a loan to a green energy company that it would not have financed absent the new legislation and lending rules.

Who authorized this loan? Congress and the Federal Reserve un-equivocally decided to lend, compelling Advance Bank to act in a manner it would not have independently chosen. Who benefits from this setup? Green energy companies gain an advantage through the Cantillon Effect by getting loans that would not have been available in a competitive market. Advance Bank benefits if the green energy firm can repay the loan, a feat made possible only by taxpayer subsidies. On the flip side, other clients of Advance Bank, including fossil fuel companies, now face a more challenging borrowing environment, needing to secure funding from alternative sources at higher costs.

Is there coercion or deception involved? The legislation mandating this loan unambiguously exerts coercion by dictating the loan terms. The loan stemmed from a Congressional decree rather than the bank's volition. Furthermore, the government's pretense that the green loan is economically and socially advantageous may constitute intellectual dishonesty. If the lending goal is a sound investment producing a loan-liquidating income stream, this loan is not legitimate.[16]

The last two examples illustrate a significant trend we identified in Chapter Three. Under our system, the money supply is always created in the commercial banks; however, money creation decisions are increasingly influenced, or even forced, by central bankers, bureaucrats, and legislatures. The relationship between commercial banks and their regulators is like a firing squad: the soldiers with rifles (commercial banks) pull the trigger, but the commanding officers (monetary authorities) are responsible for the outcome.

In the next chapter, we'll examine the causes of two real-world asset bubbles that caused much harm and destruction. This will be a journey to the "dark side" of money creation, enabling us to see the damage done by central banks and other monetary authorities when they seize the authority to make money-creation decisions.

5   BAD MONEY CREATION: THE STATIST WRECKING BALL

The malignance of government money creation;
The real meaning of inflation; The 1980s Japanese bubble;
The QE bubble; Pandemic QE and CPI inflation; Summary

The malignance of government money creation

Chapter Four illustrated that money creation in the hands of private, competitive banks is productive and non-inflationary. By contrast, this chapter's theme is that money creation caused by government actions or policies brings about unwanted price increases as well as many other adverse economic consequences.

In pursuit of this theme, this chapter has three tasks.

First, we will define inflation in a way that will improve our understanding of the entire inflation phenomenon. Inflation is properly defined not as an increase in prices but as an *increase in the quantity of money caused by government action*, and I will fully justify this definition.

Next, armed with this definition, we'll examine two important inflationary events from recent history—events that did not immediately cause conspicuous increases in consumer prices and are therefore not even called "inflationary" by most economists.

The first great inflation event was the famous Japanese asset bubble of the 1980s, which culminated in a severe financial crash in 1989 that Japan has still not fully recovered from, almost 35 years later.

The second event is the era of Quantitative Easing, initiated by the U.S. Federal Reserve under Chairman Ben Bernanke in 2009 and lasting until mid-2022. This unprecedented monetary expansion caused massive asset price increases followed by the most significant surge in consumer prices in 40 years, with many other adverse effects that still have not been fully understood by mainstream financial pundits.

Finally, based on these two case studies, we'll draw some critical general conclusions about inflation's consequences.

The real meaning of inflation

"Inflation" is widely regarded as the foremost economic problem of our time, but inflation means different things to different people.

According to my *Oxford English Dictionary*, the *OED*, dated 2002, "inflation" is defined as:

> (Unduly) great expansion or increase; *spec.* (a) **economics** (undue) increase in the quantity of money circulating, in relation to the goods available for purchase; (b) **popularly** inordinate general rise in prices leading to a fall in the value of money.

The first definition (a) is close to my own: an "undue" increase in the quantity of money. However, notice that this is much different from the second popular definition—an "inordinate general rise in prices"—which is closer to the definition most economists use today.

In recent years, economists at the Fed and other central banks have narrowed the popular definition even further. They now say inflation is not just an increase in general prices but in "consumer prices," as measured by their official price index. The Fed uses the Personal Consumption Expenditures" index (PCE), which is similar to the well-known Consumer Price Index (CPI). For example, if the PCE increases year-over-year by four percent, the Fed will declare that "the inflation rate is four percent" or just "inflation is four percent."

Moreover, the Fed now says a PCE rise of over or under 2% per year is undesirable, while an increase of 2% is desirable. So, consumer price inflation of 2% is good, they say, while rates higher or lower than that are not good.

But is this definition helpful in conceiving inflation? Does it further our understanding of how we experience an "inflationary" economy? Does it help us understand price increases? In other words, does defining inflation as an "increase in consumer prices" serve a positive cognitive purpose? "The purpose of a definition," said philosopher Ayn Rand, "is to distinguish a concept from all other concepts and thus to keep its units differentiated from all other existents."[1]

"Differentiation" requires identifying the essential or most fundamental characteristics of the concept we are considering. To take a classic example, we define "man" as the "rational animal" because our rational faculty fundamentally differentiates human beings from all other animals. If we said, "Man is the mammal with an opposing thumb and forefinger," that might be true, but it would tell us practically nothing about the *essential* difference between a human and an ape.

To illustrate the problem further, what would you think of a doctor who, noticing his patient has a high body temperature, immediately diagnoses "fever" and plunges the patient into an ice bath? He would lower the patient's body temperature all right but also might kill him in the process. Defining the patient's illness as an increased body temperature obscures understanding of the problem. Any doctor who treated a sick patient this way would be rejected as a quack, as he is assuming a mere symptom is a fundamental problem.

Instead, we'd expect our doctor to go beyond taking the patient's temperature. He would conduct a battery of tests and notice all other relevant symptoms the tests reveal. Relying on his knowledge and experience, he would find the common denominator, the cause, of all the symptoms he observes. Perhaps he would diagnose dehydration, a bacterial infection, a virus, or a cancer. These underlying causes would determine how he defines the disease, rather than dismissing it as a "fever."

In the same way, if we define inflation simply as an "increase in consumer prices," then anything that increases consumer prices must be a cause of inflation. We then lose the ability to differentiate between price increases caused by an increase in the quantity of money, by a decrease in the quantity of goods sold, or by a mere change in consumer preferences. For instance, one could claim that price increases due to hurricanes or earthquakes, which cause temporary shortages of goods and raise prices in the short term, are an example of "inflation," and therefore in the same category as price increases caused by a flood of new money. Obviously, the two are very different. Should both be called "inflation"?

This kind of muddy definition provides cover for politicians and economists to blame inflation on supply chain disruptions related to the COVID pandemic, or on energy shortages caused by Russia's invasion of Ukraine. This is convenient, because if they can blame the inflation on some external event, they can disavow responsibility for it. They can also more easily justify rationing or price controls under the guise of "fighting inflation," as if it is some kind of natural disaster instead of something of their own making.

As an example, here is an economist from a prestigious investment bank, Morgan Stanley, who literally blamed "inflation" on a cyclical weather pattern. The headline reads, "A Headwind for Policy Normalization: Morgan Stanley Adds El Nino to List Of Inflation Risks." The article then stated, "El Nino most directly affects consumer inflation as food and energy commodities prices pass through."[2]

Morgan Stanley feels this is valid because they define inflation as increased consumer prices. Bad weather can temporarily raise the prices of some items, so an El Nino must be inflationary!

Many years ago, Ludwig von Mises deplored this "dangerous semantic confusion":

> There is nowadays a very reprehensible, even danger-
> ous, semantic confusion that makes it extremely diffi-
> cult for the non-expert to grasp the true state of affairs.
> Inflation, as this term was always used everywhere and
> especially in this country, means increasing the quantity
> of money and bank notes in circulation and the quan-
> tity of bank deposits subject to check. But people today
> use the term "inflation" to refer to the phenomenon
> that is an inevitable consequence of inflation, that is the
> tendency of all prices and wage rates to rise. The result
> of this deplorable confusion is that there is no term left
> to signify the cause of this rise in prices and wages … .
> Those who pretend to fight inflation are in fact only
> fighting what is the inevitable consequence of inflation,
> rising prices. Their ventures are doomed to failure be-
> cause they do not attack the root of the evil.[3]

If it's misleading to define inflation as an increase in consumer prices, what is a good definition? The *OED* says it is an "undue" in-crease in the quantity of money, which implies "unnecessary" or "un-just." How do we determine what is "undue"?

In our Chapter Four discussion of the Cantillon effect, we learned that any increase in the quantity of money spent on specific goods will tend to elevate those specific prices above what would have oc-curred in the absence of the increased money. However, we also saw that money creation in a free market is self-limiting due to natural market forces. This means banks operating in a free market cannot create an "undue" amount of money, at least not for a prolonged pe-riod, because any tendency toward excessive expansion will self-cor-rect.

If banks operating in a free market cannot create excessive money, we are left with the fact that only government intervention in the banking system can enable a prolonged or persistent increase in the quantity of money. This fact leads us to a better, more useful definition of inflation, developed by George Reisman in his great work *Capitalism*.

> Inflation itself is not rising prices, but an unduly large
> increase in the quantity of money, caused, almost invar-
> iably, by the government. In fact, a good definition of
> inflation is: *an increase in the quantity of money caused
> by the government.* A virtually equivalent definition is
> an increase in the quantity of money in excess of the
> rate at which a gold or silver money would increase.[4]

This is the most fundamental definition of inflation I know of, with all credit to Professor Reisman. I also use the term "unproductive money creation," which I believe is roughly equivalent to "money creation caused by the government." I say this because there can, of course, be individual instances of unproductive money creation (i.e., bad loans) in a free market, but bad loans cannot be a lasting or systematic characteristic of free-market banking because of its self-correcting nature.

In addition to unwanted price increases, there are other important consequences of excessive money creation caused by the government, which we are about to explore with historical examples. The purpose of this excursion into financial history will be to spotlight some of the many malignant consequences of government-caused money creation. In reviewing this history, we'll be like the good doctor who notices his patient has a temperature but delves deeper and discovers many adverse effects arising from a fundamental cause. Some of these effects are unseen at first, and some of them are even more destructive than rising consumer prices, but all of them arise from unproductive money creation caused by the government's policies or actions.

To appreciate the damage that government money-creation decisions can do, let's examine two prominent, modern examples of asset bubbles that occurred over an extended period. As we dive in, recall the Cantillon Effect, which tells us that prices will go up first at the point where the new money is spent. If the new money is spent first on investments, like commercial real estate or stocks, these prices will rise first. If the new money is spent first on consumer items like airline tickets or refrigerators, consumer prices will rise first.

The 1980s Japanese bubble

As our first example of bad money creation, let's review the Japanese property and stock market bubble of the 1980s, examining both its causes and effects.

Japan Stock Market Index (JP225) 37664 -1438 (-3.68%)

(data as of August 15, 2024. TradingEconomics)
https://tradingeconomics.com/japan/stock-market

This is a chart of a price index of the 225 largest stocks in the Japanese stock market. Notice that Japanese stock prices went almost vertical in the mid-1980s, peaking in late 1989. The market then crashed abruptly. It took until 2024, nearly 35 years, for Japanese stocks to recover to their 1989 price level. If you watch stock prices you know this is one of the great asset bubbles in financial history. To tell the story of this famous bubble, I will rely mainly on the work of Professor Richard Werner, an Oxford economist I hold in high esteem.

First, a little background on Richard Werner. Werner is a remarkable scholar who speaks and writes fluently in German, English, and Japanese. Prior to and during the Japanese bubble, he was an investment analyst covering the Japanese market for the investment firm Jardine Fleming. In the early 1990s, he conducted research inside the Bank of Japan. In 2003, he published an explanation of the Japanese financial bubble, *Princes of the Yen*. Fourteen years after the stock market crash, Japan was still reeling from its devastating effects, but no one seemed to understand what had happened. *Princes* provided the explanation, becoming a Japanese national best-seller, for a while outselling even *Harry Potter*. There is also a video version of *Princes*, available online, which I highly recommend, and which is a major source in the account that follows.[5]

We start the story with some basics on the structure of Japan's financial industry. Following World War II, Japan's financial regulations and monetary policy were governed by the same system that had run its wartime economy. Japan's Ministry of Finance (MOF), roughly equivalent to the U.S. Treasury Department, oversaw fiscal matters, while the Bank of Japan (BOJ), the central bank, took care of monetary policy. Under the law at the time, the BOJ answered to the MOF for most policy matters, including interest rate targets. MOF engaged in a fair amount of central economic planning by developing an industrial policy. This was different from financial governance in the Western nations, which did not officially engage in central economic planning.

Within just a few decades after the war, Japan staged an amazing economic recovery. The BOJ played a key role in the initial recovery by creating enough new cash reserves to buy out the banks' holdings of worthless war bonds, putting the banks on a solid financial footing. The BOJ created these new reserves like all central banks in the post-gold era: it conjured cash reserves out of thin air and used them to purchase bankrupt bonds or bad loans at face value, thus neutralizing and monetizing this debt.

The basic pre-war financial system was still intact but with an important difference: Japan's system of allocating bank lending to favored industries, which had built a war-fighting machine capable of projecting power around the world, was redirected to a peacetime footing. During the decades following the war, the BOJ continued its wartime policy of allocating credit to its subsidiary banks, a system known as "window guidance." Under this system, the BOJ gave its member banks quotas for lending, dictating (or strongly encouraging) how much each bank could lend and which economic sectors (steel, autos, chemicals, etc.) should receive the new money. There was some room for flexibility, but the BOJ fundamentally controlled where the new money flowed, especially at the industry sector level.

This was the war economy system adapted to the production of consumer goods for export and domestic consumption. A 1951 amnesty on war criminals returned most of the banking bureaucracy to their previous positions, so the system retained its technical banking expertise. Simply put, the Japanese wartime "money factory" (the commercial banks) converted from financing tanks and submarines to financing factories for peacetime goods.

Japan flourished under this system during the 1950s, 1960s, and most of the 1970s, and its citizens' quality of life improved rapidly. For example, in 1959 alone, Japan's real economy expanded by 17%, an almost unheard-of rate of growth, unprecedented (as far as I know) in modern economies. While impressive, this growth was not wholly unexpected for a productive, enterprising population rebuilding an economy that had been utterly ruined by war.

The rate of money creation under this system was high, typically seven to ten percent per year, according to BOJ statistics available from the US Federal Reserve. However, this rate of money production resulted in only moderate consumer price increases because Japan grew its production so fast. For the most part, the production of industrial and consumer goods kept up with the production of money.[6]

However, when the US abandoned the gold standard in 1971, the dollar fell hard against the yen and other currencies, making Japan's exports less competitive in price. To protect its export markets, the BOJ wanted to weaken the yen. Using its "directed lending" architecture, the MOF and BOJ began aggressively expanding bank lending in the early 1970s, causing annual money supply growth that sometimes exceeded 25% per year.

The resulting devaluation and inflation caused a jump in the stock market. In the 18 months following August 1971, when Nixon announced the abandonment of gold, Japan's stock market more than doubled. I identify the early 1970s as the birth of the asset bubble that eventually blew up in the following decade.

In the 1980s, the world's central banks, led by the U.S., called for reform. The Americans argued that the Japanese banking system was subsidizing Japanese export industries to the detriment of US companies. In *Princes*, Werner documents the international pressure, especially from the USA, to abolish the war economy banking system and adopt US-type policies. These recommended reforms included a more Western-style, independent central bank structure. The BOJ agreed with this position and was eager to assert its independence from the Ministry of Finance. But the tradition-minded MOF disagreed, making change very difficult politically.

According to Werner, the BOJ leaders concluded that real change could only occur in the wake of a financial crisis. So, the BOJ set about engineering one, believing that was the only way to convince citizens and interest groups of the need for structural change in the government and the economy.

Werner's interpretation of the BOJ's motive is somewhat provocative, but what is not controversial is that in the 1980s, the BOJ started aggressively increasing window guidance toward the real estate sector. Average annual growth in loan quotas grew to 15% by the late 1980s, exceeding what even the bankers asked for. As Richard Cantillon would have predicted, the result was a big boom in real estate and stock market prices.

Look back at the stock market chart to see the parabolic rise of stock prices from 1984 to late 1990. Real estate price increases were even more extreme. Quoting from the *Princes* video:

> "Between 1985 and 1989, stock prices rose by 240%.
> Land prices increased 245%. By the end of the 80s, the

garden around the imperial palace in Tokyo was valued
equally to the entire state of California. The market
value of only one of Tokyo's 23 districts, the central
Chiyoda Ward, exceeded the value of the whole of Canada. Although Japan has less than 4% of the land area of
the USA, its land was valued at four times that of the
US."

By the late 1980s, speculative fervor took over. Traditional man-
ufacturers started playing the markets—these were company hedge
funds (the "Zai Tech") using borrowed money to make speculative
investments. Sometimes, their investment gains exceeded the profits
from their regular business, as in the case of the car maker Nissan.

Shiny new buildings rose in the cities. The labor market boomed
so much that there was worry about a serious labor shortage. Companies enticed new workers by giving them lavish vacations. According to interviews, corporate life became a continual holiday.

Media articles on the "new Japanese economy" famously (and incorrectly) identified the cause of the apparent prosperity as high and
rising productivity. Books on Japanese management techniques
based on ancient Samurai war strategies were best sellers. As often
happens, market observers were confusing brains with a bull market.

Still, the BOJ increased window guidance to property every year.
The only way to fulfill these expanded lending quotas was to increase
unproductive lending. BOJ offered bankers more than they wanted
to lend against property and stocks, and eventually forced the banks
to increase their loans. According to an interview with one banker,
"A side effect of increased window guidance loan increases was that
the banks increased lending even when there was no loan demand."
The BOJ was force-feeding its banks like a farmer feeds a barnyard
goose.

Quoting again from the *Princes* video:

"Like all bubbles, the Japanese bubble was simply fueled
by the rapid creation of new money in the banking system …. When [Toshiko Fukui, head of the Banking

Department at the Bank of Japan] was asked by a journalist, "Borrowing is expanding fast, don't you have any
intention of closing the tap on bank loans?" he replied
"Because the consistent policy of monetary easing continues, quantity control of bank loans would imply a
self-contradiction. Therefore, we do not intend to implement quantitative tightening."

From 1987 onwards, it was not borrowers seeking loans, but
bankers pursuing potential customers. Anecdotes from this period
abound. Young people in their 20s on modest salaries were given
loans for second and third homes. Bankers pursued clients like street
peddlers. According to one interviewee: "If a newlywed couple
wanted to buy a house, banks would offer double the amount they
asked for." To push the loans, bankers made increasingly exaggerated assessments of land value, which made the loan-to-value ratios
look better.

The average Japanese citizen knew something was wrong. People
in the street called it "excess money." From the *Princes* video:

"Only economists, analysts, and those working in the financial markets or for real estate firms knew better.
They dismissed such simplistic analysis. Land prices
were going up for far more complicated reasons than
just excess money, they claimed. Ordinary people
simply did not understand the intricacies of advanced
financial technology."

The bubble eventually spilled over into international investments
as wealthy Japanese took their money abroad. Japanese collectors
dominated the art world in the 1980s. Japanese tycoons made high-
profile purchases, like The Rockefeller Center, Columbia Pictures,
and Pebble Beach Golf Course. Hawaii real estate soared due to Japanese demand. In 1986, Japanese money bought a staggering 75% of
all new US treasury bonds sold at auction.[7]

Importantly, it was not only the absolute level of money growth
that caused the bubble, but the direction of spending of the new

money that was supplied first to the real estate sector and then to stock investors, but *not* towards firms that invested in the production of consumer goods.

Recall the three-hundred-year-old wisdom of Richard Cantillon: prices rise first on items on which new money is spent. If new money is continually re-spent in the commercial property universe—that is, if the proceeds from property sales are reinvested in other properties—it might take years for this money to "escape" to be spent on non-property commodities. If, at the same time, new money is being created and spent in the property market, it's clear that property prices must rise right along with the new money.

A similar thing happened in the USA during the early 2000s housing boom. The process consists of lending (injecting new money) into an asset class that is rising in price because of previous injections of new money. It was the same process that fueled the mortgage lending and house price booms in the United States and the United Kingdom in the 1980s and again in the 2000s.

The stock market boom in the 1920s had developed the same way. In the United States, banks loaned against stocks as collateral. Stock investors usually buy stocks, and that is what they did with their new money. As each bank took the stock price as a valid collateral value, it created new money to buy more stocks. With more money entering the stock market, the owners of stocks kept buying more stocks, so stock prices had to rise. The principle remains the same. Lather, rinse, repeat.

It's been said that easy money is a virus that turns investors' brains to mush. As in most financial bubbles, in the latter stages, widespread misunderstanding contributed to the continued unwarranted expansion of money. According to Werner, "Each bank thought it was safe to accept a certain percentage of the value of the stock as collateral, but it was the actions of all banks together that drove up the overall market."

The Japanese asset bubble continued inflating right through the late 1980s. Viewed over the long term, the inflation in the value of

Japanese real estate was staggering. According to Werner, "In Japan, total private sector land values rose from 14.2 trillion yen in 1969 to 2000 Trillion yen in 1989." This is an increase in prices of 140 times in 20 years, which equates to a rate of increase of about 28% per year.

Then suddenly, in late 1989, the party stopped. At his press conference as the 26th governor of the Bank of Japan, Yasushi Mieno said, "Since the present policy of monetary easing had caused the land price rise problems, real estate lending would now be restricted." From the video:

> He looked around, looked at the bubble, asset prices rising, the gap between rich and poor getting bigger. Let's stop it. His name was Mr. Mieno and he was a hero in the press because he fought against this silly monetary policy. But the fact was, he was deputy governor during the bubble era, and he was in charge of creating the bubble.

Almost overnight, land and other asset prices stopped rising. In 1990 alone, the stock market dropped by 32%. Then, in July 1991, window guidance was abolished. Bankers were now left almost helpless because they did not know how to make their lending plans anymore. Without window guidance, they had no idea how much to lend, or to whom. As banks began to realize that the majority of the JPY 99 trillion in bubble loans was likely to turn sour, they became so fearful that they not only stopped lending to speculators but also restricted loans to anyone else, even those deserving of credit.

Without new money to feed its rise, the stock market continued to collapse, and with it many of Japan's highly indebted companies. Many listed companies went under. Between 1990 and 2003, 212,000 companies went bankrupt. In the same period, the stock market dropped by 80%. Land prices in major cities fell by up to 84%. Five million Japanese lost their jobs and did not find employment for years. Suicide became the leading cause of death for men between the ages of 20 and 44. According to anecdotal reports, people were hanging themselves and going missing on a daily basis.

But BOJ Governor Mieno found a silver lining in the catastrophe, saying it made the population conscious of the need to implement economic transformation, by which he meant central bank independence. By Werner's account, Mieno had created the bubble, and Mieno popped the bubble.

In the years following the bust, several recovery remedies were tried. The MOF pressured the BOJ to lower interest rates to spur lending, but that didn't work even when rates were pushed to near zero. With no appetite among businesses to borrow, the BOJ was pushing on a string.

Next, the MOF tried to devalue the yen versus the dollar to stimulate exports. But the BOJ sold assets to raise yen to buy dollars, decreasing the quantity of money in the economy, which was deflationary in an already deflating economy. So, despite the BOJ's intervention in the currency market, the yen did not weaken.

Then, the MOF tried fiscal stimulus, which was supposed to increase loan demand. But they were funding government spending through taxation. With no increase in the money supply, the asset price implosion continued.

By Werner's account, the BOJ refused to engage in the necessary money creation that would alleviate the crisis, deliberately prolonging the recovery just to get the structural changes they wanted. Finally, in 1998, the Princes of The Yen at the BOJ got their wish and became independent of the MOF. But this had come at great cost to the Japanese people.

Werner sums up the bubble, echoing my Chapter Four comments on speculative bank lending.

> Asset inflation can go on for several years without major observable problems. However, as soon as the credit creation for non-GDP transactions stops or even slows, it is 'game over' for the asset bubble: asset prices will not rise any further. The first speculators, requiring rising asset prices, go bankrupt, and banks are left with non-performing loans. As a result, they will tend to

reduce lending against such asset collateral further, resulting in further drops in asset prices, which in turn
create more bankruptcies.

What conclusion can we draw from the famous Japan asset bubble? As Werner puts it, "central banks hold obscure, independent
powers that are not always well understood." But we do know their
main weapon is the power to cause the banks to create new money
and distribute that money to specific recipients who spend the new
money in specific markets.

To conclude on the 1980s Japan financial bubble: For years, new
money was knowingly directed by a central monetary authority into
property markets. This caused a large and rapid increase in property
prices that spilled over into the stock market, international investment, speculation, and gambling. The consequences of this misdi-
rected credit were many years of distorted price signals, malinvestment, and wasted capital. When credit creation was withdrawn, the
bubble burst, followed by years of deflation, stagnation, and severe
economic and social hardship, not to mention widespread poverty
and suicide.

In such situations, the best option, in my view, is to let markets
repair the economic damage through free market price discovery and
creative destruction. But the truth is, once a credit bubble has been
created, there are no painless recovery options.

Our second example of harmful money creation, caused by government action, is the era known as Quantitative Easing, the 13-year
period from 2009 to 2022.

The QE asset bubble

Quantitative Easing (QE) started in 2009 in the aftermath of the great
housing bubble and continued until mid-2022. This period saw the
rapid price rise of practically every asset class, including land, houses,
commercial real estate, bonds, stocks, and fine art. Some have called
it the "everything bubble" to describe its effects. I call it the "QE asset
bubble" to identify the bubble's cause, which was a massive central

bank asset purchase program. Later in this chapter, I will also refer to the final QE surge during the COVID panic as "Pandemic QE," but this was really part of the same grand monetary policy.

Quantitative Easing is unique in financial history (to my knowledge) in that it was executed by a coordinated effort of all the world's major central banks. This massive asset purchase program was conceived and led by Ben Bernanke, Chairman of the Federal Reserve from 2006 to 2014, and continued by his successors, Janet Yellen and Jerome Powell, until May of 2022. Ultimately, colossal asset purchases became the policy of all major central banks. The QE asset bubble provides a great learning opportunity because it is recent, very visible, and far-reaching. This is bad money creation at its worst—or at least, as bad as it can get without causing a total collapse of confidence in the currency.

The first seeds of the Fed's QE policy were planted in November 2002, right after the bursting of the tech stock bubble and the ensuing recession. In a speech to the National Economics Club entitled "Deflation: making sure it doesn't happen here," Ben Bernanke, then head of the Federal Reserve Bank of New York, outlined some creative ways in which the Fed, in cooperation with the Treasury, could "stimulate" the economy in a crisis. Here is one of several policies he proposed:

> Of course, in lieu of tax cuts or increases in transfers, the government could increase spending on current goods and services or even acquire existing real or financial assets. If the Treasury issued debt to purchase private assets and the Fed then purchased an equal amount of Treasury debt with newly created money, the whole operation would be the economic equivalent of direct open-market operations in private assets.[8]

The title of this speech was "Deflation: Making Sure 'It' Doesn't Happen Here." Bernanke was worried about the prospect of falling prices. His proposal, that the US Treasury should raise the price of "existing real or financial assets" with newly created money sounds a

lot like the government printing money to nationalize private industry. This is what Latin American dictators are famous for. Bernanke
was describing the pattern the Treasury and Fed would follow twenty
years later during the Pandemic phase of quantitative easing, from
2020 to 2022.

Fast forward from 2002 to 2009 and the Great Financial Crisis.
With asset prices crushed and the economy not recovering as fast as
Fed Chair Bernanke wanted it to, he was ready with a pilot version
of the plan outlined in that 2002 speech. The Treasury was not yet
ready to purchase "private assets"—that would come years later during the Pandemic—so Bernanke's plan was to buy assets the Fed was
already legally authorized to buy, that is, government-guaranteed
bonds. He announced a plan to conduct standard open market purchases, a routine monetary operation, in very large amounts—hundreds of billions in Treasury bonds and government-guaranteed
mortgage-backed securities, a policy that soon became known as
"quantitative easing."

As Bernanke explained in a now famous Op-ed to *The Washington Post* in November 2010, entitled "What the Fed Did and Why,"

> … Easier financial conditions will promote economic
> growth. For example, lower mortgage rates will make
> housing more affordable and allow more homeowners
> to refinance. Lower corporate bond rates will encourage
> investment. And higher stock prices will boost con-
> sumer wealth and help increase confidence, which can
> also spur spending. Increased spending will lead to
> higher incomes and profits that, in a virtuous circle, will
> further support economic expansion.[9]

From the text, it's clear Bernanke understood that "lower bond
rates" and "higher stock prices" would benefit the owners of financial
assets. If investors felt wealthier, he thought their confidence would
trickle down to the Main Street economy, creating a "virtuous circle"
of economic improvement, a kind of rising tide that would lift all
boats. Of course, this never happened. What actually happened was

that the rising tide of money lifted Wall Street's yachts but submerged many smaller vessels.

Once the Fed got QE underway, all the major central banks around the world joined in with almost identical policies. Some, like the Chinese, Japanese, and Swiss central banks, even purchased equities. (For details, see my December 2015 article in *The Objective Standard*—"Central Banks Move Beyond the Fascist Frontier.")[10]

At first, the consequences of the new money flowing into the investment markets were small and unnoticed by most. But Wall Street soon caught on. By 2012, many hedge fund managers understood the game but didn't say much publicly. One manager, David Tepper of the Appaloosa Fund, finally broke the silence at an investment conference in May of 2015. As reported by *Barron's*, Tepper commented,

> "… four major central banks (of the US, the EU, China and Japan) are pumping liquidity into the system" and "will create another tailwind for equities, even after six years of central-bank fueled growth in stock markets," Tepper said, "It's kind of hard to fight money . . . Don't fight the Fed. Now you've got four Feds. Don't fight four Feds."[11]

David Tepper's personal income in 2013 was $3.5 billion. This windfall was not unique to him. The entire investor class hit the jackpot, as these kinds of gains were repeated year after year.

As in the Japan bubble, the problem was not just the absolute increase in the quantity of money, but that the new money was directed to specific investors who bought specific assets, driving up their prices. During the first 11 years of QE (January 2009 to January 2020) M2 money supply increased at a rate of just under 6% annually, not much different from the average rate over previous decades. The money supply grew because the aggressive activity of the Fed offset weak lending activity at the commercial banks.

Like many others, I expected a higher rate of increase in the CPI during the first few years of QE, but I was not sufficiently mindful of the Cantillon Effect.[12] At first, I and many others didn't understand that the new money was being handed to investors, then spent and re-spent on stocks and bonds in a partially closed system that did not allow the new money to spill out into consumer prices. Nearly all the new QE money was directed to the financial markets, specifically to the owners of bonds, stocks, and mortgage-backed securities, who used it to buy more investment assets. This is why interest rates dropped, stock prices soared, mortgage rates dropped to 3%, and house prices soared. If there were a "Richard Cantillon Award" for market foresight, David Tepper would have won the prize.

In retrospect, it's not surprising that new money can stay bottled up in the investment markets for a long time, with very little money "leaking" into consumer prices. If you think about it, money can leave investment accounts to be spent on consumer goods when investments are liquidated to pay the investor, such as when pensions are paid, or when you take a distribution from your 401(k) plan, or when asset managers spend their fees and bonuses, which are typically a percentage of investment assets. This "leakage" is usually a small percentage of the total investment account. As asset prices rose, benefitting wealthy asset owners, we did see big increases in the prices of the things rich people spend money on, like yachts and luxury homes. But even this leakage was tiny compared to the quantity of money pumped into asset prices.

Increased productivity, much of it from international trade, was another reason consumer price increases were modest during the post-crash years. From 2009 until the pandemic-related surge in money supply began in 2020, the price of consumer goods increased at less than 2% per year compared to its long-term average (post-gold era) of 4.0% per year.[13] A larger supply of consumer goods, offered against a demand for consumer goods that was subdued by a modest amount of new money entering the consumer sector, means consumer prices grew more slowly than they might have otherwise done, even with the broad money supply growing at nearly 6%.[14]

With occasional pauses, QE continued for 13 years and accelerated during the Pandemic, fueling the asset bubble. Every time the

Fed tried to scale back on QE or raise short-term interest rates, the stock market faltered, and the Fed responded with renewed bond buying. Fearing a collapse in asset prices, the Fed found itself in a kind of trap, finding it unacceptable to stop the asset inflation. The word on Wall Street became "buy the dip" because you could be sure the Fed would step in with more money when the market faltered. The Fed's bankers saw little downside to this because, by their understanding, "inflation" was not a problem since consumer prices were rising at a slow rate.

How much new money was created due to QE? Below are two charts from the Federal Reserve that tell the story. The first is a graph of M2, or broad money supply. It shows that during the 12 QE years (2009 to 2022), the money supply increased by $14 trillion, or 175%. Most of this increase came during the "pandemic phase," 2020 to 2022. This explosion of money was unprecedented in the history of the United States

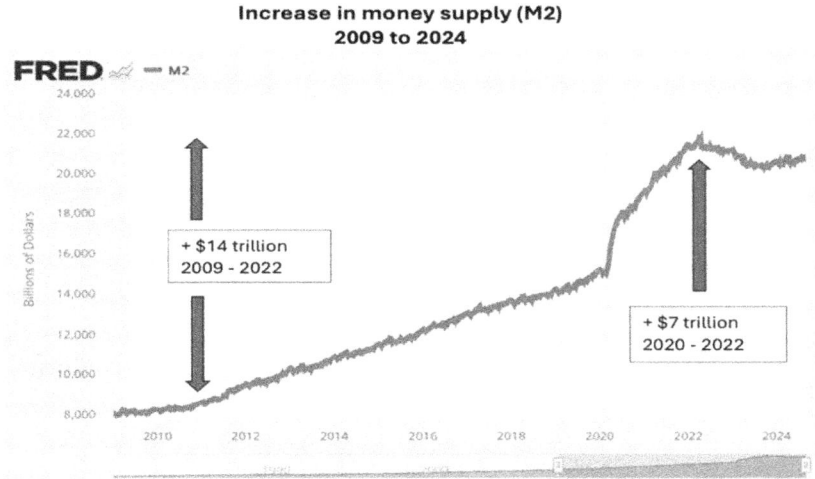

Increase in money supply (M2)
2009 to 2024

The second graph depicts the growth of the Fed's assets during the QE period.

Fed ownership of bonds
2009 - 2024

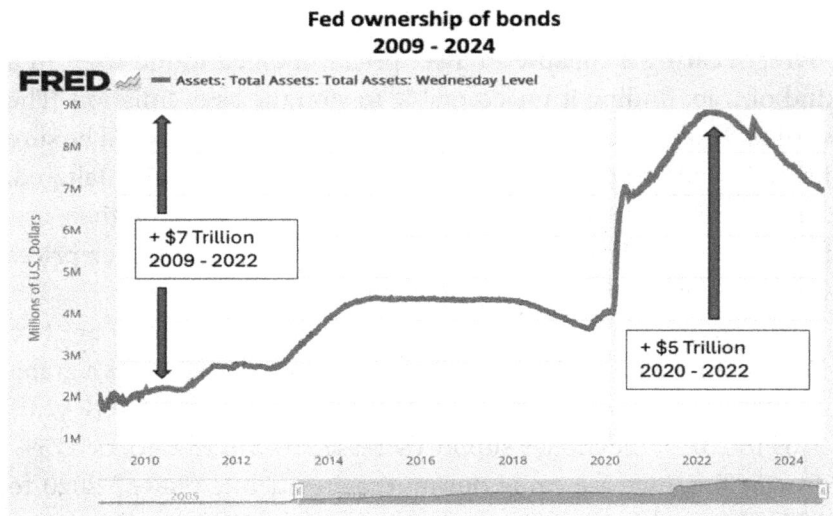

Let's summarize the conclusions from these two graphs. In the 13-year period of 2009 to mid-2022, M2 increased by $14 trillion, from about $8 trillion to $22 trillion. During the same period, Fed assets increased by $7 trillion. Every dollar of this $7 trillion increase in Fed assets was matched by an equivalent increase in new bank deposits. Thus, the Fed's QE program produced $7 trillion—half of the $14 trillion of new money (M2) created in this period. About $5 trillion of this increase was due to the "Pandemic QE" phase, starting in March 2020 and peaking in mid-2022.

Because QE pumped most of this new money into the investment markets, asset prices rose just as Richard Cantillon would have predicted: From 2009 to 2022, stocks, bonds, house prices, and commercial real estate prices soared. As one example of the inflationary effect of this new money, during the QE years, the S&P 500 index rose 425% from January 2009 to January 2022. That's an average annual compounded gain of 13.6% compared to the long-term average of 10.2%.

House prices were similarly affected. According to Fed data, the median house price more than doubled during the 13 QE years.[15]

Ben Bernanke and his proteges, Janet Yellen and Jerome Powell, continued QE year after year because they thought they were creating a "virtuous circle." But what were the real economic effects of massive money creation and soaring asset prices? Let's consider some of the leading problems associated with this kind of unproductive money creation, things that were going on right under the central bankers' collective nose.

Unjust economic inequality. One of the glaring negative consequences of the QE bubble was the unprecedented extent of unjust economic inequality. I am not referring to the normal differences in income and wealth that occur in a free market due to differing preferences, ambitions, and abilities. I am speaking of the economic injustices that occurred due to the central bank's policy of funneling free money specifically to the investor class. Through its massive bond purchases, the Fed created trillions of fresh dollars and handed them directly to the players in the investment markets.

It's easy to understand how QE benefited the rich at the expense of the poor. As we saw in Chapter Five, QE pumps up asset prices (stocks, bonds, and real estate) and crushes interest rates. Higher asset prices and low interest rates directly benefit those who own assets. On the other hand, the "asset poor," through no fault of their own, are left behind.

Perhaps the most obvious victims of ultra-low interest rates were the traditional, conservative savers, the bedrock providers of capital in a free economy. Wall Street prospered from QE, but on Main Street, suppressed interest rates made the honest saver an endangered species. To the same extent that early recipients of fiat money prospered from these easy money handouts, traditional savers suffered an equivalent decay of their purchasing power.

For example, consider an average worker who wants to provide an income of $50,000 for his retirement. Over a lifetime, this worker might be able to save $1 million, which, at a typical interest rate of

5%, would provide his annual income. But to generate a $50,000 income when interest rates are near 1%, as they were for years under QE, this worker would have to save $5,000,000, a sum that puts financial security beyond his reach. (See my August 8, 2021, Substack essay, "Unmasking Inflation," which illustrates how the Fed's preoccupation with consumer prices hides the broader effects of inflation.)[16]

So, the wealthy reaped a windfall, while the poor and middle class were unable to accumulate wealth without speculating in the stock market. Many pundits blamed this condition on the failures of "capitalism." But true capitalism is a system of justice. The economic inequalities inherent in a truly capitalist system are appropriate because they are consequences of different people's individual choices, encompassing vastly different thoughts, goals, choices, and efforts. However, soaring asset prices and near-zero interest rates cannot happen in a truly capitalist system; they can only happen in an economy where the government creates unproductive money.

Malinvestment. Artificially low interest rates distort normal investment judgment and encourage speculative borrowing, resulting in non-productive investments and wasted capital. This problem is known as "malinvestment," which comes from the fact that price distortions and low interest rates caused by asset inflation make accurate risk assessment impossible, which in turn undermines productive investing.

It's been said both Zombies and Unicorns feast on cheap money. "Zombie" companies are the walking dead that could not exist without artificially low interest rates. "Unicorns" are companies founded on hope and prayer that can get money only when it is practically free. Both kinds of companies waste scarce capital, but both are very hard to identify and kill off in a world distorted by ultra-low interest rates.

The Fed's suppression of rates also undermines credit analysis, making it difficult for lenders to distinguish between deadbeats and creditworthy borrowers. And this, in turn, leads to further market distortions—which, in turn, encourage the Fed to attempt further corrections—and so on. James Grant, editor of *Grant's Interest Rate Observer*, put it this way:

> Interest rates … are universal prices: They discount future cash flows, calibrate risks, and define investment hurdle rates. So, interest rates are the traffic signals of a market-based economy. Ordinarily, some are amber, some are red, and some are green. But since 2008 they have mainly been green.[17]

To put it in concrete personal terms: You may own your home and your car, and you may have a 401(k) or an investment portfolio consisting of stocks and bonds, but the market value of every one of those assets, as well as the purchasing power of the cash in your bank account, is being manipulated in some way by the central banks when they manipulate money creation and interest rates. You are still free to sell your assets and purchase others, but, whether you realize it or not, your decision-making processes are being heavily influenced by the garbled price signals from a rigged market. It's economic central planning hiding in plain sight.

Stagnant real wages. Unproductive money creation is also a cause of stagnant real wages. Contrary to the claims of central bankers, there is no consistent data proving suppressing interest rates increases growth or employment. Business owners always have limited funds, and when they make investment decisions, they must choose between investing those funds in labor (more employees or higher wages) or capital (machines, buildings, etc.). An artificially low interest rate biases investment toward capital rather than labor, because financing capital projects (like machinery and technology that lead to automation) with borrowed money becomes comparatively cheap. So, in fact, artificially suppressed interest rates may result in lower wages and higher unemployment than would exist in an unhampered market.

This is not to say that labor and capital are naturally antagonists. In a free market, they exist in harmony because unhindered wages and interest rates will constantly adjust to real economic demand. Labor and capital compete for investment to the extent one can substitute for the other. But in an atmosphere of interest rates pushed artificially downward, capital investment gets an abnormal advantage.

Now consider the sum of these effects on the poor and lower middle class—let's call them the working class, who mostly live paycheck to paycheck. Their real wages and salaries are suppressed, reducing their ability to save. Because interest rates are so low, what little they can save accumulates slowly. Their meager savings are further eroded by continual increases in the prices of consumer goods, where they spend most of their money.

Rising asset prices do not benefit workers who do not own any assets. Even when consumer prices increase slowly, the declining value of money negatively impacts everyone, particularly the working class. For them, the only substantial asset is their paycheck, and they do not have appreciating assets to offset the losses caused by inflation. Furthermore, real production in the economy often stagnates due to misallocated investments, exacerbating the working class's struggle with stagnant living standards. Wage earners witness wealth accumulating on Wall Street for seemingly no valid reason, making their situation feel increasingly unjust. They find it difficult to connect hard work with financial success. As a result, they almost feel compelled to invest in areas where they lack expertise to improve their financial situation.

Runaway government spending. By purchasing trillions of dollars in government debt with newly-created money and crushing interest rates in the process, the Fed signaled Congress and the Administration that borrowing and spending were virtually free. Consequently, Congress borrowed and spent like there was no tomorrow. I'll devote all of Chapter Six to what is perhaps the most intractable problem associated with inflation: unpayable sovereign debt.

Beyond these visible effects, other unseen consequences of bad money creation are the lost opportunities for productive investment that never materialized. What life-serving investments were *not* made because new money directed scarce labor and materials to government cronies or wasteful social schemes? What careers were *not* launched, and what innovations were *not* developed because monetary authorities steered capital away from productive use? We will never know.

Pandemic QE and CPI inflation

At the start of 2020, key economic indicators (like unemployment, CPI inflation, and GDP growth) signaled a promising future. However, the global panic triggered by government lockdowns led to a swift downturn as the stock market plummeted, business activity ground to a halt, and unemployment soared. A microbe called SARSCov2 was the spark, but the government's ham-fisted response was the flame that burned down the economy.

The economic crisis of 2020 came from Washington, not Wuhan. After years of low interest rates, our pre-virus financial structure was highly leveraged, with many problems—debt-ridden balance sheets, over-priced assets, and a gaggle of "zombie" companies kept alive by a near-zero cost of borrowing, to name a few. And where did this unstable structure come from? For the most part, it came from the Fed. During the QE years that preceded the lockdowns, the Federal Reserve created money to buy government bonds and to squash interest rates.

How low did rates sink? A scan of the authoritative *History of Interest Rates* by Sydney Homer and Richard Scylla reveals that in no time in the last *4000 years* have interest rates ever been as low as they were during the QE era.[18] The "wealth effect" from rising asset prices, said the Fed's learned council, would dribble down from the affluent to the less fortunate, boost consumption, and, finally, arouse a sleepy economy.

All that was a financial fairy tale. Instead of reviving the masses on Main Street, years of QE and low interest rates pumped up asset prices while weakening the financial structure.

But loans have deadlines and must be repaid or refinanced to avoid default. When an economy stops, as it did when the government sent everyone home, the loans don't go away. Lenders demand cash that leveraged borrowers in marginal businesses cannot generate. Many heavily indebted companies were ill-equipped to handle the panic selling, the collapse of asset prices, the closing-up of credit, and the scramble for cash that followed the shutdown. The brilliant civil servants at the Fed and Treasury responded by doing what they do best: conjuring up more money.

The Fed and the Treasury accomplished this through another radical expansion of the money supply. A variety of Pandemic "stimulus" programs, passed by Congress and immediately signed by both Presidents Trump and Biden, authorized various ways to get new money into the hands of investors, small businesses, and consumers. From mid-2020 to mid-2022, about $5 trillion of stimulus money was paid out to consumers and businesses, most of it borrowed by the Treasury and immediately monetized by the Fed.

Economist Jim Bianco penned an op-ed in Bloomberg that highlighted the abnormal collaboration between the Fed and the Treasury:

> To put it bluntly, the Fed isn't allowed to do any of
> this. The central bank is only allowed to purchase or
> lend against securities that have a government guaran-
> tee. [So] The Fed will finance a special purpose vehicle
> (SPV) for each acronym to conduct these opera-
> tions … . In essence, the Treasury, not the Fed, is buy-
> ing all these securities and backstopping of loans; the
> Fed is acting as a banker and providing financing … . In
> other words, the federal government is nationalizing
> large swaths of the financial markets. The Fed is provid-
> ing the money to do it … .[19]

It would have been just as accurate to say, "The Fed is requiring the commercial banks to provide new bank deposits to the sellers of the Treasury bonds, converting this new debt into new money, thus funding the Treasury's profligate spending." As usual, the new money was being manufactured in the commercial banks, even though the Fed and Treasury were calling the shots.

Some of the stimulus was in the form of checks sent directly to consumers, sometimes called "helicopter money." Some payments were in the form of guaranteed or "forgivable" loans to individuals and businesses from special purpose companies set up by the Treasury. Some of the programs allowed the Fed to buy bonds from private companies like Apple and AT&T, just as Bernanke had suggested twenty years earlier in his 2002 speech.

In all, about $5 trillion in payments went out. This additional wave of new money, which I call "Pandemic QE," was an acceleration of the QE program already in place. It eventually ignited the consumer price inflation that practically no one saw coming—not the Treasury, not the Fed, and not most private economists, who for months insisted that the rising CPI inflation was "transitory."

Consumer Price Index annual percentage change

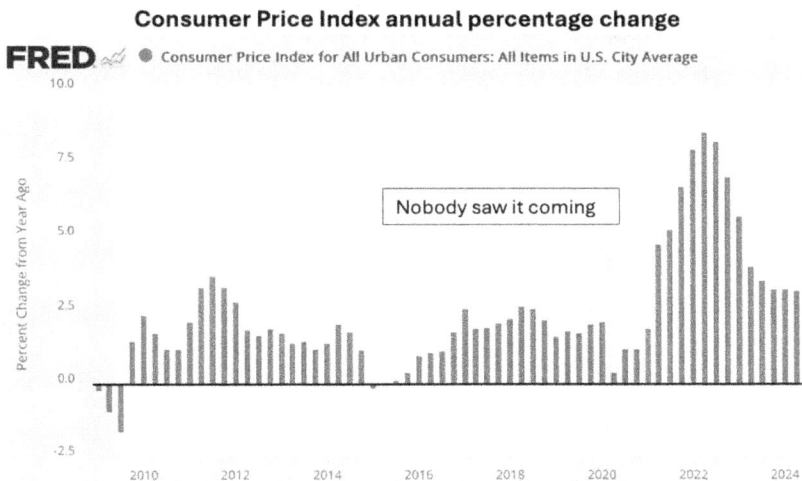

FRED — Consumer Price Index for All Urban Consumers: All Items in U.S. City Average

Nobody saw it coming

Indeed, during the first decade of QE (2009 to early 2020), consumer prices, as measured by the CPI, advanced modestly, at 1.5 to 2% per year, even as the Fed was busily creating lots of unproductive money. So why did the CPI jump so suddenly in 2021? The answer is that during the Pandemic QE period, the new money was directed not only to Wall Street, but also to the folks who spend their money on consumer goods, the same goods whose prices make up the CPI and the PCE.[20]

It was clear that purchasing more Treasurys and mortgage-backed securities would not get money to individual citizens and small businesses, but only to professional investors, which is how it had worked during previous QE campaigns. But the intellectual groundwork for expanded QE had been laid. Recall that, in 2002, Ben Bernanke had suggested a partnership between the Treasury and the Fed to get money directly into the hands of the public. That's why the Treasury had to get involved with its special-purpose lending companies, funded by the Fed, just as Ben Bernanke had suggested nearly two decades earlier.[21]

In a nutshell, Congress approved massive new spending designed to get new money directly into the hands of consumers and corporations. It's a variation on QE, and here's how it works: The Treasury borrows trillions of dollars from investors, providing the Treasury with the money it needs for its stimulus (giveaway) program. Recall that sending money to the Treasury (from investors buying Treasury bonds) moves deposits and reserves out of the banks and into the Treasury's General Account (TGA) held at the Fed. To counter the loss of bank deposits, the Fed simultaneously purchases an equivalent amount of bonds from private investors, creating new bank deposits to replace the money that went to the Treasury.

The result is that the public still holds the same amount of Treasurys and bank deposits as before the stimulus. What has changed is that the Fed now owns a lot more bonds, and the Treasury has a lot more new money to spend. The Treasury sends out trillions of dollars in checks from the TGA, which are deposited in the bank accounts of consumers and small businesses, who buy consumer goods and, in addition, invest in the stock market. In this way, the Fed's

Pandemic QE program sent massive amounts of new money to both Wall Street and Main Street.

As this stimulus money hit consumers' bank accounts, they spent much of it on the items that comprise the consumer price index. Within a year after the stimulus started hitting consumers' bank accounts, the consumer price index jumped and kept rising, shocking nearly all government economists, including Janet Yellen and Jerome Powell, who had assured us inflation would be "transitory." The irony was that after years of complaining that QE was not creating enough consumer price inflation, they finally got their wish, in spades, with the largest CPI increases in 40 years.

From 2009 to 2020, new money directed to Wall Street raised the prices of financial assets like stocks, bonds, and real estate. From 2020 to 2022, the Pandemic QE money surge was directed to both Wall Street and Main Street. Thus asset prices continued rising, but now the inflation included the items Main Street spends money on: eggs, cars, rents, and everything else in the consumer price index.

Who would have thought? The Treasury and Fed conjured massive amounts of new money and handed it to consumers, who duly spent that new cash and jacked up consumer prices. Why didn't the Fed and Treasury see CPI "inflation" coming? Because, mired in their statistics, they ignored fundamental causation and failed to consider the Cantillon Effect. As the feisty Frenchman might have said if he had been alive, "Le duh."

Summary

Japan's asset bubble and the QE bubble are superficially different, yet they have much in common. In both cases, excessive money was created in the banks at the direction of the central monetary authority. In both cases, the new money was directed toward buying assets, resulting in higher asset prices. In both cases, higher asset prices raised collateral values, justifying increased leverage and more money creation, resulting in even higher asset prices. The asset owners got richer while the poor were left behind.

In both cases, monetary authorities were confident about their actions because they misunderstood inflation: to them, the asset bubble was not "inflation" because consumer price increases were rising moderately. In both cases, the money pumping went on for years, spawning a deep speculative fervor that sucked in otherwise innocent people, damaging tens of millions of lives.

Let's conclude this chapter with a couple of summary points.

First, a correct definition of inflation—an increase in the quantity of money caused by the government—helps us identify *all* the adverse effects of unproductive money creation, not just unwanted price increases. These effects include unjust wealth distribution, malinvestment, stagnant growth and wages, runaway sovereign debt, and the eventual corrosion of public morality.

Second, government monetary authorities cause inflation and all its adverse effects by seizing control of the money creation decisions usually made by commercial bankers and then directing that new money to groups who benefit unjustly. In 1980s Japan, they did it by commanding the commercial banks to lend wantonly to the property sector. In the USA, from 2009 to 2022, they did it by commanding the commercial banks to participate in massive purchases of government bonds, a program called "quantitative easing," directing new money first to the Wall Street investor class and ultimately to Main Street consumers and businesses.

To close this chapter, I'll let the great Henry Hazlitt have the last word on inflation:

> [Inflation] discourages all prudence and thrift. It encourages squandering, gambling, and reckless waste of all kinds. It often makes it more profitable to speculate than to produce. It tears apart the whole fabric of stable economic relationships. Its inexcusable injustices drive men toward desperate remedies. It plants the seeds of fascism and communism. It leads men to demand totalitarian controls. It ends invariably in bitter disillusion and collapse.[22]

In Chapter Six, we'll examine what eventually became the most urgent consequence of excessive money creation: the ballooning sovereign debt of most governments, epitomized by the United States government's overwhelming, unpayable financial obligations.

6 UNCLE SAM'S UNPAYABLE DEBT

Why U.S. national debt is unpayable; The real national debt;
How politicians view the debt problem, Government's four
cash flow levers; Financial repression is inevitable

Why U.S. national debt is unpayable

Chapter Five detailed how the Federal Reserve "monetized" $7 trillion in government debt by purchasing government bonds with newly printed money. Apart from enriching Wall Street by pumping up stock prices, one of the significant effects of this unprecedented bubble was to drive nominal interest rates down to the lowest levels in recorded history. For most of the Quantitative Easing (QE) era, the "real" yield on the US Treasury 10-year bond (measured by subtracting the annual CPI increase from the nominal yield) was between zero and one percent. At times, this "real" yield dipped into negative territory.[1]

"Real" Yield on US 10-year Treasury

"Real" yields go negative

Source: FRED Economic Data, St. Louis Fed

Near-zero interest rates were too enticing for our elected politicians, who are so fond of borrowing and spending. Already adept at self-deception, they were easily seduced into a financial stupor that made them act as if their spending spree, paid for by borrowing virtually free money, could go on forever. The Fed's irresponsible money creation enabled their foolish spending project.

Judging by their recent actions, Congress is still entranced. Despite interest rates rising sharply since 2020, Congress continues its radical spending spree, racking up ever-higher amounts of debt to pay for it. The federal debt has exploded, and its rate of increase is accelerating to warp speed, as illustrated by the graph below.

Federal Debt Rate of Growth is Accelerating

$ Trillions

36.0	
32.0	
28.0	
24.0	
20.0	
16.0	
12.0	
8.0	
4.0	

11.2%

7.4%

6.3%

1992 1994 1996 1998 2000 2002 2004 2006 2008 2010 2012 2014 2016 2018 2020 2022

Source: FRED Economic Data, St. Louis Fed

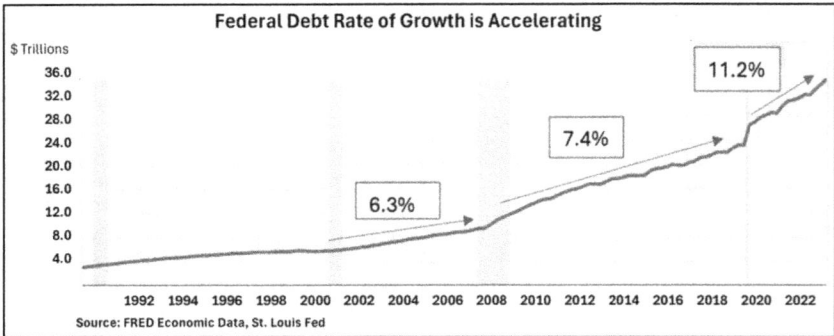

As of July 2024, the US government's total debt has reached $35 trillion. At the current rate of increase, Uncle Sam's debt will reach $70 trillion by 2031!

This surreal growth in spending and borrowing could not have happened without the collaboration and encouragement of the US Federal Reserve. By monetizing much of the new debt and sending interest rates to rock-bottom levels, the Fed dissolved the customary link between taxing and spending, making the new debt feel painless.

But the onset of pain has only been delayed. In this chapter, I aim to demonstrate that the US government's total financial obligations are already so large that they can only be repaid in dollars of diminished purchasing power.

I'll assess the US government's debt dilemma in two parts. Initially, I'll present the known facts of the United States' financial obligations, demonstrate how absurd they are, and explain why these obligations cannot be paid in current dollars. Subsequently, I'll examine this debt predicament from the point of view of professional politicians to determine their realistic options for addressing the debt problem. Why is this important to you? Because by anticipating our politicians' probable response to our burgeoning debt, investors can take defensive actions in advance.

(Spoiler alert: the political options for dealing with excessive debt will not be favorable for traditional savers and investors. Sorry.)

Let's start by asking a fundamental question: How big is the national debt, and how fast is it growing? You can visit https://www.usdebtclock.org to get an up-to-date number. As of July 31, 2024, the "debt clock" recorded that the total US debt to date is just over $35 trillion. The additional debt added in 2024 alone is over $2.0 trillion and growing rapidly.

"35 trillion," or 35,000,000,000,000, or "thirty-five times ten to the twelfth power," is the kind of number usually reserved for a quantum physics class, so let's quantify US debt from the average person's perspective. The debt clock tells us that $35 trillion is $103,000 per US citizen, most of whom pay no taxes. Calculated per taxpayer, the debt translates to approximately $267,000.

With the average US household income at $77,000 per year, $267,000 of debt per taxpayer seems like an impossible burden. Moreover, the debt is rising so fast that it's out of date as soon as you read the current number. The numbers spin like a perpetual slot machine.[2]

The real national debt

But it gets worse. The government's $35 trillion Treasury debt, often called the "national debt," is only a fraction of the US government's actual financial obligations. $35 trillion is what the government owes to the current owners of Treasury bonds, those investors who have already loaned money to the government. This is called the "funded" debt. But there's also a massive amount of "unfunded" debt significantly larger than $35 trillion.

Wait. What? Sorry, once again. We need to explain the nature of this unfunded debt and estimate its magnitude. Understanding this unaccounted-for obligation is crucial as it presents a far more significant challenge than the $35 trillion funded debt alone.

The U.S. Congress has made open-ended future commitments that are often taken for granted. These primarily involve pledges for future "entitlements," such as Social Security, disability payments, Medicare, and Medicaid. Approximately 70% of the annual federal budget is allocated to fulfill these entitlements, which are legally binding promises enshrined in federal law, with yearly adjustments for cost-of-living increases based on changes in the consumer price index.

These future obligations are distinct from the "funded" Treasury debt because the government has not yet levied taxes or borrowed funds to cover them. Consequently, these future obligations stand apart from, and in addition to, the "national debt" owed to the investors who loaned to the government and now hold Treasury bonds. The primary cause of our persistent and expanding deficit spending lies in these recurring commitments that still need to be paid for.

Because our elected representatives have consistently been unable to gather enough tax revenue to cover these recurring costs, the Treasury pays for the shortfall by borrowing from investors in the Treasury market. For example, suppose legislation mandates that the Treasury spend $6 trillion in the current year, but the IRS can only collect tax revenues and fees amounting to $4 trillion. In that case, the Treasury must borrow the remaining $2 trillion (the "deficit") in the bond market, which then adds to the "national debt."

The US government has operated at a deficit annually for the past four decades, except for a small surplus in 2000. The chart below shows these deficits have grown significantly since the 2008–9 financial crisis.[3]

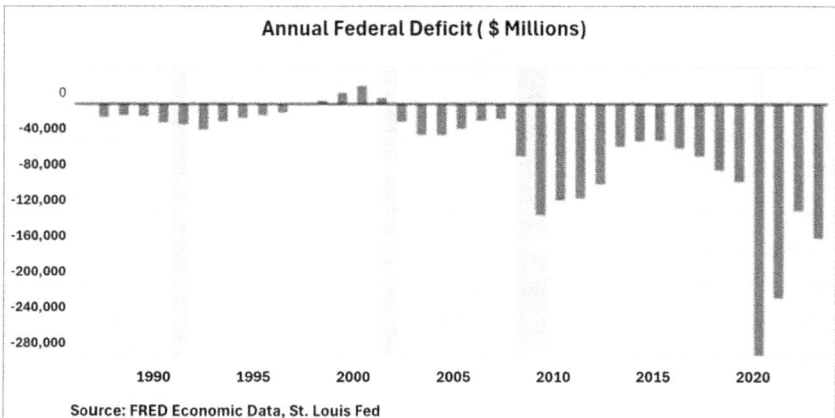

Annual Federal Deficit ($ Millions)

Source: FRED Economic Data, St. Louis Fed

US government deficits are expected to remain high for the foreseeable future. The Congressional Budget Office (CBO), known for consistently underestimating the deficit, projects that the US government deficit will average $2.0 trillion annually until 2033.[4]

Large amounts of debt from accumulated deficits are not new to the US or other sovereign nations. For example, to pay for World War II, the USA and many other nations borrowed much more from their citizens than they could raise by collecting taxes. The World War II borrowing binge paid for "one-time" costs—planes, ships, and soldiers' wages. But when the war was over, we scrapped the tanks and planes, and the soldiers transitioned from destructive combat to constructive civilian occupations. The borrowing requirements ended when the war ended. Therefore, while the wartime debts were sizeable, they were also finite liabilities that could be gradually paid off with collected taxes.

Our current deficit spending differs from a wartime deficit because it is being used to fund unknown, open-ended future obligations. Today's annual deficits are based on the promise to pay the retirement, disability, and medical benefits of every US citizen, including everyone alive today and yet to be born, cradle to grave, *with no known limitations*. Social Security has cost-of-living escalators built-in by law, but the escalation formula is based on CPI inflation, which is unknown in advance. Moreover, future medical and disability benefits are not just promises to pay money but to provide physical goods and services with no known limit on their dollar cost. For example, it's impossible to know the future dollar cost of the government's promise to pay for future emergency room and end-of-life care for every US resident, including the unborn.

Although we can't predict the exact expenses the government will incur in the future, we can make some rough guesses based on today's costs. So, let's look at a shorthand method of estimating the value of the US government's "unfunded" financial obligations. The goal here is not to precisely assess the nation's unfunded debt but to demonstrate that these obligations are far greater than we can realistically afford.

To estimate the size of America's unfunded liabilities, we need to make a few reasonable assumptions. The problem is like calculating the value of future retirement benefits in an employee pension plan. Many pension funds offer members a lump sum payment at retirement instead of future payments. The retiree can take one large payment today, invest it conservatively, and pay for all his future retirement costs with the proceeds from the investment. With a few simplified assumptions, we can make the same kind of estimate of the present value of the US government's future financial obligations to all its citizens.

First, we must estimate the annual expenditures not covered by taxation. By definition, this is the annual deficit. To ensure we are not being alarmist or overstating the problem, let's assume a $1.5 trillion annual deficit in today's dollars. This is even less than the current CBO deficit forecasts, which historically have been too low. So, if anything, our estimate of the annual deficit is too optimistic.

Second, we must assume an annual rate of inflation. The annual deficits are equal to the cost of "entitlements" funded by borrowing, and these entitlement costs have built-in inflation escalators. For our example, let's assume just 3% yearly inflation, which may be too low, given that the long-term average annual increase in the Consumer Price Index is about 4.0%.[5] A CPI inflation rate higher than 3% would raise the cost considerably, so again, this is a conservative assumption.

Finally, we must assume a reasonable rate of return on investment. We'll assume an annual return of 5%, roughly the same as nominal GDP growth.

So, here is our estimate stated as a Finance 101 "word problem": Invest a lump sum of money today (PV) that will earn 5% annually and pay for $1.5 trillion in annual benefits in today's dollars for a very long period in the future, assuming 3% yearly inflation. The question before the class is: What lump sum investment today would be needed to do this? In Finance 101, this is a classic "present value" problem.

Deriving the entire calculation would be time-consuming, so let's use a well-known formula called the Gordon Growth Model: PV = D/ (r-g).[6]

PV = "present value," i.e., a lump sum investment required to pay for future deficit spending.

D = annual deficit spending, equal to the dollar value of the government's unfunded yearly expenditure in today's dollars.

g = annual growth rate of the deficit spending, also equal to the inflation rate

r = annual investment rate of return on a lump sum investment

PV = \$1.5 T / (5%-3%) = <u>\$75 T</u>

By this calculation, the "present value" of the future unfunded debt is \$75 trillion. To be clear, this is the lump sum you would have to invest today to earn the retirement, disability, and medical benefits promised to Americans in the future.

Add to this the \$35 trillion in debt already incurred, and our government's total financial obligations are \$110 trillion in today's dollars!

Other credible estimates of the US government's unfunded liabilities are much higher. For example, in 2023, a study from the Cato Institute placed the present value of the unfunded debt at \$80 trillion. Adding the funded debt brings us a total debt of \$115 trillion. Openthebooks.com estimates total US debt, funded and unfunded, at \$175 trillion.[7]

Although all these estimates are only approximations, they are instructive. *Their value is to demonstrate that the investment required to fund future benefits, even in a conservative scenario, is an impossible sum.* Can anyone seriously imagine financing a lump sum of \$75 trillion, let alone \$175 trillion? \$75 trillion is almost three times the annual US GDP and well over three times the US broad money supply.[8]

Or compare Cato's estimate of $115 trillion in unfunded debt to all the money in the world. Today's worldwide broad money supply is around $125 trillion, and the global annual GDP is about $110 trillion. Even if it were possible to invest all the money in the world to fund US future deficits, there would not be enough money to do so, and there would not be nearly enough investment opportunities.[9]

These massive future entitlements are "unfunded" due to the simple fact that *they cannot be funded!* All the world's balance sheets combined will not pay for them. Even if we could somehow steal the wealth from other countries, there is probably not enough wealth in the entire world to pay for the promises American politicians have made to all Americans, living and unborn.

The absurdly high present value of these future deficits proves that Congress is deceiving Americans by promising they can consume more wealth than the world can provide.

So the next question is, what will our elected politicians, who created this mess, do about it?

How politicians view the debt problem

Some politicians and media figures often use dramatic metaphors such as the "debt bomb" to characterize our extensive federal debt, insinuating that this escalating debt will eventually trigger a catastrophic financial explosion that wrecks everything it touches.[10] But most politicians who speak in these terms are exploiting the debt problem for shock value rather than doing anything about it. Despite their apocalyptic metaphors, no "bomb" is going to explode. There will be periodic financial crises, but it's doubtful that any single financial event will crash the dollar or render our government unable to function.

What we are facing is more like a debt swamp—once you step in, you gradually find yourself sinking and struggling to move forward. Economic progress grinds to a halt, and it's tough to identify the point where there's no going back to dry ground.

Our elected leaders are responsible for creating this intractable debt problem and will be tasked with finding solutions to resolve it. To anticipate how they will act, we must understand their career incentives.

We can simplify the career behavior of politicians as a series of recurring steps:

Step 1: Politicians make promises to get elected.

Step 2: Politicians tax and borrow to pay for their promises.

Step 3: Politicians get re-elected and make additional promises to get re-elected.

Step 4: Politicians tax and borrow more.

Step 5: Return to Step 1.

To fulfill their promises, politicians throw public money at social problems, real or imagined. From wiping out sickness and poverty to stopping the seas from rising, politicians promise to solve all kinds of unsolvable problems by spending hundreds of billions in public money. (Your money!) They obtain this money by taxing the public and borrowing from investors. The process keeps them in office because throwing other peoples' money at unsolvable problems is popular with enough voters to get heavy-spending politicians reelected year after year.

The repetitive cycle of promising, spending, and campaigning encourages politicians to adopt a short-term time horizon regarding the nation's finances. Politicians do not make a living like ordinary people. They do not have to raise a crop year after year or plan a multi-decade business strategy. Politicians give away other peoples' money for a living, so they are constantly on the lookout for more of it.

Problems arise when the cost of keeping their promises rises faster than their ability to gather tax revenue. When politicians run out of taxpayer money, they borrow money from savers and investors by issuing Treasury bonds. When they run out of bond buyers willing to buy their bonds at market-determined interest rates, central banks step in to monetize some of the government's debt,

allowing the politicians to borrow more. In other words, the un-
checked spending of politicians encourages the government to resort
to inflation, which I defined in Chapter Five as money creation
caused by government action.

The leading example of inflationary money creation in contemporary America is the Fed's massive debt monetizing during Quantitative Easing from 2009 to 2022, covered in Chapter Five. In that
13-year episode, the Fed bought vast amounts of government bonds,
creating huge quantities of new bank deposits. These new deposits
were then recycled into more Treasury debt, financing the most significant budget deficits in history.

David Stockman, a former budget director under Ronald Reagan,
summarizes the Fed's role in facilitating irresponsible spending and
increased debt:

> Someday historians may wonder how such a disaster
> came to pass, and surely the Fed's culpability will be
> hard to miss ... By monetizing massive amounts of the
> public debt during the last two decades, it allowed the
> debt to explode while crippling the bond yield signaling
> mechanism that might have at least given Washington's
> politicians fair warning.[11]

Our elected officials may publicly complain about our absurdly
gargantuan debt, but they know that the government's debt problem
is very different from the problems a typical person or corporation
faces. The reason is that, unlike an ordinary citizen, the government
never has to pay off its debt.

Why is this? No lender will lend to a human being in perpetuity
because no one lives forever. If a borrower dies in debt with no
money in his estate, his debt dies with him—a very bad deal for the
lender! But the US government, in theory, will "live" forever. For instance, if the US Treasury borrows money in the bond market for ten
years, it can borrow again in ten years, paying off the principal of the
old loan and borrowing again, ad infinitum. This is called "rolling
over" or "refinancing" the debt, similar to rolling over a mortgage

loan. The difference is that the government can roll over debt continually without ever paying off the principal.

This is why politicians are not moved to take action when confronted with absolute debt numbers like "$110 trillion in total debt." Their problem is not the massive amount of debt. Their major financial concern is finding enough money to keep their promises and roll over the debt for the next election cycle.

In other words, elected politicians are motivated by short-term cash flow, not the nation's long-term financial health.

Government's four cash flow levers

Let's look at each element of the government's cash flow equation to see where politicians will likely concentrate their efforts. When confronted with a cash flow shortfall, they must apply some combination of the following options, each designed to reduce cash outflow or increase cash income. (These options are listed in order of the potential effect they would have on the budget, not in order of likelihood of adoption.)

1. Reduce or default on promised entitlement payments.
2. Increase taxes.
3. Increase borrowing.
4. Reduce interest costs.

Option one: *Reduce or default on promised entitlement payments.* A majority (70%) of annual government spending consists of entitlement benefits (social security, disability, Medicare, and Medicaid) that must be paid by law, with built-in inflation escalators. The only honest response to a shortfall in the ability to pay entitlements would be to say, "Oops, sorry, we miscalculated, and you cannot have what we promised you because we don't have the money." Conceivably, Congress could then improve cash flow by delaying Social Security and Medicare benefits until age 80 instead of 65.

An invasion of friendly Martians is more likely to happen. The torches and pitchforks come out when you tell people they will not get their healthcare, disability, or social security. Default on obligations may be the honest alternative for an insolvent government, but it's an inferior strategy for the politicians in power. If you haven't noticed, no one in Congress or any presidential candidate ever dares to discuss this possibility. Instead, they fall over themselves to assure voters that their Social Security or Medicare benefits will *never* be reduced.

The truth is that these entitlements cannot be paid in full, so politicians will want to *appear* to pay these entitlements to the people who elected them, at least in nominal dollars. So, the nominal payouts to most voters will not be reduced, but they may be reduced for people whose votes do not matter. For example, Congress may reduce social security payments to wealthy people because they don't have enough votes to affect an election. However, cutting entitlement payments to the rich will not be enough to solve the cash flow problem. Chapter Seven will cover this option in more detail.

Option two: *Raise taxes.* How about simply raising tax rates to get more money? Can Congress increase taxes enough to cover their deficit spending?

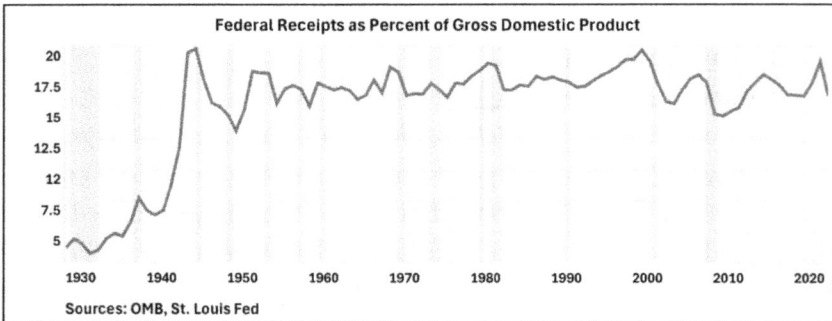

Federal Receipts as Percent of Gross Domestic Product

Sources: OMB, St. Louis Fed

The problem with this idea is that raising tax rates isn't likely to bring in much extra revenue. For the last 80 years, federal tax receipts as a percentage of the US GDP (a proxy for America's collective income) have been relatively constant at between 15 and 19 percent and never higher than 20%, even though marginal tax rates have varied from 28% to 90%! Higher tax rates don't necessarily result in higher tax receipts because if tax rates on income get too high, people will produce less taxable income.[12]

It's worth pointing out that tax receipts drop sharply during recessions (gray-shaded areas in the graph above), and typically, government deficits go way up during these periods as the government increases spending to help people through hard times. That's why recessions increase the deficit and the total debt numbers faster than usual.[13]

The question for politicians is, what tax rate will gather the maximum revenue? A zero-tax rate results in zero tax revenue. A 100% tax rate also delivers zero revenue because people stop working and earning when they can't keep any money they earn. Somewhere between zero and 100 percent is a theoretical optimum tax rate that will give the government its maximum revenue. That point is at the top of this theoretical curve, known as the Laffer Curve, named after the economist Art Laffer.[14]

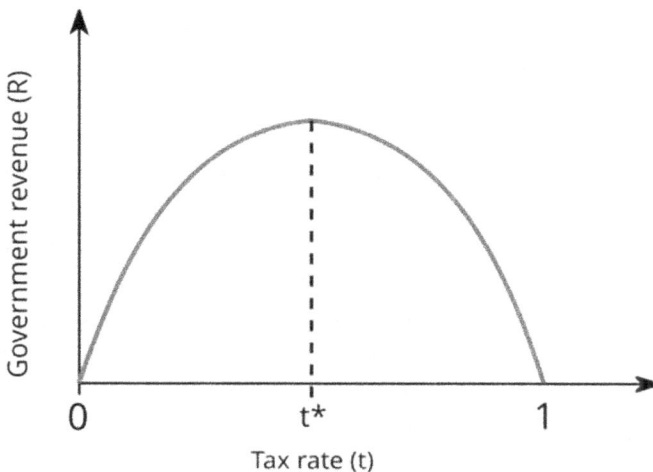

We have historical examples of this principle in action, such as when the United Kingdom reduced tax rates in the 1980s, and tax receipts went up a few years later. Another example was after the fall of Communism when the Russian government slashed corporate taxes and raised tax revenues substantially. At a moderate tax rate, citizens and corporations felt they were getting something for their tax money, so they were willing to pay rather than spend a lot of energy evading taxes.

The main takeaway from the Laffer Curve is that although we cannot always know the "optimal" tax rate from a politician's point of view, politicians know they cannot continually raise more revenue simply by increasing the income tax rate. Based on history, a reasonable assumption is that the Treasury can sustainably gather a maximum of 20% of GDP in total revenue.

If the government cannot collect taxes above 20% of GDP, the obvious way to increase tax revenues is to grow nominal GDP. An inflating GDP will produce an expanding tax base, increasing tax revenue. Consequently, an inflating GDP (which requires an inflating Consumer Price Index) is advantageous to the government as long as the people don't complain too much about rising prices.
It's also worth noting that when the government stimulates the stock market, as it did during the QE era, higher stock prices lead to higher capital gains taxes, which are a significant source of tax receipts.

So far, the government's best chance of increasing revenue is to adopt policies that inflate GDP and boost the stock market.

Option three: *Increase borrowing.* The ballooning federal debt demonstrates that the Treasury has always been able to borrow to fund its deficits. But can this continue indefinitely? To answer, we need to know how they have gotten away with it so far.

As we saw earlier, the fundamental limit on the government's borrowing is its ability to pay interest on its debt. However, increasing debt typically means paying higher interest costs. Why has the government been able to radically increase its debt and still afford to pay the interest?

The answer is that, for the four decades prior to March 2020, interest rates reliably sank like a rock in a tub of honey. As the debt increased, declining rates offset the expected growth in interest costs. It's similar to refinancing a house with a cheaper mortgage loan: You can afford a more expensive home with a 3% mortgage than a 6% mortgage.

The following three charts tell the story graphically.

Falling interest rates, which reached the lowest level in history …

Yield on 10-year Treasury Bond

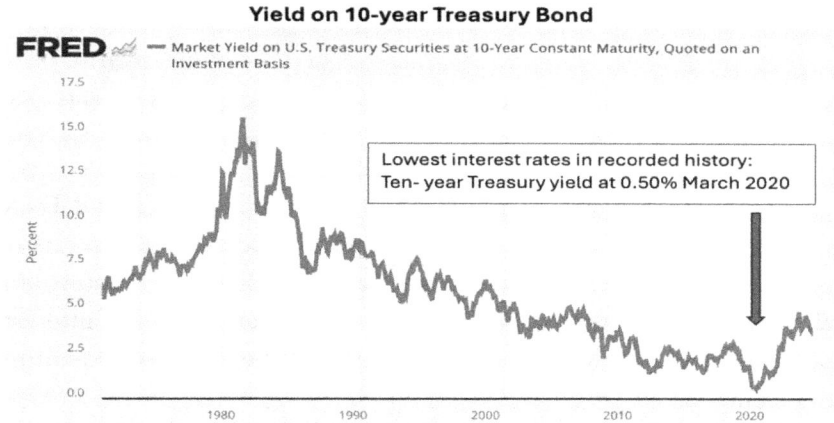

... offset the rising US sovereign debt (spurred by runaway spending) …

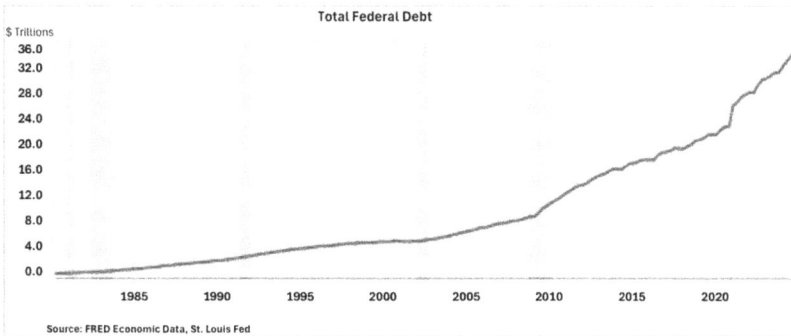

... resulting in record low interest costs as a percent of national income (GDP) between 2001 and 2021.[15]

Interest as Percent of GDP

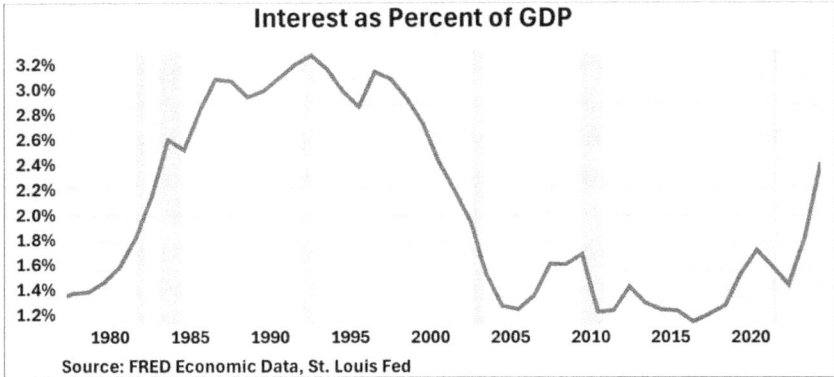

Source: FRED Economic Data, St. Louis Fed

These low and declining interest costs led Vice President Dick Cheney to famously say in 2003, "Reagan proved deficits don't matter." This self-evidently foolish statement would be true if you could always borrow at near-zero interest rates. However, normal interest rates and higher interest costs have changed the cash flow equation in recent years.[16]

It's likely that many foreign Treasury buyers, like Japan and China, saw America's problem of rising interest costs years ago. Central banks that habitually invested their countries' trade surpluses into US Treasury bonds have either stopped increasing or are actively decreasing their Treasury holdings. Perhaps their reasons are partly geopolitical, but I doubt they would have stopped lending to Uncle Sam if they thought Treasurys were a good investment. China, once a significant owner of Treasury debt, is gradually replacing its Treasury holdings with gold. All else equal, less demand for Treasurys results in higher interest rates.[17]

What will be the consequences if the US government attempts to continue increasing its spending and borrowing while interest rates rise on an expanding amount of debt? Higher interest rates on an ever-expanding quantity of debt will cause total interest costs to skyrocket. In fact, this is already happening.

As of Q2 2024, annualized federal government interest payments have topped $1 trillion, exceeding the Medicaid and Defense annual spending.[18]

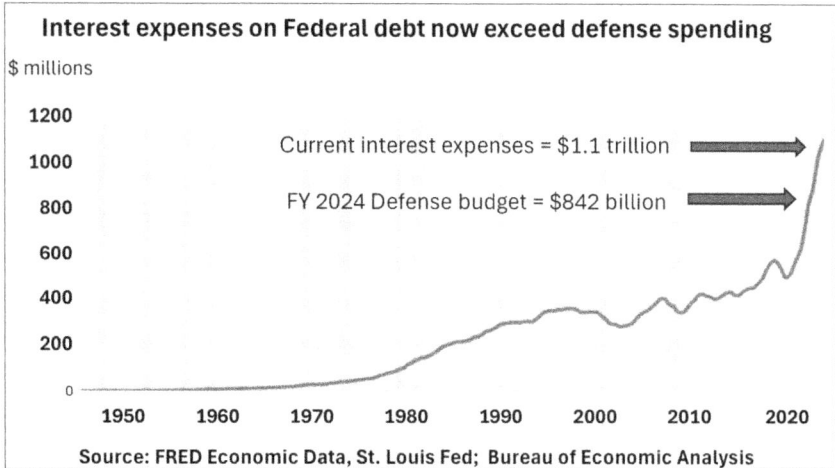

Interest expenses on Federal debt now exceed defense spending

$ millions

Current interest expenses = $1.1 trillion

FY 2024 Defense budget = $842 billion

Source: FRED Economic Data, St. Louis Fed; Bureau of Economic Analysis

Can interest rates reverse course and decline, giving our government a reprieve? I believe this is very unlikely. As we'll see in the next chapter, there are good reasons to think market interest rates, which have risen rapidly in the last four years, will stay higher for longer.

Because of rising debt levels and higher interest rates, interest costs are beginning to dominate the federal budget. In 2021, a nonpartisan think tank called the Committee for a Responsible Federal Budget (CRFB) projected spending on large government programs based on Congressional Budget Office data. At the time of the study, the yield on the 10-year bond was 1.6%. Even assuming only modestly rising interest rates, CRFB's projections show interest costs overtaking defense, Medicare, and Social Security spending within 20 years.[19]

Quoting from the CRFB study:

> "Over the long term, interest costs will continue to outpace growth in other budget areas. Interest will exceed total non-defense and discretionary spending by FY

2032. It will go on to become the largest federal government line item – exceeding the cost of Social Security
and Medicare – by 2045. *By that point, spending on net
interest will consume about 90 percent of all income tax
revenue.*" [Italics added.]

Fig. 7: Projected Spending on Large Government Programs (Percent of GDP)

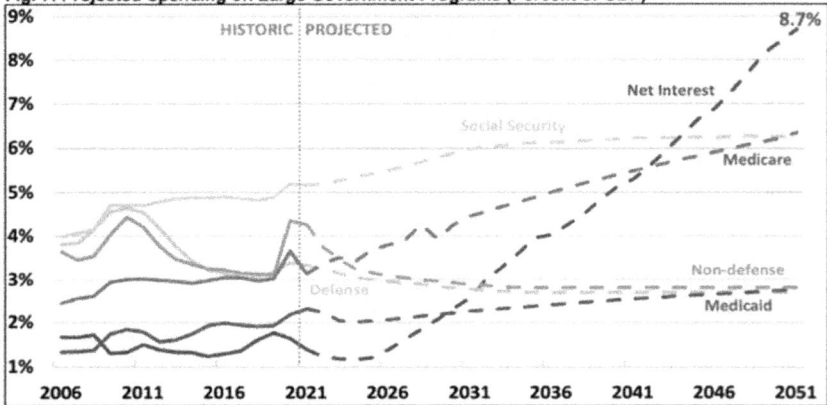

Source: Congressional Budget Office and CRFB calculations.

The referenced CFRB study was published in 2021. Based on their
analysts' assumptions, interest costs would surpass Medicaid payments around 2028 and defense spending around 2031. However,
only three years after the study was published, the government's
cashflow problem was already worse than the CFRB estimate. As of
July 2024, when this book went to the publisher, annual interest costs
exceeded defense spending, years ahead of the CFRB projection.

Seemingly out of the blue, after decades in which deficits seemed
not to matter, rising interest costs have set a trap in which interest
payments threaten to overwhelm the political cash flow equation. At
some point, lenders in the bond market will conclude that a government selling bonds to pay interest on its old bonds is like a snake
eating its tail—in other words, unsustainable.

The bond market will sniff out the problem before we get to that
point. If you were lending money to someone who could pay the

interest on his loan only by borrowing more, would you continue lending to them? At some point, possibly soon, Treasury investors will require much higher interest rates to invest in additional Treasury bonds. However, higher interest rates are ultimately self-defeating because they will raise interest costs even more, increasing the pressure on the government's cash flow.

The snake can eat its tail for a while, but not forever.

This problem exists because American voters permitted politicians to make promises that cannot be kept in the long run. Given the politicians' incentives, we should have expected it. Driven by the immediate demands of election cycles, our leaders prioritize the short term, neglecting the imperative of long-term solutions. Year after year, they escalate borrowing to pay for entitlements, thereby ballooning deficits, compounding debts, inflating interest costs, and hastening the next fiscal crisis. But as long as they think the government can pay the interest costs, they are incentivized to keep the system going for one more budget cycle, hoping for a miracle.

When our government runs out of bond buyers at reasonable interest rates, and the government is borrowing solely to pay interest on existing debt, who will buy more US debt? Houston, we have a problem.

The interest cost dilemma brings us to Option Four.

Option four: *Reduce interest costs*. Somehow, the government is going to have to reduce its interest costs. Interest costs are a function of 1) the amount of debt outstanding and 2) the interest rate on that debt. Short of defaulting on government debt, it's impossible to reduce the outstanding debt without reducing the principal, which I do not believe will happen. This leaves reducing the interest rate paid on government debt as the only remaining option for balancing the cash flow equation.

The problem with this idea is that a worldwide market determines interest rates on Treasury debt. The Fed can manipulate this market for a while, as they did during the QE years, but that policy has already backfired, as years of excessive money creation have caused consumer prices to soar.

Therefore, if the Fed once again implements quantitative easing to force interest rates lower by monetizing the government's deficits, the result will likely be more consumer price inflation and, ultimately, even higher market interest rates. At this point, the government's appetite for debt has overwhelmed the Fed's ability to monetize it without causing much higher consumer prices, which is politically unacceptable. The debt trap is set.

If the Fed becomes unable to control interest rates by intervening in the bond market, what alternatives will the politicians have? Short of admitting they are broke, reneging on promised entitlements, and resigning in disgrace—which will not happen—they will be forced to address their cash flow problem by the most expedient means. What will that look like?

We have already seen why politicians are unlikely to materially reduce entitlement payments, which account for 70 percent of the annual budget. They may be able to inflate GDP and stocks and thus raise more tax revenue. They will talk about moderating their borrowing, but significant deficits are already baked into the entitlement cake.

Interest costs are thus the linchpin of the planners' cash flow equation. The government must limit interest costs by lowering the interest rate on Treasury debt. Normally, interest rates are determined in a competitive bond market, but as bond markets become increasingly wary of U.S. government debt, they will require higher interest rates. Therefore, reducing interest rates can only be done by the force of law or the "nudge" of financial regulation.

Financial repression is inevitable

Considering their four cash flow options, the government's emphasis will have to be on Options Two and Four: stimulating nominal GDP to raise the tax base while suppressing nominal interest rates to lower interest costs. In macroeconomic terms, this will probably mean suppressing interest rates to a level below the nominal GDP growth rate.

Economists have a term for this policy mix: "financial repression." Financial repression punishes savers through currency debasement while restricting their ability to save through interest rate suppression. Its implementation is already underway in other economies, such as Japan, and we are likely to see much more of it in the USA, starting soon and lasting for many years.

In Chapter Seven, we'll detail the various legislative, policy, and regulatory actions the government may use to implement financial repression.

7 THE ARSONIST AND THE FIREMAN

What is financial repression? Knowing your enemy;
Limit entitlements; Increase taxes; Keep on borrowing;
Reduce interest costs; Capital controls; Can financial repres-
sion work?

What is financial repression?

In Chapter Six, we learned that the Fed created trillions in new money under a program called "quantitative easing." By taking money creation decisions into their own hands, Washington's monetary masters purchased massive amounts of Treasury bonds, flooded the investment markets with new money, drove interest rates to their lowest levels in recorded history, and triggered the worst consumer price inflation in forty years. A dollar in 2024 is worth at least 20% less than a dollar in 2020. "Quantitative seizing" might have been a better name for their program.

At the same time, seduced by the Fed's near-zero interest rates, Congress commenced an orgy of spending and borrowing. The debt seemed free at the time. But now that interest rates have returned to normal levels, the government faces an intractable funding crisis.

How can the government solve this debt dilemma? In preview, this chapter will propose that the politicians who hijacked money creation to inflate the national debt will now try to neutralize it with—you guessed it—more money creation. Money creation, the igniter of debt, will come back disguised as the eradicator of debt. The arsonist will return in a fireman's uniform.

The government's financial policies will result in "financial re-pression," a peculiar combination of high inflation and low "real" in-terest rates, enacted through many new laws, policies, and regula-tions. What will financial repression mean to the average saver and investor? Financial historian Russell Napier, who has been warning about financial repression for years, portrays it succinctly:

> Financial repression is stealing old peoples' money slowly.[1]

Financial repression is best illustrated with a real-world example.

A close friend—we'll call him Joe—is 72 years old. He spent 40 years working as a high school teacher and coach before retiring in 2016. His wife, Paula, is also a retired teacher. They own a pleasant, cozy home in the Midwest. Their retirement plans are focused on leading a peaceful and tranquil life. Joe plays golf several times weekly and enjoys tending to his orchard, while Paula enjoys her book club and connecting with neighbors. Although they travel oc-casionally to visit friends and family, most of their time is spent in and around their home.

After retirement, their financial situation was stable for a few years; however, after the government implemented monetary "stim-ulus" measures during the COVID lockdown, consumer prices rose significantly, substantially impacting Joe and Paula's way of life. Their day-to-day costs, including groceries, fuel, insurance, healthcare, and other expenses, have surged by more than 25% over the past four years. Like many pension schemes, Joe's retirement plan does not account for increases in the cost of living.

In 2023, Joe recognized the problem, projecting that in the next 10 to 15 years, he and Paula might have to sell their house and rent an apartment. In response to this dilemma, Joe returned to work, in-creased his earnings, and reduced his time on the golf course. Given his excellent health and capabilities, Joe secured a teaching position that provides additional income and professional satisfaction. Of course, not everyone in a similar situation may have the same opportunities as Joe.

Now that Joe is working again, his income is increasing. However, due to inflation, the purchasing power of his dollars is decreasing each year. Even though Joe is now more productive than he was in the pre-inflation period, a substantial portion of his increased output is depleted by elevated prices and taxes. In essence, Joe is now working much harder to maintain a constant standard of living.

Joe and Paula exemplify the impact of financial repression. As we'll shortly see, financial repression is imposed through various government policies, laws, and regulations formulated to embezzle Joe's earnings and savings. Joe and Paula are directly feeling the effects of this control, precisely as the government intended. The government needs more money, and financial repression is how they will get it.

Like an overdrawn derelict, our government needs cash to maintain its spending habits. But unlike the derelict who must beg for money, our government has coercive power. Consequently, we can expect our money-hungry politicians to use the carrot and the stick – the "nudge" and the "whip"—to ensure the continuous cash flow necessary to fulfill their commitments and avoid being thrown out of office.

Knowing your enemy

The objective of this chapter is to predict the government's maneuvers. As Sun Tzu stated in *The Art of War*, "To know your enemy, you must become your enemy," which, in this context, implies understanding the mindset of politicians driven by political interests. If we know what they believe they must do to keep their jobs, we can take defensive action to mitigate the adverse effects of their actions.

Let's review the strategic options open to our elected and appointed officials, whom we refer to collectively as "the government." These people include Congressional lawmakers, regulators at the Federal Reserve, regulators in the Treasury Department and its subagencies, and still other regulators such as the Federal Deposit Insurance Corporation (FDIC).[2]

In Chapter Six, we learned that the government has four "fiscal levers" it can pull to achieve its cash flow objectives. Each lever suggests a parallel strategy to increase revenue or reduce cash costs. These strategies are:

1. Limit entitlements.
2. Increase taxes.
3. Continue borrowing.
4. Reduce interest costs.

While considering these options, ponder this: If you were a politician who had led your government to the brink of financial collapse, with your primary objective being to stay in power, what steps would you consider taking? How would you procure the funds required to honor your campaign promises and secure reelection for another term?

Limit entitlements

First, you would try to renege on the financial commitments you know you cannot pay. It's well-known that the US government debt is out of control due to the legally mandated spending on Social Security, Medicare, and disability care—entitlements that absorb 70% of the federal budget. These entitlements and their automatic cost-of-living escalators are so deeply written into the public's expectations that they are known as "non-discretionary" spending—as if our elected officials have no power to cut them.

Career politicians across the spectrum rarely discuss cutting entitlements because it is political suicide. This sentiment was captured in a 2012 statement attributed to former Luxembourg Prime Minister Jean Claude Juncker: "We all know what to do. We just don't know how to get re-elected after we do it."

Rather than self-destruct by making drastic cuts, the government will cautiously trim benefits to groups whose votes won't matter in the next election. For example, the wealthy will almost certainly receive lower Social Security benefits and higher Medicare premiums. Conversely, essential voting blocs such as unions and minority groups are more likely to receive promised entitlements.

The government tends to shave benefits discreetly when it believes the public is not looking. One reliable technique is to change the method of calculating the mandatory cost-of-living increases written into the laws governing social security and disability payments. According to the U.S. Census Bureau (2023), 74% of Americans receive government benefits linked to BLS inflation numbers.[3] Capping the increases in these programs is an important source of "savings" for the government. Therefore, it's not surprising that the Bureau of Labor Statistics (BLS) systematically understates CPI inflation to control the cost-of-living escalators built into social security and disability programs.

The following chart reveals the deception in the BLS statistics. Shadowstats.com, an inflation monitoring research group, evaluates consumer price index adjustments using the 1980 methodology. Using the old approach, today's CPI inflation (upper line) is almost twice as high as the official published rate (lower line). [4]

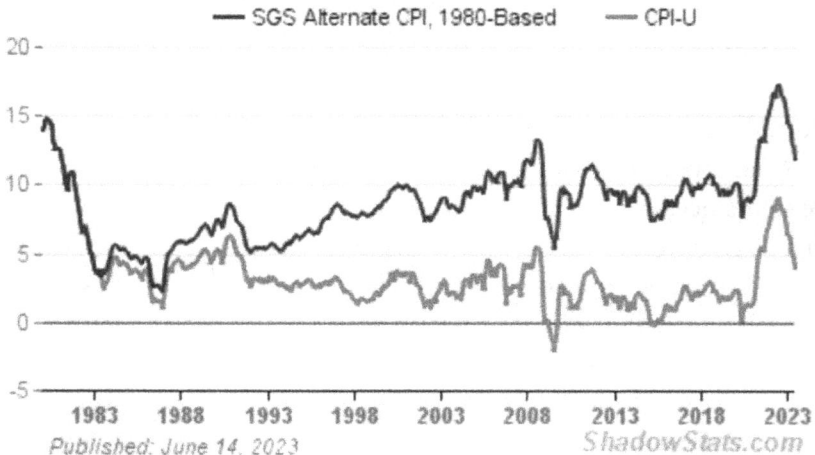

Consumer Inflation - Official vs ShadowStats (1980-Based) Alternate
Year to Year Change. Through May 2023
— SGS Alternate CPI, 1980-Based   — CPI-U

Published: June 14, 2023   ShadowStats.com

The current method of calculating the CPI incorporates mathematical routines like "substitution" and "hedonic pricing," which are complex and contentious topics beyond the purview of this discussion. The key takeaway is that the Bureau of Labor Statistics is motivated to downplay CPI inflation. For instance, if the government can increase your Social Security benefits by five percent while your actual cost of living surges by ten percent, it allows the government to save money by withholding the funds it had initially committed to provide.

As the late Charlie Munger said, "Show me the incentive, and I'll show you the outcome." We should expect entitlements to be quietly and selectively reduced whenever the politicians can get away with it. The BLS has played its part in financial repression and will continue to do so.

Grant's Interest Rate Observer documents the BLS's record:

> Is there not one federal institution that has contributed consistently, over 40 years, to the reduction in the measured inflation rate? Why, yes ... It's the very institution that compiles, amends, and modernizes the Consumer Price Index. Out of 25 such updates since 1983 ... only 4 gave rise to an upside revision in the reported price data. The Bureau of Labor Statistics is that steadfast agency ... In general ... the more sophisticated the indices become (as, for instance, in the substitution of owner's equivalent rent for house prices, which occurred in 1983), the more favorable the appearance of the reported inflation data.[5]

However, try as they might, the BLS's little "soft" defaults on financial commitments can only provide minor budgetary relief that will fall far short of closing Congress's financial gap. The real money will be found by boosting tax receipts.

Increase taxes

Expect the government to implement various measures to increase tax revenue, all while treading carefully so as not to enrage the masses. New incremental revenue sources will include taxes on the wealthy, "sin" taxes, estate taxes, and possibly a nationwide sales tax. But, as we'll see, the biggest potential for increasing taxes lies in expanding the base of taxable income through inflation.

Taxes on the wealthy. The affluent will likely feel the pinch from a hike in capital gains taxes, hitting owners of assets like stocks, bonds, and real estate. Anticipate a strategic move to tap into this lucrative revenue source, albeit cautiously, to avoid snuffing out investment enthusiasm among the wealthy. Watch for the emergence of a modest "wealth tax" aimed squarely at the nation's wealthiest individuals. Moreover, Congress may focus on curbing tax deferral strategies, like the Section 1031 exchange program, which shields real estate investors from capital gains taxes for prolonged periods. Another potential measure is taxing substantial stock market transactions primarily affecting high-income individuals.

Taxes on "sinners." Additional "sin" taxes will likely be levied unless many voters oppose them. Taxes on "vices" often garner public approval under the guise of discouraging undesirable social behavior. The famous 1998 "tobacco settlement," which provided a permanent source of revenue to Medicaid from tobacco sales, was a prototype revenue generator.[6] Additional taxes on liquor, recreational drugs, and gambling will all be fair game.

A new variant of the sin tax might be environmental taxes, including higher gasoline taxes or potential carbon dioxide emissions taxes. These taxes might be tolerated by the public because we are supposed to be ashamed of using "scarce resources" or because we are supposed to believe carbon dioxide is burning up the planet. If enough voters accept this dishonest environmentalism, we can expect the government to cash in with a new carbon tax.[7]

Taxes on the dead. There may be some attempts to install more punitive estate taxes, but these are likely to fail. Estate taxes are unpopular, and some states have even provided ways to avoid them entirely. For example, Wyoming and South Dakota have a legal arrangement called a Dynasty Trust that allows a person to avoid all estate taxes for up to 1000 years. To avoid starting a stampede to these states for estate tax relief, I suspect legislators will not press too hard on increasing estate taxes.[8]

Taxes on nonprofits. Taxes on non-profits are not likely but possible, as there are some calls to tax universities and hospitals, which look and act more like businesses than charities.

National sales sax. Another possible tax initiative could be a nationwide Value Added Tax (VAT), a national sales tax on merchandise. A few presidential candidates have floated this idea, but it is getting minimal political traction. A VAT would have to be implemented cautiously because an aggressive VAT could backfire by stifling nominal GDP and lowering the income tax base. If such a tax is implemented, expect it to start very small.

Expanding the tax base. Congress can increase taxes incrementally in many ways. However, new taxes alone cannot provide the massive revenue needed for our ballooning government spending and deficits. As discussed in Chapter Six, a significant revenue increase necessitates expanding the tax base, which is contingent on growth of the nominal Gross Domestic Product (GDP).

In their efforts to expand nominal GDP, politicians are likely to adopt the critical strategy of allowing price inflation to "run hot," thereby inflating both nominal GDP and the income tax base. The downside to this strategy is inflation and all its unwelcome consequences. Nevertheless, if the public becomes accustomed to persistent inflation, a swiftly expanding nominal GDP could serve as a substantial and increasing reservoir of tax income over a long period.

A proven method to increase tax revenue involves merging high inflation with a "progressive" income tax structure akin to the one in the U.S. In a progressive income tax setup, as your earnings grow, a higher percentage of your income is taxed. The underlying principle is that high earners should contribute to the government at a higher rate simply because they earn more. (While I disagree with this principle, our primary job here is to predict government actions, not protest their policies.)

For our discussion, the critical thing to understand is that a progressive income tax schedule is designed to take more of your *real* wealth through a process called "bracket creep," which I will now illustrate with the graph and explanation below.[9]

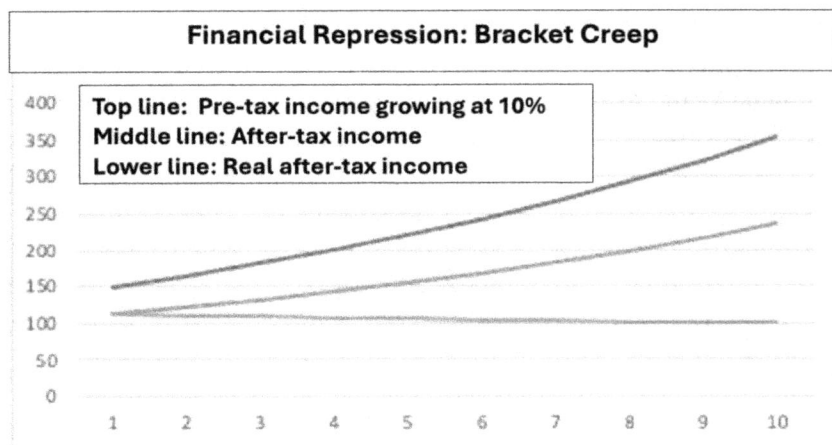

Financial Repression: Bracket Creep

Top line: Pre-tax income growing at 10%
Middle line: After-tax income
Lower line: Real after-tax income

Source: HardmoneyJim, February 18, 2023

Let's imagine a household earning $150,000 per year and assume a progressive tax schedule like the one currently in place in the USA. The example is somewhat simplified to make the calculations obvious, but the analysis's outcome is realistic.

Assume the first $50,000 of your annual household income is taxed at 15%. Next, income between $50,000 and $100,000 is taxed at 25%. Then, income between $100,000 and $150,000 is taxed at 35%. Finally, all income above $150,000 is taxed at 40%. That's a simple progressive tax schedule that's not materially different from today's.

Next, let's assume a period with significant inflation (expected under financial repression) in which the prices of goods, services, and gross income grow at 10% per year for ten years. Without taxes, your growing income would keep up with your increasing cost of living, as all costs and prices would rise at 10% per year.

But as we're about to see, "bracket creep" enables the Treasury to covertly take more of your actual wealth as your inflating income moves into a higher tax bracket. That's because more and more of your rising income is pushed into a higher tax bracket, even as your dollars are losing purchasing power due to inflation.

In this hypothetical example, here is a summary of what happens over ten years:

1. Your annual pre-tax income (top line) rises from $150,000 to $354,000, creating an illusion of prosperity—after all, look how fast your income is increasing!
2. Your annual after-tax income (middle line) rises from $113,000 to $233,000.
3. Because of "bracket creep," the total tax you pay as a percentage of your annual pre-tax income rises from 25% to 33%.
4. Your take-home pay adjusted for annual price inflation (lower line)—declines from $113,000 in year one to about $100,000 inflation-adjusted dollars in year ten. Note the downward slope of the lower line in the graph.
5. The percentage of gross income you keep after tax declines from 75% to 66%. That's why the middle line rises slower than the upper line.
6. Over ten years, the government "progressed" from taking $37,500 in taxes to $121,000 yearly. This is an annual growth rate of 12.5% versus inflation of 10%.

All of this is a bad deal for the taxpayer but great for a money-hungry government. They needed your inflating tax base to pay for their entitlement promises in depreciating dollars. Because of bracket creep, the government took a bigger portion of your real wealth by reducing your inflation-adjusted income from $113,000 to $100,000.

Inflation-induced bracket creep drains wealth from the most productive earners—those with growing incomes—and most people don't even realize it is happening. If the government can grow nominal tax receipts faster than the growth rate of its committed entitlements, it will be paying down its debt through inflation.

This is the treadmill of financial repression. Yes, progressive taxation in an inflationary economy is surreptitious and unfair, but remember, from the politicians' point of view, this is precisely how financial repression is supposed to work. Because they need your money.

This tactic is currently working. As of June 2024, recent consumer price inflation has elevated nominal GDP to $28.2 trillion and annual tax revenues to $4.9 trillion, marking record highs for both figures. While taxes are insufficient to cover a $7 trillion (and increasing) annual federal budget, a rapidly increasing nominal GDP plays a crucial role in sustaining the influx of funds into the government.

Boosting nominal GDP. How can the government keep CPI inflation "running hot," that is, continue inflating GDP year after year? It must ensure that banks continue creating fresh money for GDP-related transactions. For example, new money spent on automobiles or home rents boosts GDP and raises the income tax base. Conversely, money spent on buying stocks and bonds does not immediately impact GDP or taxable income, although inflating asset prices eventually increases government revenue via capital gains taxes.

So, the question becomes, how will our government encourage or require the banks to create enough new money to spur the growth of nominal GDP (and consequently the tax base)?[10]

One traditional method of boosting GDP is stimulating the housing market. Although rising house prices do not directly affect GDP, related spending on house rents and household goods does have a significant impact.

And, just in time for the 2024 election, we're about to see a surge in housing-related stimulus. In March 2024, the Federal Housing Finance Agency (FHFA), also known as Freddie Mac, unveiled a new initiative enabling homeowners to take out a second mortgage on their homes. Freddie Mac will guarantee these loans, making them risk-free for lending banks and cheaper for borrowers than traditional second mortgages. The program can potentially create between $800 billion and $1.5 trillion in new money, providing a swift boost to GDP-related activities.[11] The policy is, of course, inflationary. Still, it is just what the doctors of financial repression ordered.

However, a program like this provides only a one-time boost to GDP. Other bold and creative money-creation programs must be invented to boost nominal GDP over the long term.

Industrial Policy and Directed Lending. A likely strategy could involve placing bank lending under the jurisdiction of a national industrial policy executed through commercial banks. Throughout history, monetary regulators have implemented a money creation scheme known as "directed lending," which entails centralized credit allocation by a governing body. This mirrors the money creation model that contributed to Japan's asset bubble in the 1980s and echoes the credit creation practices that propelled the wartime economies of Germany and Japan in World War II.

An industrial policy entails guiding or incentivizing banks to provide loans to industries crucial to the government's goals. In the coming repression, I anticipate a rise in bank lending to vital sectors such as communication systems, infrastructure development, renewable energy, and workforce training initiatives. The government will likely encourage bank loans towards "public-private partnerships," emphasizing the essential nature of these projects for stimulating economic revival and asserting that only the government can orchestrate the needed transformations.

To boost lending towards these preferred projects, the government will offer various incentives, including tax benefits, regulatory leniency, and, most significantly, guarantees on bank loans. With the government's assurance of profits, banks will lend, even at low interest rates, till the cows come home.

Politicians love this setup as it grants them the authority to allocate new funds without the need for increased taxation or borrowing. This affords them financial authority without being held accountable for unpopular spending and borrowing programs. Moreover, the GDP inflation generated by the influx of new money expands the nominal tax revenue base, alleviating the government's financial constraints.

Only a modest amount of taxpayer money is needed to "guarantee" that the bank will be repaid if the loan defaults. Therefore, there is a "de minimus" impact on the federal budget except for a potential "contingent liability" in case of loan failures. Since these corporatist loans resemble standard, market-based loans, their inflationary implications will not be widely understood by the general public. While some of these loans may encounter difficulty, most will not be allowed to default and instead will be renegotiated or extended ("rolled over") as banks will have faith in government backing. In extreme cases, the Fed can step in with new bail-out money.

At root, loan guarantees would mirror what the Fed did under their "bank term funding program" (BTFP) when Silicon Valley Bank (and several other banks) collapsed in March of 2023. Under that program, the Fed purchased the bank's Treasury bonds, which had depreciated due to a rise in interest rates, at their total face value. In a "guaranteed" lending program, central bank money creation is the ultimate source of the loan guarantees, just as it is the ultimate source of all bank bailouts.[12]

In a semi-free, mixed economy like ours, "directed lending" is a central planner's dream because, on the surface, it looks a lot like free enterprise. Expect the government to use it as much as possible.

How might an industrial policy with directed lending be implemented? A specific example, while hypothetical, will help explain.

Suppose Congress decides to address the increasing threat posed by the expanding Chinese navy. Congress concludes that the American shipbuilding industry, previously outsourced to China and other nations, must be rejuvenated and returned to the USA. To initiate this large-scale project, Congress establishes a "development bank" dedicated to re-shoring the industry. This bank could be a "public-private partnership" involving the Treasury Department and private equity investors as shareholders.

This is not a new idea. Historically, numerous countries have set up development banks to finance emerging or favored industries. Development banks typically receive government guarantees to cover potential loan losses. In the present example, they would extend loans to the shipbuilding sector under highly favorable terms to fund new ports and the supporting infrastructure. Borrowers would be required to source labor and materials from the USA or designated friendly nations. The new ships would be sold to the US Navy, friendly foreign navies, US-based shipping companies, and other interested parties.

Undoubtedly, rebuilding the US domestic shipbuilding industry would entail significant costs over many years. Because of all the new money created, such a project would be inherently inflationary, driving up nominal GDP as the new money was spent on materials and labor bought from within America.

A GDP-inflating banking policy aligns with multiple government goals during financial repression. Therefore, this kind of policy will likely get support from politicians across the political spectrum. Industrial policy will be justified by appeals to patriotism, the national interest, rebuilding the national defense, or various "emergencies." In a Democrat administration, they might be dubbed Patriot Banks, while a Republican president might label them "MAGA banks." Such initiatives might not be explicitly labeled "industrial policy," but that is precisely what they will be.

Because they usually come with government guarantees, directed lending programs are susceptible to corruption and misallocation of resources. Despite this risk, not all funds distributed through such programs will be misused, and some might even be used effectively. Looking back at history, even controlled economies like those of fascist Germany and Imperial Japan achieved a high level of productivity, at least temporarily.

Consequently, directed lending initiatives can be expected to produce a mix of productivity, corruption, and inefficiency. Nevertheless, the primary economic impact of directed lending is to sustain financial repression by enlarging the nominal tax base, enabling the government to eat away some of its debt through inflation.

Local governments may also engage in the practice of creating money and boosting GDP. In 2019, California introduced a law allowing local governments to establish "publicly owned" banks. Rather than obtaining funds through municipal bonds, state and local governments can steer bank lending toward municipal ventures. With loan guarantees provided by local taxpayers, significant funds could be made accessible for such projects.[13]

What would the Fed's role be in a financial repression strategy? Could the Fed engage in direct lending to businesses? While we cannot rule this out entirely, direct lending by the Fed would raise concerns due to its obvious central planning nature, sparking controversy. Instead, the central bank could provide additional liquidity to specific industries when required. Perhaps they would call it "selective QE," in which the central bank buys the bonds of selected companies or industries to reduce their funding costs and shield equity investors from bankruptcy. We already have a precedent from the COVID stimulus program, in which the Fed purchased the bonds of healthy private companies like Apple and AT&T. The apparent purpose was to keep their bond prices high, signaling confidence in the bond market.

Predicting the destination of new funds under an industrial policy or any directed lending scheme will be essential for making sound investments in an age of financial repression. In Chapter Eight, we will explore investment strategies in more detail.

Continue borrowing

Even under the best circumstances, the US government will need to borrow increasingly more enormous sums in the coming years. Traditionally, major lenders to the US government have been foreign nations such as Japan, China, and the United Kingdom. These countries accumulated US dollar reserves by maintaining a trade surplus with the US. A significant portion of these surplus dollars, essentially representing the profits from non-US businesses, were channeled into US Treasury bonds. These lenders viewed Treasurys as secure, easily convertible to cash, and not highly susceptible to significant devaluation due to inflation.

Over time, foreign investors have expanded their ownership of Treasury securities; however, the growth of US debt has significantly outpaced the growth of foreign ownership. Consequently, the proportion of the debt held by foreign entities has been decreasing over the years. For instance, although total US debt surged from $18 trillion in 2015 to $35 trillion in July 2024, the percentage owned by foreign investors decreased from 34% to 23%.

This shift away from foreign financing is due partly to geopolitical realignments (such as the escalating tensions with China and Russia) and partly to foreign investors' growing concern that the US Treasury bond may not be the risk-free asset it was once thought to be. As foreign buyers retreated, the Federal Reserve stepped in and monetized a significant piece (over 20%) of the new US debt issued from 2015 to 2024.

Foreign Holdings as Percent of US Debt

Source: Federal Reserve data, graph by author

As explained in Chapter Six, the reduction in foreign investors' lending share is occurring just as the government's need to borrow is exploding. Thus, as foreign investors fade away, the government must turn to US domestic investors to meet its growing funding needs.

In speculating on potential funding sources, we can segment domestic Treasury bond investors into four main categories: the Federal Reserve, US commercial banks, non-bank US financial institutions, and the general public. Let's examine these potential lenders to determine how they might be incentivized, persuaded, or compelled to lend to the US government at rates below the level of CPI inflation.

The Federal Reserve: Buyer of Last Resort

Can we expect the Fed to purchase massive quantities of Treasurys as it did during the QE period? A repeat of QE on that scale seems improbable, as the Fed is now constrained by the consumer price inflation it caused during the "Pandemic QE" monetary expansion. This is why, as of May of 2022, the Fed has been reducing its Treasury holdings through its "quantitative tightening" (QT) initiative, which is supposed to correct the inflationary consequences of the QE period.

However, the Fed will always have some involvement in monetizing Treasury debt. Even under its current cautious projections, the Fed foresees increasing its Treasury holdings by $2 trillion by 2034. Nevertheless, the Fed cannot repeat its massive QE debt monetization program without risking new asset bubbles and uncontrolled CPI inflation—the very issues it is trying to counteract. Therefore, don't expect massive Treasury purchases by the Fed *unless* another crisis requires the Fed's intervention to avoid a deep recession.

Who, besides the Fed, will invest in Uncle Sam's debt?

US Commercial banks: big potential monetizers

US commercial banks, the primary creators of new money, represent a significant, untapped funding source for the government. While banks have not held substantial government debt in recent years, their Treasury holdings doubled from $800 billion to over $1.6 trillion during the COVID crisis, indicating capacity for further expansion.

The government will likely increasingly turn to commercial banks to buy its Treasurys. Historically, many governments in dire financial situations (e.g., banana republics) have exploited the private banking sector to monetize debt to fund their government's spending and borrowing. This practice became evident to me as a banking analyst in 2002, when I witnessed Argentine banks constantly buying government bonds amidst rising inflation.

Furthermore, there is a relevant historical example in the United States. Following World War II, US government debt constituted 40% of US banks' assets, in contrast to the current figure of around 7%. During the post-war period, commercial banks created money by purchasing government bonds, effectively inflating away the burden of war-related debt.

Revisiting this approach holds significant potential. Using 40% as a benchmark and considering that US commercial bank assets are around $23 trillion, the banks could purchase more than $8 trillion in new debt, matching the scale of the Fed's QE program.

To encourage banks to purchase Treasurys, regulators would have to ease current bank capital and liquidity requirements. Currently, US banks are bound by a rule stipulating that their "capital" (akin to net worth or the difference between all assets and liabilities) must not fall below three percent of total assets. This rule limits how much banks can invest in Treasurys without additional capital.

A potential solution is for regulators to permit banks to exclude Treasury bonds from calculating their 3% capital ratio. This would free the banks to load up on Treasurys, as they could simply create the money (deposits) needed to buy them from investors in the open market. By focusing on highly liquid T-bills and short-term notes, the banks would be assured of risk-free profits.

If you think this sounds like quantitative easing done by commercial banks instead of the Fed, you are thinking accurately.

There's already some movement in this direction. In March 2024, the International Swaps and Derivatives Association (ISDA), a financial industry trade group, sent a letter to the Fed and other bank regulators asking that banks be allowed to permanently exclude on-balance-sheet Treasurys from total leverage exposure. If approved, this request will open the door to more extensive Treasury holdings by the banks.[14]

Other regulations could be modified or eased to enable banks to increase their holdings of Treasurys. These modifications might involve changes in "risk weightings," liquidity requirements, safety evaluations, and other pertinent factors.

Given the intricate nature of banking regulations, a more detailed discussion is beyond the scope of this chapter. But it's reasonable to speculate that commercial banks, the leading creators of money, will probably assume a more pivotal role as lenders to the government.

Non-bank financial institutions

Another significant group of potential Treasury buyers comprises US non-bank financial entities, sometimes called "savings institutions." This category encompasses pension funds, 401(k) plans, insurance companies, mutual funds, exchange-traded funds (ETFs), some hedge funds, and non-bank lenders—institutions that pool funds from savers or investors for investment purposes. Collectively, these entities manage assets totaling at least $60 trillion. Although they lack money-creation capabilities, they present an attractive lending source for a government that needs money.

Let's think like bureaucrats to devise ways the government could encourage or require these entities to expand their Treasury holdings.

Fiduciary regulations could be changed. For instance, the government could require 401(k) plans to allocate 25% of their investments to government bonds to maintain their tax-exempt status. (No such requirement currently exists.)

Regulators could also introduce policies restricting certain "high-risk" investments, like emerging market stocks or junk bonds, from tax-exempt retirement accounts. Such adjustments would steer more funds toward low-risk options like US Treasurys.

Furthermore, targeted tax incentives could be introduced to encourage specific institutions to prioritize Treasurys. For instance, in 2017, legislation offered pension funds additional tax benefits for investing in Treasurys. Pension funds now hold around 14% of US Treasurys among non-Fed and non-foreign entities, and there remains potential for further growth.

Likewise, regulators could mandate that diverse investment institutions (such as mutual funds, ETFs, and others) restrict their stock purchases to "manage risk," leading to increased investment in Treasury bonds.

There are other ways these institutions could be encouraged to hold government debt. For instance, the US Treasury could issue long-term, non-tradable securities to public pension funds, mirroring its existing arrangement with the Social Security Trust Fund. This move would help the Treasury Department in its regular funding operations by removing a portion of its debt from the competitive bond market.

Additional "incentives" might involve changes in investment rating methodologies. For instance, a higher proportion of government bonds could be required to achieve a AAA rating in an investment portfolio.

Moreover, imposing a transaction tax on equity trading could elevate stock trading expenses and prompt some institutions to shift their investments toward government bonds rather than stocks.

If you use your imagination and "become the enemy," you can probably think of other possibilities.

Individual savers and investors

Expect the government to encourage individual citizens to invest directly in Treasury bonds. This is already possible through a user-friendly platform, www.treasurydirect.gov, where investors can buy Treasurys directly from the government for as little as $1000.[15]

To further coax individual investors into Treasurys, labor regulations could be implemented to endorse an automatic Treasury savings plan. This initiative could become a standard "benefit" provided by every HR department during new employee open enrollment. By structuring it as an "opt-out" savings scheme, employees would be encouraged to automatically allocate a portion of their monthly earnings towards purchasing Treasury bonds. Such a program might even become mandatory for all 23 million US government employees.

Regulators could "encourage" individual investors to buy more government bonds in many ways. For example, they might say: "Nice IRA you got there. You must now invest 25% of your retirement funds into US Treasurys if you wish to keep accumulating your retirement plan tax-free."

Selective price controls could also nudge investors into government bonds. For example, controlling landlords' ability to raise rents would make investing in Treasurys more attractive.

The bottom line on government borrowing: As foreign investors flee Treasurys, expect the US government to use both the carrot and the stick to find new domestic buyers of its bonds.

Reduce interest costs

There are only two possible strategies for minimizing interest expenses: reducing the debt owed or lowering the interest rate. Since significantly reducing the outstanding debt is impossible without defaulting—an inconceivable scenario for a government that relies on continual borrowing—the primary method to control interest expenses must be curbing interest rates.

Typically, interest rates are determined by continual trading in a competitive bond market. This process, known as "price discovery" in the credit markets, ensures that interest rates align accurately with lending risks. However, as discussed in Chapter Six, Uncle Sam will soon be unable to afford rising market interest rates. If he reaches a point where he cannot sell bonds in the market at low interest rates, Uncle Sam will run out of money.

Confronted with this imminent challenge, Uncle Sam has a few options to reduce the interest rate he pays on debt. One option is for the Fed or the Treasury to intervene in the bond market, disrupting the standard price discovery process. A second option is to reduce rates through legislative or regulatory measures, employing various tactics ranging from persuasion and propaganda to direct enforcement measures to suppress interest rates.

Let's first look at market intervention tactics the Fed and the Treasury can employ using their legal authority. A repression technique sometimes used by monetary authorities is called "yield curve control" (YCC).

The term "yield curve" denotes a range of market interest rates on bonds based on their maturity dates and principal repayment schedules. A "normal" yield curve of interest rates on US Treasury bonds looks like this:

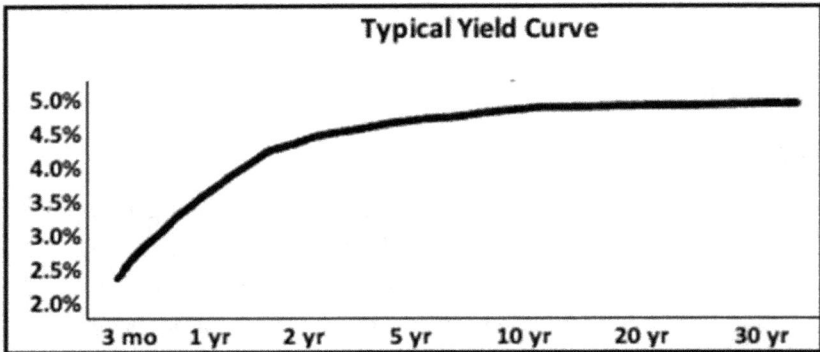

Typical Yield Curve

The yield, or interest rate paid to the bond owner, is on the vertical scale. The time until maturity (when the bond pays off the principal) is on the horizontal scale. This structure of interest rates reflects the uncertainties and risks of lending to Uncle Sam over the short and long term. As you might expect, interest rates on bonds that mature many years from now are usually higher than those that mature in a few months or years because the uncertainty associated with changing interest rates increases with the bond's maturity.[16]

YCC consists of a monetary authority intervening in the market to control interest rates at specific points on the yield curve. A prominent example is the YCC strategy the Bank of Japan (BOJ) has used to suppress the yield on the ten-year Japanese government bond. Since 2012, the BOJ has controlled the Japanese government bond (JGB) market by purchasing a substantial amount of the government's ten-year bond issuances, thereby suppressing rates along the entire yield curve. Currently, the BOJ holds such a large portion of the ten-year bond that, on some days, there is no trading activity at all in the ten-year. This dominance by the BOJ prevents the competitive bond market from discovering an actual market interest rate.

Japan's implementation of YCC very clearly illustrates financial repression. The 10-year and similar bonds serve as a crucial avenue for savings among the Japanese population. The 10-year Japanese Government Bond (JGB) yield is approximately 1%. In contrast, Japan's Consumer Price Index (CPI) is increasing at a rate of 2–3%. Consequently, the cost of living is surging faster than Mrs. Watanabe's ability to grow her savings. This situation epitomizes genuine financial repression, a strategy deemed essential by the Japanese government due to the country's holding the world's highest debt-to-GDP ratio. This problem amplifies Japan's sovereign debt challenges beyond even those faced by the USA.

The Federal Reserve is unlikely to push US interest rates down to Japan's rock-bottom levels; however, it could use YCC to impose a ceiling on long-term rates to help manage interest expenses.

According to Charles Peabody, a veteran banking analyst at the New York research firm Portales Partners, the Treasury Department is already implementing a limited form of YCC. For example, among the Treasury's many manipulative "tricks" is the new practice of borrowing more in T-bills (very short-term debt) instead of selling longer-term bonds, where the bond market is increasingly less willing to buy at low interest rates. From Peabody's May 2, 2024 letter:

> This is a clear indication that Treasury is worried about the growing illiquidity in the Treasury market. Put another way; Treasury is issuing more Bills [short-term debt] to buy back coupons [longer-term debt]. Sounds like YCC to us! [Brackets added.][17]

The Treasury can manipulate interest rates at the margin. Still, only the Federal Reserve has the enormous financial resources required to execute a comprehensive YCC strategy over a long period because only the Fed can create unlimited money to intervene in the bond market. As the government's financial challenges escalate, as they are bound to do, YCC will likely be put into effect. They may not call it "yield curve control," but that is what it will be.

In addition to market intervention via YCC, monetary authorities can influence interest rates through various legal or regulatory means. Congress could take legal actions, while the Federal Reserve, the Federal Deposit Insurance Corporation, the Comptroller of the Currency, or the Consumer Products Safety Commission could exert regulatory pressure.

What other legal or regulatory actions could be used to suppress interest rates while diverting investors to Treasurys? If, like Sun Tzu, you "become the enemy," you can imagine some possibilities.

For instance, one method authorities could employ is to cap the interest rates banks provide on deposits. To illustrate, consider a scenario where customers are limited to earning a maximum of 2% on bank deposits, whereas they can secure perhaps 4% on Treasury bills (or through money market funds that invest in Treasury bills). In such a situation, one would expect many bank customers to shift out of bank deposits into Treasury bills.

Capital controls

Of course, if the US government suppresses interest rates, US investors will look abroad for a better yield or a currency that can be invested in for a higher return. Therefore, expect the government to install capital controls to limit the transfer of funds out of the USA. "Invest American" will likely become the government's patriotic (propagandistic) slogan. The objective will be to trap investors' money in the USA, where it is more likely to be invested in Treasury bonds or spent in domestic industries to boost nominal GDP.

As just one example, tariffs on imports, already a fact of life for American businesses and consumers, discourage investment capital from leaving the country. Expect additional and increasing tariffs, especially against our New Cold War enemies or their allies.

Can financial repression work?

Is it possible for financial repression to devalue US government debt to a more sustainable level? History suggests it is achievable. For example, between 1944 and 1950, France managed to decrease its debt-to-GDP ratio from 180% to 50%. This was primarily achieved through rapid inflation, nearing hyperinflation levels. Following this period of significant financial turmoil, France grew rapidly and rebuilt its war-ravaged economy. Nonetheless, I am skeptical that France's approach, which bordered on hyperinflation, is a viable solution for the US debt problem.

Another historical example may provide better insight. Renowned economic historian Russell Napier has documented that in the decades following World War II, the United Kingdom, burdened with substantial war debts, inflated those debts away over 35 years. The UK achieved this by maintaining high inflation and nominal GDP growth while pushing savers into low-yield government debt. Between 1945 and 1980, the UK reduced its debt-to-GDP ratio from 238% to 50%, enabling it to re-enter the competitive bond market. From the government's perspective, financial repression "worked." Nonetheless, the broader population, particularly the middle class, bore a significant financial burden as their standard of living stagnated for decades.[18]

The current debt crisis facing the US government is unsustainable. The crux of the matter is this: while the government will seek to raise taxes wherever possible, more than incremental tax hikes are needed to resolve their cash flow issues. The most viable avenue to enhance cash flow lies in boosting tax revenues through an inflating GDP and herding domestic investment into government debt at artificially low interest rates—a strategy known as financial repression. Short of resorting to outright default or hyperinflation, financial repression is the sole escape from the debt problem the government finds itself in.

Let us summarize financial repression's essential components. The government will increase taxes within an inflating tax base, trigger currency devaluation via inflation, and push interest rates below the rate of consumer price increases. These policies will restrict the individual's ability to accumulate wealth by traditional saving. Furthermore, the government will install capital controls to discourage investors from pursuing better returns overseas. Collectively, these strategies will impede wealth accumulation by channeling the individual's wealth to a government that needs money to pay down debt. Drawing from the post-war British model, these policies will likely persist for a prolonged period and impact all Americans significantly.

For financial repression to succeed, the government must rely on coercion, public complacency, and widespread ignorance. You may have to comply with their policies, but you don't have to be ignorant of their intentions, which are to make you pay for their past financial sins.

How will you react to financial repression?

Some, like my friend Joe, who we met at the beginning of this chapter, will delay retirement, work extra jobs, earn more money, pay more taxes, and rely less on pensions and government entitlements.

Others, unable or unwilling to continue working, will choose to cut back on consumption and accept a lower standard of living.

Still others will be the frogs in the simmering pot who ignore their rising cost of living until they are hit by an unexpected disaster, like sickness or injury, and suddenly realize they no longer have sufficient wealth to weather the storm.

Your fundamental goal should be to avoid becoming the oblivious frog in the pot. For those who are still in their working years and willing to think creatively, there is a positive path forward.

The investor's task is to craft a savings and investment strategy that enables us to avoid the worst effects of financial repression and potentially thrive in the new economic landscape. This will be the focus of Chapter Eight.

8 HOW TO DEFEAT FINANCIAL REPRESSION

*A parable of repression; The new investment environment;
Investing under financial repression; Avoid long-term bonds;
Active versus passive investing; Sensible investing principles;
Should you own Bitcoin? Why everyone should own gold;
Where to find help*

A parable of repression

What's the real purpose of the government's financial repression policies? To put it bluntly, the purpose of financial repression is to transfer physical wealth from wealth creators to the government. A short parable will illustrate the process.

Imagine yourself as a farmer running a successful dairy business. You keep your milk stored in a large, refrigerated tank until it is sold to customers by the gallon. Unbeknownst to you, a government official decides to tax you without your knowledge. Under the cover of night, he visits your farm and secretly draws off milk to settle his debts and reward his cronies. To cover his tracks, he refills the tank with water, creating a diluted version of your milk that appears unchanged, making the theft virtually undetectable. Unaware of the diminishing quality of your product, you continue to sell the watered-down milk. Over time, your customers start to complain that the taste of the milk isn't as good as before, and products like butter and cheese made from your milk lack their usual quality. Your customers' children are losing weight because the diluted milk is less nutritious.

Our allegory has many real-world parallels in an era of financial repression. If you have a business, you and your employees will work harder than ever but keep less of the real wealth you create. If you are living off your savings, you have been a wealth creator in the past, but now more of your accumulated wealth will be siphoned away right under your nose. The theft is indirect and surreptitious. Unless you discover the nature of this theft, you will not understand what is happening to your livelihood.

The first seven chapters of this book were dedicated to explaining how the government has used reckless money creation to pay for its reckless spending and must now use money creation to seize the wealth needed to pay back its debt. Although you cannot entirely avoid this theft, you can take action to mitigate its effects and possibly even prosper. This final chapter presents strategies to help you defend yourself against financial repression while accumulating wealth and safeguarding your savings.

The new investment environment

Financial repression is a crucial feature of a new investment environment that will be radically different from that of the last several decades. This new environment will require a new approach to saving and investing.

Often, the environment you are immersed in is hard to see—you cannot see the forest because you are surrounded by trees. The following story by the late David Foster Wallace illustrates the problem.[1]

Two young fish are swimming along one day, and they meet an old fish swimming the other way. The old fish nods at the two young fish and says, "Good morning, boys. How's the water today?" They all continue along their paths for a while, and then one young fish looks at the other and says, "Hey, what the hell is water?"

The young fish are not aware of the water they are swimming in, and neither are most investors. Most investors do not appreciate that they acquired their investing habits in a sea of expanding money and credit, declining interest rates, high and rising asset prices, and the speculative excesses that accompanied this period. These investors never noticed the strong current pushing them along from behind, assuming their easy investment environment was normal. As we enter the new era, they may still be expecting a favorable current when none will be there, and they may fail to notice that the water they are swimming in is getting murky.

Market prices can change abruptly, but the changes in the investment environment that cause these price movements are usually gradual, sometimes glacial, and difficult to notice if you are looking for day-to-day signs of change. The elements of change include many factors, such as money creation, interest rates, government policies, technological progress, and international relationships, including the possibility of war. Changes in these elements are not always immediately followed by changing prices—this takes time. Therefore, practically everyone evaluates today's prevailing conditions by extrapolating the conditions of the recent past. Very few seek to know how changing conditions will affect the evolving investment environment.

Let's describe the benign environment we have been swimming in for the last couple of decades and contrast it to the repressive environment we are now entering. Then, based on our understanding of this new investment world, we'll consider how to approach saving and investing in the future.

What do we observe? First, we are shifting from stable consumer prices to rising prices. Second, a prolonged period of easy money (rapid money supply growth and declining interest rates) has transitioned to a tighter policy designed to counteract consumer price inflation. Third, an era of international economic cooperation and increased trade is being replaced by heightened political tensions and a new Cold War. Let's consider each of these changing economic factors in turn.

First, the old environment of stable consumer prices has given way to rising prices.

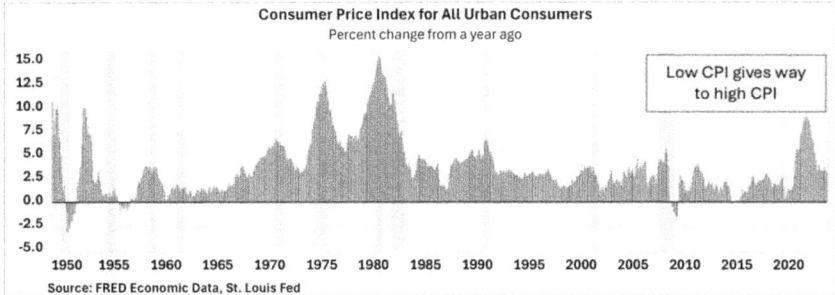

Consumer Price Index for All Urban Consumers
Percent change from a year ago

Low CPI gives way
to high CPI

Source: FRED Economic Data, St. Louis Fed

The graph illustrates the annual rate of consumer price inflation since 1971. From the early 1990s, particularly from 2008 to 2020, a low yearly increase was an important feature of the investment landscape. This was also a period of exceptional asset price increases. Low CPI inflation was OK for wage earners, but the combination of low CPI inflation and soaring asset prices made investors feel complacently rich.

In the new environment, as often happens during an inflationary surge, living costs rise faster than wages. This is because wage increases are typically sticky, lagging consumer price increases. When CPI inflation accelerates, the price-wage gap widens quickly. Most people will have to "run a little faster"—meaning they will have to work harder, longer, or at multiple jobs—to maintain their standard of living.

Even a moderate increase in consumer price inflation can have a significant negative impact on consumers. If consumer prices go up by the Federal Reserve's target rate of 2% annually, the purchasing power of a dollar decreases by half in approximately 35 years. However, historically, the actual CPI inflation rate has rarely remained as low as 2%. The average annual CPI rise in the post-gold standard era is around 4%. At that rate, the value of a dollar will diminish by over 60% in just 25 years and by nearly 85% over 50 years. Hence, in an environment where CPI inflation hovers around historical norms, saving money by hoarding dollar bills proves to be a losing proposition.[2]

Why was CPI inflation so muted from 2009 to 2020? There were two reasons. First, the Fed's massive multi-year QE program put trillions of dollars into the hands of professional investors, who then bought more investments, driving up the price of financial assets. Very little of this new money got into the hands of those who primarily spend on consumer goods, so consumer prices did not inflate nearly to the extent that asset prices did. This phenomenon, known as the Cantillon Effect (as discussed in Chapter Six), was actively at play during this timeframe.

Second, consumer price increases were subdued because the cost of producing them was restrained by the increasing efficiency of expanding global trade. As Adam Smith might have said, the growing specialization of production from international trade improved productivity and helped keep consumer prices low. To put it concretely, cheap labor from China and elsewhere kept consumer product prices low, benefiting US consumers.

However, the "off-shoring" trend is reversing as international tensions heat up in what looks like a new Cold War. As manufacturing centers move back to the USA ("reshoring") or to friendlier trading partners ("friend-shoring"), the quantity of cheap goods will decline, the cost of labor and materials will rise, and productivity could experience a setback. As these supply networks restructure, we should expect higher annual consumer price increases compared to the era of expanding global trade.

These on-shoring and friend-shoring trends will have important implications for investment opportunities as labor and supply networks shift to new locations. The companies that profited from low-cost, efficient global trade will be squeezed, while players in the new network will benefit from the new trends.

Let's move on to the second dimension of change in the investment environment: The era of "super-easy money" (strong money supply growth plus low and declining interest rates) has ended.

Easy money's effect on investing is best illustrated in graphic form. "Easy money" refers to both the quantity of new money available for investing and the cost of borrowing it. Lots of new money (rapidly rising M2) available at low cost (low or declining interest rates) constitutes easy money. The graphs below show why March 2020 to March 2022 was marked the easiest monetary policy in US economic history. Interest rates were suppressed to near zero while the broad money supply exploded upward. It doesn't get much "easier" than that!

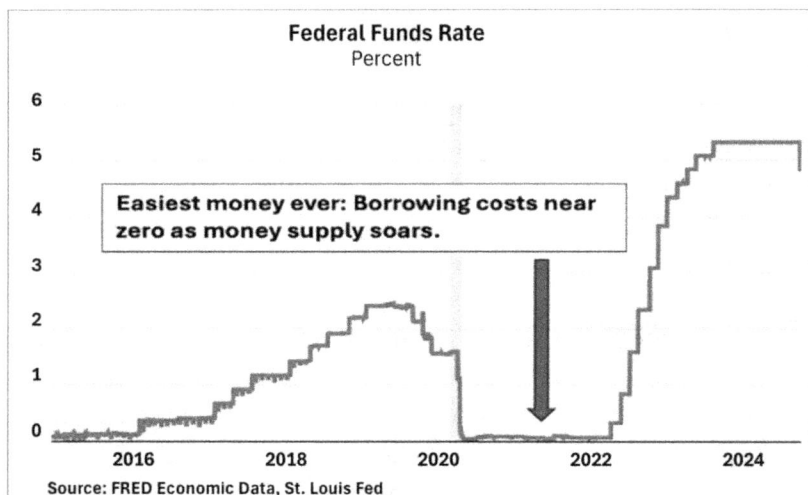

Federal Funds Rate
Percent

Easiest money ever: Borrowing costs near zero as money supply soars.

Source: FRED Economic Data, St. Louis Fed

Money Supply and Stock Market

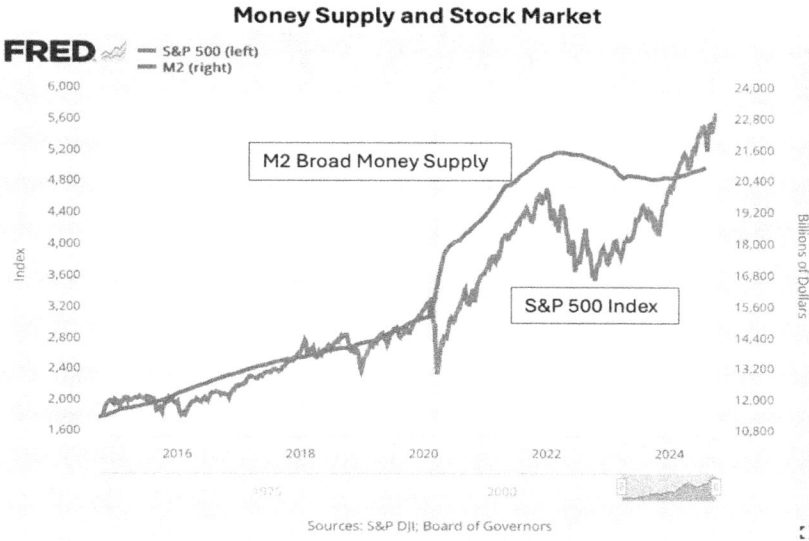

In the second chart, the upper line (right scale) represents broad money supply (M2), while the jagged lower line (left scale) indicates the S&P500 stock index. It is evident that stock market valuations were influenced by the infusion of new money into the financial system between March 2020 and March 2022. During this period, the Federal Reserve injected approximately $7 trillion of new money, leading to a doubling of the stock market within two years.

Notably, a temporary peak in the S&P500 index occurred in January 2022, topping out when the Fed announced it would respond to the rising Consumer Price Index (CPI) levels by hiking rates and tightening the money supply.

A 10-month stock market correction followed as the Fed "tightened" aggressively, raising short-term interest rates from .25% to 5.5% over two years while allowing its balance sheet to decline, causing M2 to decline. The market reacted to tighter money, declining by 22%.

M2 bottomed around August 2022 and began growing slowly again due to a gradual increase in money creation in the commercial banks, which offset the Fed's shrinking balance sheet. The gradual resumption of money growth and the realization that the Fed was nearing the end of its rate hikes signaled "green" to stock investors.

From the correction bottom in October 2023 till this writing, the SP500 has risen by 50% in anticipation of Fed rate cuts. I would add that this latest rally in the SP500 is exceptionally narrow, with most of the gains driven by a few "mega-cap" high-tech stocks, especially those related to the latest Wall Street fad, "artificial intelligence."

My point is not to denigrate AI, which is a revolutionary technology, but to point out that sheer market momentum is driving the market higher during 2024. Other than the 7–10 hottest technology stocks, recent gains in the SP500 index have been modest at best. Historically, these kinds of narrow market advances have not ended well. When the growth of money available to buy stocks slows, the broad stock market also slows, as it must, and new highs become increasingly fragile and hard to maintain.

For stock prices to rise continually, there must be a continuous inflow of new funds invested in the stock market. This can pose challenges when the money supply expands slowly, especially if the freshly injected funds are not promptly channeled into stock investments. As the Federal Reserve begins to wind down its tightening measures, the growth of the M2 money supply will resume. However, in the future, central banks may not channel significant amounts of new funds directly into the stock and bond markets as they did between 2009 and 2022. Financial repression will require that new money be directed first to GDP transactions, boosting GDP-related prices. Consequently, stocks may continue to advance, but not at the rate of recent years.

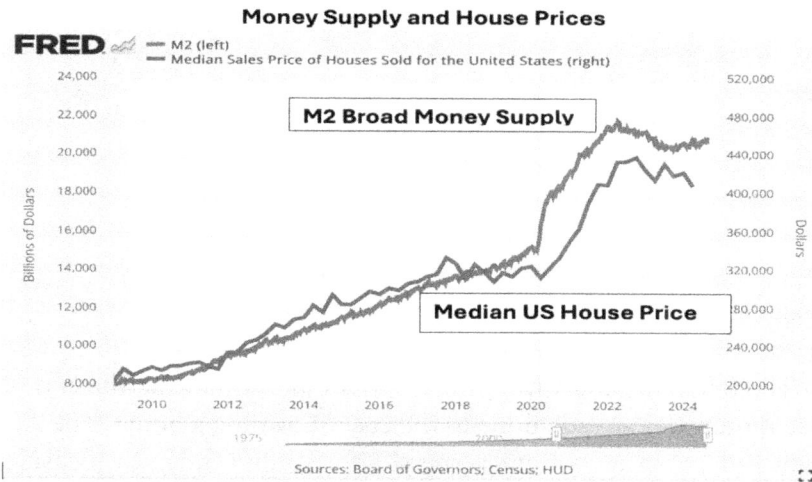

All markets need a continual inflow of new money to continue advancing, and this principle applies equally to the housing market. This graph from Fed data shows what easy money did for house prices during the Pandemic QE. Note the steep price rise of 50% in 30 months from 2020 to 2022. Like the relationship with stocks, the close relationship between easy money and rising house prices is no coincidence.

The following chart shows the evolution of 30-year mortgage rates. During Pandemic QE, the Fed pushed 30-year mortgage rates down to below 3%, an all-time low. With ultra-low rates and lots of new money sloshing around, it's not surprising that house prices jumped 50% in thirty months.

The Fed stopped buying mortgage-backed securities in March 2022, and mortgage rates promptly began rising, reaching 7.8% in October 2023 and abruptly ending easy money in the housing market. The US median house price peaked in Q4 22 and now seems to be rolling over slowly, although as of this writing, house prices have not fallen precipitously.

US 30-Year Mortgage Rates

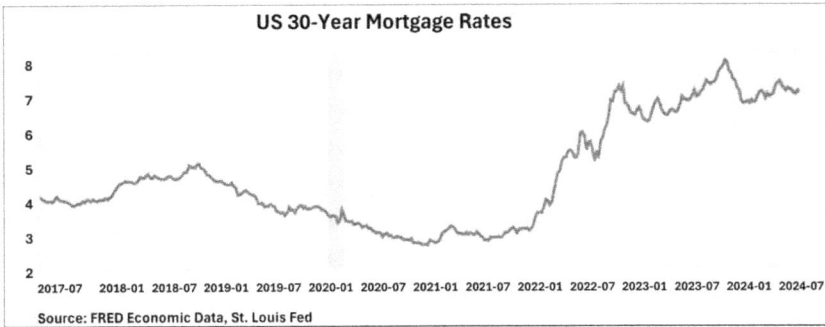

Source: FRED Economic Data, St. Louis Fed

The following chart from the Atlanta Fed shows what the end of easy money has already done to the cost of owning a home. The Atlanta Fed publishes a homeowners' affordability index to measure the burden of purchasing a home on the average household. The major inputs into this index are household income, mortgage interest rates, and house prices.[3] Note how affordability has plunged since the Fed started raising interest rates and stopped buying mortgage-backed securities early in 2022, marked by the arrow. Note also that affordability is the worst since the early 2000s housing bubble (2002 to 2007).

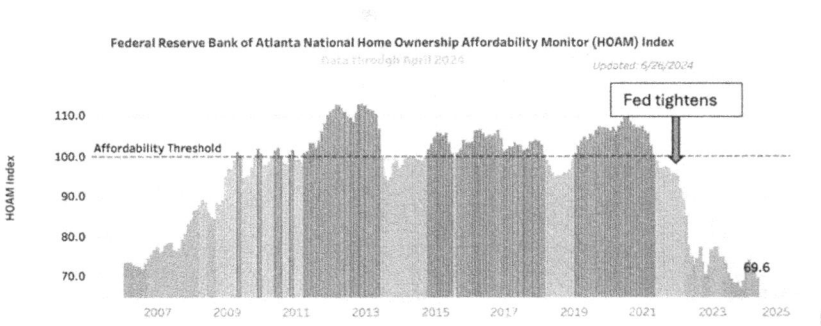

Federal Reserve Bank of Atlanta National Home Ownership Affordability Monitor (HOAM) Index

To state the affordability problem slightly differently, in 2020, when mortgage interest rates were three percent, the cost to own an average home was about 28% of median household income. Two years later, after house prices had gone up 40% and mortgage rates spiked to nearly 8%, the percentage of median household income required to own a home had reached 44%. This percentage exceeded the previous record set during the 2006 housing bubble. [4] This reading is an extreme condition that will be corrected by a combination of lower mortgage rates, lower house prices, and higher household income, but the adjustment may take years. Until that time, exercise caution when shopping for a new house! I'll have more to say about the importance of buying a home later in this chapter.[5]

These housing statistics illustrate that an easy money environment elevates asset valuations, while a restrictive monetary policy typically exerts downward pressure on asset prices. If my hypothesis that monetary conditions will not remain as lenient as they were over the past two decades proves true, then engaging in speculative investment decisions based on rising asset prices may no longer be the cakewalk it has been in the recent past.

The third dimension of the new investing environment is heightened political discord, both domestically and internationally. Signs of increasing political unrest are everywhere, as populist candidates are gaining traction in Europe and the USA. Unlike the comparatively stable political environment that prevailed during the previous investment era, the new era is marked by escalating political unrest and surging crime.

In the United States, incidents such as the January 6, 2021, Capitol riot, the 2020 "BLM riots," anti-Israel demonstrations, and the attempted assassination of Donald Trump illustrate the widening political divide and social turmoil. In Europe, there are parallel populist protests against green energy taxes and raising the retirement age. The parallels to the period of the 1960s to the early 1980s are unmistakable: divisive rhetoric, lack of political consensus, rising crime, and political violence.

On the global stage, tensions among major powers are rising, a departure from the previous era marked by more harmonious diplomatic and economic ties. Financially, this escalating friction manifests as a gradual shift away from the dollar as the dominant global reserve currency as our adversaries seek alternative means to conduct their trade transactions. Should this shift persist, its repercussions will likely impact nearly everyone, although the effects will be indirect and not always obvious.

In Chapter Seven we saw that foreign investors have already begun to turn away from buying Treasury bonds. Financial repression will exacerbate that trend. As the USA runs up its debt and interest costs, it will have to borrow at suppressed interest rates that are not particularly attractive to investors. Suppressed US interest rates tend to lower the dollar's value relative to other currencies. Given a declining dollar, an energy exporter, like Saudi Arabia or Russia, would be less inclined to invest their export surpluses into US Treasury bonds. Consider the perspective of a non-US oil exporter who gets paid in dollars. How should he invest his profits? If Treasury bonds earn 4% while the price of oil is rising at, say, 8%, he is better off leaving his oil in the ground. Or perhaps he would rather hold trade surpluses in a currency that is not depreciating, like gold.

This example illustrates how lowered interest rates and currency devaluation can impact global trade. It stands to reason that nations such as Russia, China, and Saudi Arabia, which have historically stored their trade surpluses in US Treasurys, would seek more appealing alternatives to safeguard their surplus revenues.

The gradual retreat from the dollar is further intensified by the US policy of "weaponizing" its reserve currency position to penalize adversaries, as witnessed in the freezing of Russia's access to US banks by the US Treasury in 2022. By weaponizing the dollar in this manner, the US provides additional motivation for trading partners to distance themselves from investments tied to the dollar, reducing demand for Treasury securities. This, in turn, exerts upward pressure on interest rates, prompting the government to intervene to suppress rates artificially.[6]

Let's sum up the differences between the investment environment we are leaving and the new one we are entering.

In the old investment environment, regular injections of cheap money into the bond market reliably raised financial asset prices and suppressed interest rates. In the old environment, you could buy a big-cap stock index fund and let the easy money do the work.

In the new environment, the era of plentiful money inflows that consistently lift stock prices may end, requiring a more discerning approach to stock selection. In the new environment, central bank money injections will be driven by financial emergencies, not routine policy. Consequently, we cannot count on systematic asset price increases year after year as we once did.

In the old environment of low CPI increases and easy money, one could accumulate wealth by investing in assets whose price increase would quickly outstrip the slowly rising cost of living. For example, you could buy a house, watch its price rise, and then tap into your new wealth by refinancing or taking out a second mortgage at a low interest rate. This gave you cash to spend on cheap consumer goods, making you feel richer. In the new environment, you'll have to wait longer for house price appreciation, and higher interest rates may not allow you to tap your home as if it were a bottomless ATM.

In the old environment, you could reap a post-Cold War peace dividend and benefit from low everyday prices, courtesy of cheap labor from emerging markets like China. In the new environment, you'll pay more for everyday consumer items because they cost more to produce.

The old environment is gone. At present, the Federal Reserve is not providing abundant, easy money but is instead allowing the money supply to expand at a more restrained pace. This approach alleviates the upward push on asset values and investment profits. While the Fed may still inject additional liquidity into the system, such actions will likely only occur in response to some perceived necessity.

That's a snapshot of the old and new investment environments. The new environment is much less forgiving. Not only will you have to contend with a rising cost of living, it will also be more challenging to compensate for it with rising asset prices. Our growing sovereign debt requires financial repression to subdue the government's interest costs, which translates to negative real rates to keep interest rates below the rate of increase in the cost of living. Negative real rates mean it's hard to accumulate savings to keep up with rising consumer prices. Stagnating wages that lag consumer prices encourage social unrest. De-globalizing trade and increased international tension imply an incremental (but not wholesale) move away from the dollar as the world's reserve currency.

Investing under financial repression

Given these new conditions, let's conserve time and mental space by thinking first about where we do *not* want to invest our savings. I suggest avoiding two investment strategies that worked in the old environment but are not likely to work in the new one.

Avoid long-term bonds

I recommend not owning long-term bonds unless you are convinced they would have good value if held to maturity. "Long term," in my view, is a maturity of over five years. Do not "rent" long-term bonds unless you want to become an expert trader. (By "rent," I mean buying a long-term bond as a temporary speculative position you intend to sell before the bond matures.) Bond investing is for experts only unless you are buying to hold for the entire term of the bond.

The 13-year period of QE, which included vast money creation and interest rates pushed to near the zero lower bound, was once dubbed by the Fed as the "new normal" monetary policy. Investors became very comfortable with this policy, which consisted of near-zero interest rates and a policy of aggressive money creation through bond purchases (QE). During this period, bond investors had a one-way, highly profitable ride, and many made a fortune by riding the wave of declining interest rates. As rates fell, bond prices rose, and capital gains were reinvested in more long-term bonds. Rinse and repeat, year after year.[7]

However, with the onset of consumer price inflation, the Fed's "new normal" policy abruptly ended. The Fed raised short-term interest rates substantially and stopped directly subsidizing the stock and bond markets through QE. As a November 2, 2023 article in the *Financial Times* makes clear, the "new normal" that had made so many bond investors look like geniuses during the QE era has given way to higher rates and vulnerable bond prices.[8]

In the new environment, some people will make positive returns on long-term bonds, but these will be expert bond traders buying and selling bonds to the "fish" at the poker table. My advice is, don't be the fish. Swimming with the sharks in the bond market is a full-time occupation!

To reiterate, if you are not comfortable holding a bond for its full scheduled term, don't buy it. Ask yourself, at what interest rate would I want to hold onto an investment for ten years, with no chance of selling it? In my experience, most people would say the rate required is 10 to 12 percent. As always, your mileage may vary.

Ten-Year Treasury Yield

Source: US Treasury, US Federal Reserve   © 2024 Bianco Research (printed with permission)

(Source: Bianco Research, Aug 30, 2024 (subscription required) https://www.biancoresearch.com/quick-comments-what-were-reading-1432/)

The above chart, courtesy of Bianco Research, shows the 10-year US Treasury bond yield, or its proxy equivalent, back to 1787. The first thing to notice is that bond yields move up and down in long multi-decade waves. Why interest rates move in this pattern is a puzzle, but the historical fact that they do is unmistakable. The latest major wave, a massive downward move from 1981 to 2020, lasted nearly 40 years—longer than the careers of most active investment professionals. Remember, as yields declined, bond prices went way up, making a fortune in capital gains for those who had bought bonds when yields were much higher. Several generations of investors grew up in this environment and have a bias for bonds built into their investment routines. However, windfall profits are not an intrinsic feature of government bond markets, i.e., not something a bond investor should count on.

I believe the latest secular bull market in bonds ended in March 2020 when interest rates reached their *lowest levels in 4,000 years of recorded history* ("4,000" is not a typo). The 10-year yield bottomed out in August 2020 at 50 basis points—one-half of one percent. As this chapter is being written (October 2024), the 10-year bond yield is about 4.0%—at the lower end of the typical historical yield range of 4 to 6%. As the interest rate has risen over the last four years, bond prices have declined significantly.

Is the bond bear market over, and are you ready to bet on a long-term turnaround? There are always temporary price rallies (interest rate declines) in a bear market, but I think it's unlikely interest rates will plunge back to 2%, and if they do, it may not be for long.

Market-based interest rates have historically compensated investors for price increases, plus a "real" return of around 2%, so long-term consumer price inflation doesn't have to be more than 3 or 4% to push bond yields much higher than in the 2010 to 2020 era. Recall that the average annual CPI increase in the post-gold era is about 4%.

Add another 2% for a "real" yield, and you need a yield of 6% to provide a modest return above CPI inflation. But even 6% may not be high enough.

Whether or not I am right about the trend of market interest rates, there is another good reason to avoid long-term bonds. As mentioned in Chapter Seven, a good reason not to own long-term bonds in an era of financial repression is that the government needs a negative real interest rate—below the CPI inflation rate—to reduce its debt burden. That means your interest payments will likely not keep up with the rising cost of living.

It's also advisable to avoid other investments that mimic or depend on the yield on long-term government bonds. For example, be careful about investing in life insurance companies' stocks. Life companies estimate their future payouts based on long-term interest rates and buy long-term bonds to match future income with those projected payouts. As rates rise, their liabilities also increase, but the value of their long-term investments declines, and they can quickly become insolvent. Please note that these cautions do not necessarily apply to property and casualty insurers, which are different animals and may do well under financial repression, depending on who manages the company's investment portfolio. Warren Buffett of Berkshire Hathaway (Geico) comes to mind.

A possible exception to this caveat against long-term bonds might be to buy "TIPS," or Treasury Investment Protection Securities.[9] The way a TIPS bond works is that both the principal and interest adjust with changes in the CPI. Initially, you get a lower nominal yield than an ordinary bond, but then, unlike a standard bond, as the CPI goes up, the principal value of the bond goes up, and the interest you receive is adjusted upward based on that increase in value. Theoretically, you get a positive "real" yield for the life of your investment. TIPS are sold in 5-year, 10-year, and 30-year durations, and several Exchange Traded Funds (ETFs) make owning TIPS easy.

However, I have two reservations about TIPS as an inflation hedge. The first is that they are adjusted based on the CPI, but as we have seen, the CPI does not adequately measure inflation, so TIPS might not realistically compensate you for your loss of purchasing power.

My second concern is that the Fed has been known to manipulate the TIPS price. At the time of this writing, the Fed owned about 25% of all TIPs, so clearly, the Fed can move their price by purchasing or selling them in the open market.

If you want to invest in "bond-like" instruments, consider making your own private loans to sound borrowers rather than lending to the government through the public bond market. For example, I know people who lend money to property developers in their local area. They always lend to people they know, and they always build a solid margin of safety into the loan. They insist on having a first lien on the property as collateral for the loan so they will be "first in line" in case of default. Additionally, they insist on a loan-to-value ratio of less than 75% as a cushion in case the property's value declines suddenly. Finally, they always record the loan and lien with an escrow office to ensure there will be no dispute on the agreed terms if they have to foreclose on the property. They typically get 10 to 12% on their investment, providing fair compensation for both credit and inflation risks. This is win-win investing—both lenders and borrowers are happy. This "do-it-yourself" approach demands attention to detail and a fair amount of homework, but the reward is an excellent return with relatively low risk.

Active versus passive investing

Another investing strategy I would avoid is passive investing in stock index funds, a practice that has gained significant popularity over the last two decades. This approach was lucrative when interest rates were on a downward trend, especially during the QE years when it was hard to outperform a passive index with active stock selection. However, looking ahead, passive investing may not be as lucrative as it once was. Let's delve into the reasons why.

Since the early 2000s, purchasing an index fund that mirrors a broad stock market index such as the S&P 500 and continuously contributing to it has been a favored savings option. Approximately 80% of equity investments in 401(k) plans are allocated to these funds. Despite sharp setbacks like the dot-com crash in 2002, the global financial crisis in 2008, and the pandemic-induced market volatility in 2020, remaining invested in the index consistently proved rewarding. Central banks' response to each market downturn was additional QE and lower interest rates, which restimulated the stock and bond markets, consistently propelling asset prices to new highs. Investors learned to "buy the dip" with every downturn, as their experience showed that asset values only increase over time.

Buying the index has worked because, under a policy of easy money, companies that would have normally failed were kept alive by falling interest rates and readily available credit. This meant that the extreme differences between sound companies and "zombie" companies were not fully reflected in their stock prices. Rapid money creation and declining interest rates undermined the regular creative destruction of capitalism.[10]

As investors flocked to index funds, index fund managers had to buy all the stocks in the index, not just the "best" stocks. Stock prices became more correlated, meaning all stocks tended to move up and down together more than in the past. In this way, easy money and passive investment undermined the stock market's normal reward and punishment system. Traditional value investing strategies, which involve buying historically undervalued companies or those with strong financial positions capable of withstanding economic downturns, became less effective and, therefore, less popular.

Other factors added to a tendency toward a more homogeneous valuation of all stocks. Some central banks, like the Japanese Central Bank and the Swiss National Bank, actively purchased large pools of stocks or stock funds (with newly created money), adding upward price pressure to the broad stock indexes. In addition, low interest rates reduced the return on new bond investments, pushing some traditional bond investors into stock index funds.

Like bond investing, passive stock index investing has worked long enough to become a habit for most stock market investors. Under easy money conditions, passive investing became a no-brainer, an effective and popular one-way ticket to becoming wealthy. Slogans like "TINA" (there is no alternative) to stocks became popular. "Get in the market, stay in the market, buy stocks for the long run, buy the dip" are all popular expressions arising from an investment strategy that worked during an era of easy money.

I suggest we will see a shift away from this "automatic pilot" mode of index investing. It may not go away entirely, but we are entering an era where passive index investing may not be the world-beater it was in the past.

A *Barron's* article from April 2024 pointed out that value investing works better during periods of normal interest rates, which bodes well for a return to value strategies. The article points out that from 1990 through April 2024, the average passive fund outperformed the average active fund when the 10-year U.S. Treasury note yield was 3.5% or lower, according to a Janus Henderson analysis of Morningstar data. However, when yields exceeded 3.5%, the average active U.S. equities fund came out ahead.[11]

A January 2023 *Financial Times* article by the eminent investment strategist Mohammed El-Erian, sums up the changing environment succinctly.

> Passive investing is particularly attractive in a world where investment outcomes are heavily influenced by a common global factor. This was the case for more than a decade as the combination of artificially floored interest rates and massive injections of central bank liquidity boosted all assets. Even zombie companies and fragile sovereigns [the debt of insolvent governments] could refinance without much difficulty... .

El Erian explains that the common global factors of low CPI in-flation and low interest rates are now shaken, requiring central banks to raise interest rates and restrict money creation. In addition, glob-alization is declining due to rising political tensions. And with this comes a shift in how and where goods are manufactured and trans-ported, raising costs. These changing conditions create new invest-ment opportunities while closing off old ones.

And I agree with El Erian's summary comments:

> In short, this is an investment world in which greater
> selectivity, smart structuring, and dynamic asset alloca-
> tion ["dynamic" means changing course in anticipation
> of new information] trump more often the lower fees
> on passive vehicles. It's a world that warrants a partial
> return to a' la carte selection after many years of fixed
> menus.[12]

What are some viable alternatives to passive index investing? His-tory provides a clue as to how different classes of assets will perform under higher inflation and interest rates. The years 1966 to 1982 were a period of high consumer price inflation, mostly rising interest rates, international political tensions, and domestic political turmoil—all of which sounds similar to today's evolving environment. What worked during these 16 years?

Total returns with dividends reinvested, January 1966 to July 1982 - U.S. assets		
		Real Return
Consumer Price Index	196%	-196%
Small company stocks	619%	423%
Large company stocks	126%	-70%
Large cap growth stocks	139%	-57%
Large cap value stocks	250%	54%
Mid-cap growth stocks	118%	-78%
Mid-cap value stocks	352%	156%
Long-term corporate bonds	67%	-129%
Long-term government bonds	61%	-135%
source: Ibbotson and Russell Napier, *Solid Ground* Aug 2 2022		

The chart shows the real (CPI-adjusted) return on various investment programs, including large and small-cap companies and bonds. Small company stocks, mid-cap value, and large-cap value stocks were the clear winners. Large company stocks and large-cap growth stocks—the kinds of stocks that populate the S&P500 index—posted negative real returns. Bonds were a disaster, barely beating cash, which underperformed the soaring CPI by nearly 200%. (This means a 1982 dollar would have bought one-third of what it would have bought in 1966.)

Investment returns under financial repression will not mirror this chart exactly because history rarely repeats; it just rhymes. I offer these data to illustrate that buying and holding an index, as many people have done successfully for years in their 401(k) plans, may not work as well in the new environment as it did in the recent past.

Value investing strategies worked then, and I think they will work under financial repression. I believe active investing is back, and value investing is an excellent active strategy. I'll elaborate on value investing in a moment.

Sensible investing principles

Let's continue with El Erian's theme, which is that you should consider picking from an *a la carte* menu of investing ideas rather than the fixed-price menu. I want to offer you a partial menu of investments that should do well under financial repression. This will not be a comprehensive menu but a list of the types of dishes you can choose from. To extend the analogy, I will recommend you eat more beef and less corn, but I will not tell you where to buy your beef or how to cook it. Here are five general recommendations I believe will work under financial repression.

Recommendation 1. "Sweat" your cash without risking it

If you have extra money sitting in a bank deposit or a brokerage account, you are probably getting less than one percent annual interest on that money. You haven't had to care about this for years because consumer price inflation was only 1-2%, so it didn't matter very much that money market and bank deposit rates were one percent or less. But today's money market rates are over 5%, and the CPI is around 3% (likely understated), so don't settle for 1% interest on your extra bank deposits. As of this writing, brokered 3-month CDs now pay 4.0 to 5.0%. Short-term Treasury notes also yield over 4.0%. There are ETFs and money market funds that invest in short-term Treasurys. They are easy to buy and sell in a brokerage account, and their fees are low. All of these alternatives to low-yielding bank deposits are safe and liquid.

Your broker may not guide you to these funds because he can't make much money doing it, so do it yourself. With this low-risk strategy, you probably won't beat the true inflation rate, but at least you'll limit its damage. Bottom line: make your cash sweat and squeeze the best short-term, no-risk return out if it.

Recommendation 2. Own your own home (but the purchase price matters!)

Home ownership is the biggest and best long-term investment most people ever make. In the USA, there are tax advantages, like the deductibility of mortgage interest, that make home ownership financially attractive.

Another significant advantage of home ownership in the USA is that your home is a secure property right. Property rights are under assault today, and financial repression policies might make it worse. However, the family home is such an icon of the American dream that I suspect your house will be the last place the government will come to plunder your wealth. Many states even have special homestead laws that allow you to keep your home in the event of bankruptcy.[13]

But be careful, don't just run out and buy any house. As previously mentioned, as of this writing, both house prices and mortgage rates are very high relative to the average household income, creating the worst "affordability" conditions in many decades.[14] This extreme condition will change over time because it must: home prices and mortgage interest rates will eventually adjust to the ability of people to afford them. I am not predicting that house prices will fall sharply or mortgage rates will plummet. However, I have little doubt that affordability will improve from its current extreme level. Therefore, waiting for better pricing and financing conditions is probably better than plunging in.

However, there are exceptions. All real estate is local and specific, so if you see a great deal you want and have the money, buy with an understanding of the prevailing industry conditions and the risk that your home's market price might decline for a while.

I would be more concerned with the right house price than securing a low mortgage rate. You cannot control mortgage interest rates. If they go up after you buy, you probably got a relatively good deal, but if they go down, you can always refinance the mortgage to your advantage.

Many people buy homes as rental investments and have built significant wealth over time. This requires a lot of commitment and work, but if you want to manage rental properties, it can be financially rewarding.

The first two recommendations—optimizing cash returns and carefully buying a home—primarily rely on diligence and discipline. Yet, in times of financial repression, prosperity hinges more on your knowledge and creativity than on austerity. The next three recommendations aim to guide you in leveraging your intelligence and ingenuity to navigate the evolving investment landscape.

Recommendation 3. If you invest in the stock market, consider a "value investing" strategy.

What do I mean by "value investing"? I mean old-fashioned stock-picking based on fundamental analysis of a company's business prospects, financial health, and price. You buy, say, the 12 best individual stocks for your portfolio. That's enough different names to get most of the benefits of diversification. You definitely don't need more than 20 stocks. They should be healthy companies representing various industries. Sometimes, nothing in any industry qualifies, and you'll need to wait until better prospects appear. In other words, holding cash may be a better option when stock prices are extremely high than taking on a new position.

Value stocks are often cheap because they are temporarily out of favor, resulting in a depressed price that will eventually correct upwards. The plunging price of a "value stock" often reflects an extreme but temporary adverse reaction that can be exploited. What follows is one of hundreds of examples from my career that illustrate this point.

In April 2010, the oil rig called *Deepwater Horizon* exploded in the Gulf of Mexico, releasing a massive oil spill that was difficult to contain. Almost immediately, the stock price of the rig's operator, British Petroleum (BP), crashed by over 40 percent. The media presented the incident as an unprecedented disaster, constantly showing disturbing videos of oil-covered wildlife on the beaches. Interviews with local fishermen implied a catastrophe that would cause unprecedented and permanent damage to the Gulf and the livelihoods of its businesses and residents. Government officials at all levels piled on with statements expressing outrage. Various environmental and government groups lined up to sue British Petroleum into bankruptcy. It was an arch example of hype, panic, and over-reaction.

At the firm where I worked, our clients held large positions in BP stock. Should we sell the stock, as many large shareholders were doing? Should we hold on to the shares we already owned? Should we buy more? And how could we know?

Fortunately, one of my partners was an excellent energy analyst who took the case apart. Looking past the media hype and the threat of bankruptcy due to lawsuits, he constructed a comparison showing how other companies had fared after similar environmental accidents. He found that the BP stock price was discounting an unprecedented scenario in the history of environmental lawsuits. He also showed that petroleum in seawater does not cause permanent pollution but is biodegradable over time. Another critical piece of information was that, despite the alleged damage to Gulf Coast fisheries, the price of shellfish along the Gulf Coast had not changed, indicating that the damage to industry and livelihoods would be minor and temporary, even in the worst case. The oil spill appeared to be a genuine problem, but it was exaggerated, causing panic among BP shareholders, many of whom impulsively sold their stock. However, our analysis showed a good chance the damage would be contained, controlled, and paid for without bankrupting the company.

As disciplined value investors, our first decision was *not* to panic and sell. As we revalued the company to reflect the likely financial damage, we found that its probable fair value was well above the stock's depressed market price. In the face of all the negative news, we bought a lot more shares. A few years later, after the share price recovered, this proved to be the right investment decision. Although the share price never recovered to its pre-spill price, we significantly lowered our average cost by buying more stock at a bargain price. This allowed us to profit nicely from owning BP.

The story's point is that if you want to become a value investor, this is the approach you must take toward the companies you invest in. Just as you don't succumb to the "fear of missing out" (FOMO) and buy wantonly, you don't panic and sell impulsively.

If you decide to get actively involved in stock investing, you must educate yourself. Start by reading *The Intelligent Investor* by Benjamin Graham, *One Up On Wall Street* by Peter Lynch, and then read Warren Buffet's annual letters to Berkshire Hathaway shareholders. All of these are readily available online. If you don't find these or similar writings interesting, my advice is to steer clear of the stock market. If you don't like it, you will not be interested enough to understand it. Don't force yourself into something you don't understand due to FOMO. There are other ways to accumulate wealth!

Value investing has been out of favor for many years, but to paraphrase Mark Twain, its death has been greatly exaggerated. Value investing never really died; it just hibernated for a few decades, and I suspect it will re-emerge as an effective strategy under financial repression.

If I could offer one little aphorism to sum up my thoughts on value investing, it would be this:

> In the stock market, the opportunity of a lifetime comes
> along about every three months.

That's from an unknown source, but I wish I had said it.

That adage contains a lot of condensed wisdom. It means if you are patient, you will eventually find excellent opportunities at bargain prices. It means you do not have to fret every time you fail to buy a rising stock because other opportunities will emerge. It implies that success depends on diligent work, regular study, avoiding speculation, shutting out the daily noise and hype, resisting FOMO, and investing in real businesses, not "the market." It means you don't have to invest in something you do not understand because, eventually, you'll find something that makes sense to you. It also implies you will make mistakes, but you do not have to regret them because you don't have to be right every time to succeed. It means investing is like an endless game of baseball—you will always get another chance at the plate. As Warren Buffett said, you can wait for the fat pitch.

To add some color to value investing, I'll now describe a specific technique that illustrates how a value approach can work. One conservative system I use is to look for stocks of companies with a solid record of paying growing cash dividends. "Dividends don't lie" is a common expression among value investors. That means it's hard for a company to disguise its financial performance if it is committed to sharing its growing profits with shareholders in cash dividends.

The dividend-growth strategy is simple in concept but not always easy to execute. Finding the right dividend-growth companies at the right price takes diligent work and patience. However, the process is straightforward and not highly technical.

First, find a company with a good track record of increasing dividends over time. It should be a solid company with a sustainable competitive advantage in its industry and product line. When the share price looks reasonable, buy some stock and start collecting the dividends. Your intention is to own this company for a long time. Don't worry too much about bottom-ticking the stock price—choose the company based on its ability to grow its dividend stream, and if the price is reasonable, it's okay to buy it.

You can reinvest the dividends directly back into the stock if you want. I prefer to let dividends accumulate and then invest chunks of cash back into my best portfolio prospects. If nothing is priced reasonably, accumulate cash for a while. (Remember, "the chance of a lifetime" will come along again soon enough.)

After you own the stock, pay more attention to its financial performance than its price. Paying increasing dividends is one excellent indicator of sound financial performance. You don't have to sell just because the stock price goes up or down. You can make portfolio changes now and then, but frequent trading is your enemy.

Here is an example of such a company that illustrates the technique. Kimberly Clark (KMB) is a well-known consumer products company (paper products) with a strong market position. It is conservatively financed (i.e., no excessive debt) and has a long-term record of steadily growing sales and rising dividends.

Suppose you bought the stock at $27.35 per share in January 2004, when the annual dividend was $1.42 per share. At that time, the dividend yield was 5.2% ($1.42 divided by $27.35). By 2024, the annual dividend was $4.80 per share, an increase of 240%, which is a compound annual dividend growth rate of 6.3%. The stock price has also risen a bit faster than the dividend, at a compound rate of 8.5% per year. As of this writing (July 2024), the dividend yield is 3.4%—the current annual dividend of $4.80 divided by the share price of $140. A 20-year chart of KMB's share price is shown below.

If you evaluate the success of this investment simply on the progress of its share price, the results are positive: The shares went up at an average of 8.5% per year, about the same rate as the S&P500 index. However, if you were preoccupied with the share price, the journey might have been upsetting because the KMB price trajectory is choppy, sometimes rising or falling precipitously. For example, in 2015, the stock price rose rapidly from $80, peaking at above $100 in

2016 and again in 2017, before falling right back to $80 in 2018. How would you have reacted to this price movement if you were concerned about the stock price? Should you have sold at $100? How would you have known selling was the right thing to do? Would you have regretted not selling at $100 after the stock retreated to $80? In my experience, preoccupation with the stock price causes investors to overreact to price changes, and overreaction is the number one reason for poor performance in stock investing.

The point is that the underlying financial performance is much more stable than the market price. This makes complete sense when you consider that the daily manufacture, transport, and sale of paper products is and should be a steady, predictable, growing business.

In contrast to the stock price chart, look at the following chart, which shows the peaceful progression of the dividend yield on the original cost. Today, you would be earning 18% annually on your original investment. And you have every reason to think this yield will keep rising year after year. Look how stable the dividend performance is compared to the stock price performance! The point is that you don't have to watch the share price all the time. You just have to check in to see if the company is maintaining its ability to raise its dividend.

Kimberly Clark Dividend Yield
On Original Cost

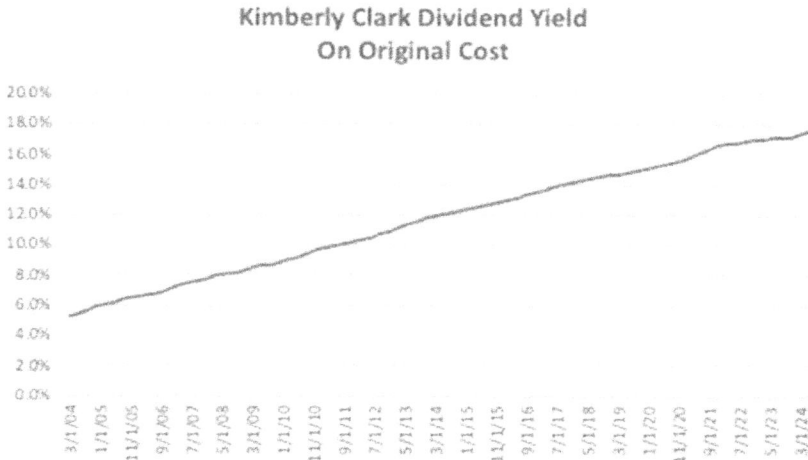

(Data and graph compiled by the author)

Plant the seedlings, tend the orchard, and watch the trees grow. The wealth lies in the company's products and how consumers receive those products. The company's wealth is shared with you not primarily due to a rising share price but from the growing cash flow paid to you in dividends. This is investing, as opposed to speculating.

It's helpful to think of investing in a *business* instead of "buying a stock." Imagine there was no stock market, only privately owned businesses. If you wanted to own a company that would provide for yourself and your family, you would like a solid business that grew steadily, provided good income, and reliably grew its profits. A chart of this progress would look like the dividend yield graph above, not like a stock price chart! You wouldn't worry much about what price your company might fetch in the marketplace, and rightly so. For actual investors, this is the way to think about the businesses you own in your stock portfolio.

I chose KMB almost at random. There are many excellent companies like this, some with spectacular long-term results. For example, my wife has owned Sempra Energy for over 20 years. The current dividend yield on her original investment is 26%. Think of this. She is getting a safe 26% return on an investment she made over 20 years ago. That yield will increase again at the end of this year when the company raises its dividend, as it has done nearly every year for a generation.

Many of these kinds of companies are available in many industries—in energy, consumer goods, industrial goods, and communications, to name a few. And these good prospects don't require mountains of research to be discovered.

Investing in these kinds of companies is a great way to save and build income for retirement. Yes, you might have made more money buying Tesla or Nvidia or even owning an index fund for a while, but investing in dividend growth stocks is a strategy for all seasons. You can sleep at night, and monitoring your investments will not waste your precious time.

Despite the demonstrated effectiveness of dividend-growth investing, it's not very popular among professional investors. Maybe you've never even heard of it. Most professional advisors will not advocate the "buy-and-hold-and-collect-the-dividend-and-reinvest-it" strategy because it will not make them a lot of money. There are several reasons for this. First, their fee structure is usually a percentage of assets under management. To justify their fees, they must make frequent—often unnecessary—buy and sell decisions. In other words, they need to look like they are adding value to your investment program, so they churn your portfolio for the optics and charge a fee. Second, a value strategy—including a dividend growth strategy—might underperform the "benchmark" stock index, sometimes for years. This was the case for the last 20 years when buying an S&P500 index fund outperformed almost all active asset managers. Underperforming a benchmark index is anathema to most stock portfolio managers, so they will likely chase performance by buying and selling, pursuing that elusive above-average share price return.

Managing your own deep-value, dividend-growth portfolio cuts way down on the trading activity, and you don't pay management fees. It can be boring for long periods, like watching paint dry. You might not make a single transaction over an entire year or more. Value investing requires more patience than expertise. It does require your attention, but not every day. This method will work in an era of average or even poor stock market returns and during moderate to high inflation.

Other value-oriented strategies can also work well. The dividend-growth approach is one easy-to-implement strategy I have used for years. Some of the information sources I recommend at the end of this chapter will provide further helpful guidance.

Recommendation 4. Consider other traditional inflation beaters

Farmland: Productive farmland usually retains its value during inflationary periods because its value depends in part on the price of the crops it produces, which move up with inflation. Farmland has some disadvantages, of course. It is not very liquid, i.e., it may be hard to sell during economic downturns or extended periods of bad weather. But if you are patient, farmland value generally appreciates well over time, and its price is not volatile like stocks. Owning farmland could also provide some "standing ground" during increasing government intrusion. The same could be true of timberland.

A working farm is too expensive for most investors, and most people don't want to do physical farm work anyway. In addition, successful farming requires many underappreciated skills that cannot be learned overnight. However, you can invest indirectly in farmland through private partnerships or publicly traded real estate investment trusts (REITs) that will fit nicely into a dividend growth portfolio. Beware, if you are shopping for a farmland REIT, understand the embedded fees and avoid paying a significant price premium over the fund's net asset value. I have had better luck with private partnerships run by reputable managers. An excellent partnership for both private and institutional farmland investing is Sower Farmland of Omaha, NE (https://sowerfarmland.com).

Commodities: You might consider investing in various agricultural and physical commodities, but only via a managed fund and only in modest size relative to your whole portfolio. Commodities investing can be expensive and volatile. It is the perfect "FOMO trap," meaning you might see the price of Platinum rising and rush to get in on the rally. Don't do that! Commodity trading is a tough, professional market. If you invest in a commodity trading fund, plan to invest in it for the long term. Evaluate your manager carefully, keep the allocation modest relative to your whole portfolio, and expect volatility.

Bitcoin: Should you own Bitcoin? Bitcoin and other cryptocurrencies have been on the scene for about fifteen years. While all crypto performance has been volatile, Bitcoin has been a spectacularly positive performer over this period.

I am not going to go deeply into the pros and cons of Bitcoin in this space. I have investigated it, weighed the merits to the best of my ability, and decided that, at this point, Bitcoin and the other cryptos are not for me. However, I am privately rooting for Bitcoin because if it succeeds, it will be because the market chose it as money, which is where all sound money originates.

I admit to not having a highly favorable opinion of cryptocurrencies as investments. Most crypto-bulls recommend them as a new form of money, but of course, they cannot yet be classified as money because they are not a "commonly accepted medium of exchange." If Bitcoin or other cryptos ever become widely accepted in exchange, I will embrace and use them. Unless and until that day comes, I will sit on the sidelines and watch.

If you invest in Bitcoin or other cryptocurrencies, keep several things in mind. First, its price in fiat currencies (e.g., dollars) has been very volatile, which is one characteristic that makes it unsuitable for use as money, at least at present. Bitcoin's price is more correlated to the Nasdaq than to gold or CPI inflation. Second, some governments do not look favorably at Bitcoin; for example, China has banned its citizens from mining and trading Bitcoin. I fear that if Bitcoin becomes too great a threat to fiat currencies, other governments will also restrict its use.

Having said all this, I acknowledge that many very knowledgeable investment advisors make a solid long-term case for owning Bitcoin. If you are interested, investigate, but do not dive into Bitcoin or any cryptos just because everyone else is doing it. Some sources mentioned at the end of this chapter (Lyn Alden and Luke Gromen, for example) have done excellent work on Bitcoin, and their opinions are worth reading.

Recommendation 5: Own gold

Why everyone should own gold

My final recommended investment strategy deserves a category all its own because gold is the most important asset you can own to counteract the adverse effects of financial repression. Other precious metals, like silver, are also acceptable, but I will confine my comments to gold because it is the only precious metal universally accepted as money for over 5000 years.

According to a 2024 report by the World Bank, gold has shown impressive performance against other asset classes over the long term, outpacing bonds and real estate, especially during periods of rising consumer prices. This makes gold an attractive investment option for diversifying away from the old environment by hedging against inflation and political uncertainty.[15]

Over 5-year and 20-year time horizons, gold performed similarly to US equities, significantly outperforming other major asset classes. Over 10-year horizons, gold returned on par with US corporate bonds but substantially lower than US equities; however, gold still outperformed all other major asset classes. It is important to note that the additional return associated with investing in gold implies considerable volatility. The risk in this volatility can be mitigated considerably by a commitment to holding for the long term.

The chart below shows gold's performance under different inflation scenarios. Note that gold outperforms handily when consumer price inflation is above 3%. If, as I expect, we are in for an extended period of above-average inflation under financial repression, gold is likely to perform well.

FIGURE 17: GOLD RETURN OVER VARIOUS INFLATION LEVELS

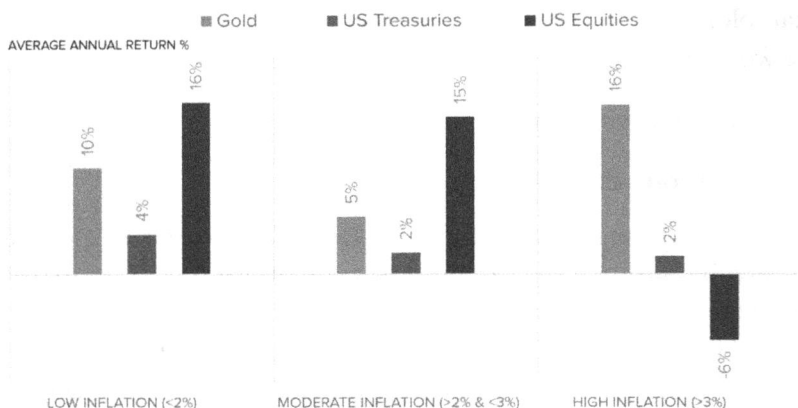

Source: Author's calculation based on Bloomberg data.
*As of 31 December 2022. Based on monthly nominal returns for gold USD spot price, Bloomberg US Treasuries Agg, MSCI US Equities and YoY US CPI since February 2003.

I believe physical gold is the bedrock asset for your regular savings plan—the "GOAT" asset, especially during financial repression. (GOAT = "greatest of all time.")

Pure physical gold, held in coin or bullion, has proved to be a reliable store of value for thousands of years. However, in recent years, gold has been eclipsed by serial asset bubbles in stocks, bonds, and real estate. Nevertheless, if I am right about the growing threat of financial repression, the performance of these traditional asset classes will be more muted in the future. Under those conditions, gold should re-establish its dominance.

One reason gold outperforms in periods of financial repression is that "real" interest rates are negative, meaning the return on bonds does not keep up with inflation as measured by the CPI. If the yield on gold is zero, but the "real" yield on bonds is less than zero, it stands to reason gold will outperform bonds.[16]

In addition, gold and gold-related investments have been neglected by institutional investors for years, but recently, gold has been gaining favor. The most telling sign is that central banks worldwide are now buying thousands of tons of gold annually, led by the Peoples Bank of China. According to the World Gold Council's 2024 Central Bank Gold Reserves Survey,

> An increasingly complex geopolitical and financial environment is making gold reserves management more relevant than ever. In 2023, central banks added 1,037 tonnes of gold—the second-highest annual purchase in history—following a record high of 1,082 tonnes in 2022.
>
> Following these record numbers, gold continues to be viewed favourably by central banks as a reserve asset. According to the 2024 Central Bank Gold Reserves (CBGR) survey, which was conducted between 19 February and 30 April 2024 with a total of 70 responses, 29% of central banks respondents intend to increase their gold reserves in the next twelve months, the highest level we have observed since we began this survey in 2018.[17]

Gold is easy to buy and easy to store. There are many reputable vendors in the USA, some of which are mentioned at the end of this chapter. I recommend owning physical gold rather than owning it through a derivative security like an exchange-traded fund. You can store your coins or bullion in a safe space like a vault in your home, a bank safe deposit box, or a certified gold vault, of which there are many around the USA and overseas. No one needs to know about your gold but you and perhaps a trusted relative or business associate.

There is much more to say about gold. For a detailed presentation on why everyone should invest in gold, see my Substack podcast and attached PDF, "Why Everyone Should Own Gold." This piece was originally published in March 2023 and re-published on July 15, 2024.[18]

I'll close my comments on gold with some wise words attributed to James Aitken of Aitken Advisors:

> [In] helping people think about an investment decision, there are three choices. Buy it, sell it, and the third, which is so often overlooked. Do nothing. If you own gold as a liquidity reserve or a store of value, you have the luxury of being able to do nothing in periods of great upheaval.
>
> —James Aitken, Aitken Advisors[19]

Where to find investment help

I retired in 2016 and am no longer in the business of providing investment advice as a paid professional. However, I still actively manage our family assets, which consist of real estate, stocks, direct loans, precious metals, and other private investments, according to the principles I've described in this chapter.

Instead of offering specific investment advice, I can best help by listing some of the information sources I use to stay on top of the economy and the investment markets. These are the news and advisory services my wife and I use to manage the investments of our family office in Jackson Hole. This is not an exhaustive list, and the names are likely to change slowly over time, but they are all excellent sources, and I believe you will benefit by checking them out.[20]

Newsletters

Jim Grant's Grant's Interest Rate Observer
https://grantspub.com/
Indispensable commentary on interest rates, stocks, and precious metals. 48 issues per year. Expensive but well worth it. *Grant's* also sponsors a fall investment conference in New York. These are true "gold-star" events. I've lost track of how many times a Grant's

Conference investment idea has paid for my subscription many times over.

Lyn Alden Investment Strategy
https://www.lynalden.com/
Lyn's offering is inexpensive and comprehensive. Her newsletter is probably the best value available for the money. She has an excellent grasp of what moves stock and bond prices. She offers solid recommendations with deep-dive analysis of industry groups and individual names. She understands money creation very well, as evidenced by her excellent 2023 book *Broken Money*. If you plan to manage your portfolio of stocks, I strongly recommend subscribing to Lyn's service.

Fred Hickey's The High Tech Strategist.
Fred doesn't use a website. His newsletter comes monthly via snail mail, or he will email it to you for an extra charge. It's inexpensive and well worth it. In addition to deep coverage of high-tech stocks, Fred covers individual gold mining stocks. His research is deep and high quality. To subscribe to The High Tech Strategist, send an email to: thehightechstrategist@yahoo.com

Luke Gromen's Forest for the Trees (FFTT)
https://fftt-llc.com/
Luke Gromen's commentary is creative, insightful, and "macro" oriented. He has a unique perspective on how money flows affect stock and bond prices and currency exchange rates.

Alasdair Macleod's MacleodFinance Substack
https://alasdairmacleod.substack.com/
is must-read material. Alasdair is a true scholar of money and banking with a correct understanding of money creation in all its details. He uses this knowledge to inform his opinions on interest rates,

sovereign bonds, and the gold price. A subscription to his Stack is inexpensive and excellent value for the money.

Russell Napier's The Solid Ground Newsletter
https://russellnapier.co.uk/
This is my favorite "macro" newsletter. Deep insight into central banks, foreign exchange, world bond markets, and mega-trends in the investment world. Russell has been a strong influence on my thinking about financial repression. His research is expensive for non-professionals but well worth it if you want to extend your understanding beyond US markets.

Grant Williams's
https://www.grant-williams.com.
Grant publishes a comprehensive newsletter called "Things That Make You Go Hmmm" (TTMYGH) that is thoughtful and entertaining. In my view, his best value-added comes from his frequent podcast interviews with famous investors. These are thought-provoking and fun to listen to while exercising or driving. His service is moderately priced and available in several tiers.

Bill Fleckenstein's
https://www.fleckensteincapital.com/.
Bill provides low-cost, common-sense daily commentary with good insight into gold-mining stocks.

David Stockman's Contra Corner:
https://www.davidstockmanscontracorner.com
Stockman, the former budget director under the Reagan administration, is a tireless crusader against central bank transgressions. David understands US monetary policy and spending as well as anyone I know. His data is impeccable. He offers great insight, and he can be a bit wordy, but his newsletter is reasonably priced.

HardmoneyJim

https://jim3c5.substack.com/.

My Substack newsletter (which will resume when I finish this book!) concentrates on money creation and its consequences, including occasional investment suggestions when I see something compelling. My primary purpose is to educate non-professional investors about how the money and banking system works, allowing them to adopt strategies to safeguard their wealth. I do not charge a subscription fee.

Traditional print and online periodicals

There is so much available. Where does one start with traditional media? I'll offer my quick take first on the traditional periodicals. I don't read them all every day—that would be impossible—but I do use all of them to do research for my investments, including articles and podcasts. These are my own opinions. Your mileage may vary.

The Wall Street Journal (https://www.wsj.com) and its sibling *Barron's* (https://www.barrons.com) offer solid, honest coverage of all aspects of investing, but coverage of foreign markets is somewhat limited.

Bloomberg (https://www.bloomberg.com) is politically biased to the left but has the most comprehensive and accurate suite of data available. It is somewhat expensive, but you can access information and data from markets worldwide.

The Economist (https://www.economist.com) is one of the oldest financial periodicals. It provides a valuable overview of the prevailing consensus on many economic issues. Like today's consensus, *The Economist* leans left.

The Financial Times (https://www.ft.com) is biased toward green energy, but the staff clearly understands money, banking, and monetary policy issues. The coverage is comprehensive.

ZeroHedge (https://www.zerohedge.com/) is a comprehensive financial news aggregator that monitors events in near real-time. ZH leans strongly to the right, which I believe is a deliberate policy designed to differentiate itself from the mainstream financial establishment. You can scan it a few times each week to get an early heads-up on emerging stories. In my experience, most reporting is responsibly written despite its rightward bias. The basic subscription is inexpensive, but a premium service is also available.

Seeking Alpha (https://seekingalpha.com/) provides a variety of research services, some for free, some by paid subscription. You can pick and choose among the offerings. Several good analysts are in the dividend-investing space, and I recommend trying them. In addition to its good analysis and commentary, Seeking Alpha provides abundant data on markets as well as individual stocks. It's a "must-have" if you manage your stock portfolio, in my view.

Sure Dividend (https://www.suredividend.com) is a high-quality research service that a friend recently recommended. Various service and information levels are available, and all are reasonably priced. *Sure Dividend* research dovetails nicely with the dividend-growth investing strategy described above.

Traditional TV media

What should one watch daily to keep up with the financial news? None of these are necessary, but I tune in most days to get a quick update on all the financial markets. Here is my take on the primary sources in the mainstream television media.

Bloomberg Television
https://www.bloomberg.com/live/us
Like its affiliated periodical, Bloomberg News, BTV is politically biased to the left. However, unlike its competitors, who are inclined to
repeat the mainstream news cycle, BTV mostly sticks to business
news. Overall, BTV offers the best in-depth financial reporting.

Fox Business News
https://www.foxbusiness.com
Fox leans right more than its affiliated periodical, *The Wall Street
Journal*. Fox tends to drift into political commentary and repeat the
mainstream news cycle instead of sticking to business and financial
news. However, some of their regular hosts, such as Charles Payne,
are very respectable.

CNBC
https://www.cnbc.com/live-tv/
There is a good reason CNBC is known among professional investors
as "Bubble Vision." Their commentary is occasionally helpful, but
mainly consists of what retail stock speculators want to hear. Just for
fun, tune in to Jim Cramer's afternoon commentary someday. In my
humble opinion, if you take Cramer seriously, you should *not* invest
in the stock market.

I usually tune into Bloomberg or Fox Business for a few minutes,
switch to the other for a few minutes, and then go on with my daily
business.

Data services

X (formerly known as Twitter)
https://x.com
In my view, every investor should subscribe to X as a "looker"
(lurker?). X is the best way to follow your favorite investment
thought leaders. A lot of financial news and emerging data breaks on

X long before it reaches other media, if it ever does. Also, the exchanges between some of the famous financial lights are often enlightening. Tweet away if you want, but be careful; active engagement in X is a time sink.

Jim Bianco, Bianco Research
https://www.biancoresearch.com/
Jim Bianco may be the most highly respected economist on Wall Street. His work is independent, not affiliated with any of the major brokerage firms, and offers high-level analysis targeted at institutional investors. His research service is expensive as it is priced for multiple users at large financial institutions. Therefore, a paid subscription may be impractical for your personal savings program, but I include Jim in my recommendation list because he is plain-spoken, honest, and very thoughtful. Jim is a genuinely original thinker with a practical orientation. Bianco Research offers many excellent thematic ideas but only some specific investment recommendations. Free trials are available: see the website. If you don't subscribe to Bianco Research, watch for Jim Bianco on YouTube and follow him on X (Twitter). He's also a frequent guest on Fox Business News, Bloomberg News, and CNBC.

Charlie Bilello
https://bilello.blog/
Bilello's weekly blog and excellent data charts are free. Data is timely and accurate. Other investment services are available as add-ons.

Wolf Richter, *Wolf Street*
https://wolfstreet.com/
This is another excellent data service, with good coverage of the housing, auto, and bond markets. The basic service, which is very good, is free.

Gold vendors: Monetary Metals & Co.
https://monetary-metals.com
This company buys and sells precious metals, enabling investors to earn interest on gold, paid in gold. *The author of this book is a director on the Monetary Metals Board.* Other precious metals vendors I have used successfully are GovMint.com https://www.govmint.com and APMEX https://www.apmex.com. Many other reputable, fair dealers can be found online.

I hope you have enjoyed and benefited from this book. If you did, you can access my regular Substack essays and podcasts—available for no charge—at HardmoneyJim https://jim3c5.substack.com/

Appendix 1: Defining Money

The definition; Two kinds of money;
Counting the money supply; M2 or "broad money";
Proposed adjustments to M2

The definition

You may have heard the "money couplet," adopted by economics teachers in the early 20th century, after William Stanley Jevons analyzed money according to its four functions.[1]

"Money's a matter of functions four:

A medium, a measure, a standard, a store."

The rhyme provides a good description of the main characteristics of money: medium of exchange, measure of value, standard of value, and store of value. These characteristics are often said to constitute the "definition" of money.

But merely listing the functions of money does not constitute its definition. A description and a definition are not the same thing. As stated in our discussion of inflation in Chapter Four, a definition should differentiate the defined concept from all other concepts. This means a definition must identify the most fundamental characteristic of the concept in question, the characteristic that distinguishes the concept from all other concepts.[2]

Without a precise definition, we will end up discussing "money" without knowing what the other person is talking about. For example, if we think of money only as a "store of value," then any financial instrument or commodity that stores value (like a Treasury bond or a barrel of oil) could be called "money."

But we can avoid this confusion. The four functions of money listed in the rhyme are not equal in importance. One of these functions is fundamental, while the others are secondary, i.e., derived from the more fundamental one. Fortunately, the most fundamental definition of money was established by Ludwig von Mises.

Mises defined money as a "commonly accepted medium of exchange" for a very good reason: money's function in exchanging goods and services underlies all the other characteristics attributed to money.

> Money is a medium of exchange. It is the most market-able good which people acquire because they want to offer it in later acts of interpersonal exchange. Money is the thing which serves as the generally accepted and commonly used medium of exchange. This is its only function. All the other functions which people ascribe to money are merely particular aspects of its primary and sole function, that of a medium of exchange.[3]

Mises argued that money as a means of exchange is elemental, and all the other characteristics (measure, standard, and store) are derivative from that. Let's look at each of the other functions one at a time. (The following explanations are mine, as I learned them from reading von Mises's *Human Action* and *Theory of Money and Credit*. I take full responsibility for any errors herein.)

Measure. Is money a measure of value? No, because money itself cannot be a "measure" of anything. In economics, the "value" of a good is measured as a price, a ratio between a quantity of money exchanged for a quantity of goods or services. This ratio—the price—is a measure of value by the specific parties of a specific economic exchange. We can compare historical prices of goods, and this helps us measure the value we want to put on a good we are buying or selling. But even in a stable economy, prices constantly change. Eggs may sell for $4 per dozen today and $5 per dozen next week. And why do we even have price data to use for economic calculation? Because we and others have exchanged money for goods and have found, through price discovery, how to measure the value of some goods versus others. We could not make such measurements of value unless we were exchanging goods and services, using money as our tool of exchange, to establish prices.

Price, not money, is the measure of value, and price is determined by exchange. By exchanging money for goods, we discover prices. To summarize: Money facilitates exchange; exchange results in prices; prices are a measure of value; therefore, money as a tool of exchange is more fundamental than the measurement of value.

Standard. Is money a standard of value? It's true that money provides a standard, that is, a unit of account (e.g., the dollar, euro, yen, etc.) that is used to express prices. This becomes obvious when we observe economic behavior. People express the price of everything in some convenient unit of money. They do not express prices in terms of other commodities – for example, we don't say it takes 50,000 bushels of corn to buy a house.

But could there be a standard of value—a monetary unit of account—without exchange? Our favored monetary unit, the dollar, was adopted hundreds of years ago by large numbers of people through voluntary exchange. But to become the *standard* unit, money first had to be commonly accepted in exchange. In America, the dollar won its place as the standard unit through actual usage, i.e., through exchange. Thus, the "commonly accepted medium of exchange," of necessity, also became the standard unit of account through custom and social practice. Consequently, the primary characteristic of money is its function as a medium of exchange, which precedes and necessitates its acceptance as a standard unit of account.

Store: Yes, money is a store of value, but only under specific conditions. Money by itself cannot store value because money's only fundamental value is derived from the useful goods it can be exchanged for. Money, then, is a "store of value" only when there are non-money goods available for exchange.

Money functions best as a store of value when there is a continuous flow of production of many goods and services in the economy. If goods are not being produced for exchange, money is of no value. Imagine Robinson Crusoe subsisting on a desert island: he obviously has no need for money. Only when goods are being exchanged in a robust economy is money a good store of value. If money is a commonly accepted medium of exchange, there must be goods available for exchange. It is the fact that money can be readily exchanged for useful goods in a robust economy that confers its ability to "store" value. Once again, we are back to "medium of exchange" as the fundamental characteristic of money.

Money is indeed a "matter of functions four," but it is able to play all these roles only because of the fundamental fact that it is the commonly accepted medium of exchange.

Two kinds of money

Mises identified two classes of modern money. First, there is "standard money," and then there is "fiduciary media," which is derived from standard money. If we are on a "gold standard," then physical gold is the standard money. Standard money constitutes full and final payment. When a debt is paid with standard money, the recipient of the money has no further claim to any party. The receipt of standard money satisfies all prior claims.

Standard money makes possible its derivative, "fiduciary media." Fiduciary media are claims to receive standard money, accepted and exchanged as equivalent to standard money but for which no standard money exists. An example will make the distinction between the two types of money clear.

Under a gold standard, suppose a bank has 100 ounces of gold in its vault, all of which were deposited by customers. Against these gold units, assume the bank has issued 100 claims on gold, in the form of banknotes or bank deposits, each representing a claim to one ounce of gold. These claims are traded in the economy as if they were gold, based on widespread confidence that the bank will promptly exchange physical gold for such claims when they are presented at the bank. This would happen when a banknote holder went to the bank teller and demanded physical gold in exchange for his banknote, or when the owner of a bank deposit withdrew his deposit in gold. In this case, the claims for gold exactly equal the quantity of gold in the bank.

So far, there is only standard money, circulating independently of the banking system, and banknotes (or bank deposits) that serve as a substitute for the standard money held by the bank. As yet there is no "fiduciary media."

Next, suppose that through its lending and investment operations, the bank issues an additional 100 claims, each representing one unit of gold. There are now 200 claims (banknotes or deposits) circulating in the economy, but only 100 ounces of gold in the vault are available for redemption. By von Mises's definition of money, we now have 100 units of banknotes (or deposits) backed by standard money and 100 additional units called "fiduciary media" circulating in the money supply. All 200 banknotes (or deposits) are accepted equally in commerce and are indistinguishable from each other. Therefore, all these banknotes are money.

Common acceptance by the public is key to the definition of money. This view is shared by economists of varying ideologies. As the neo-Keynesian J.K. Galbraith put it, money is precisely what most people think it is:

> The reader should proceed … in the knowledge that money is nothing more or less than what he or she always thought it was—what is commonly offered or received for the purchase or sale of goods, services, or other things. [4]

Because all the banknotes and deposits, covered and uncovered, are a "commonly accepted medium of exchange," all meet the definition of money.

In today's fiat bank reserve system, standard money is no longer a natural commodity like gold or silver. Instead, standard money consists of dollar units "made up" by the central bank. Standard money, or full and final payment, consists of 1) paper currency and coin circulating in the economy independent of the banking system and 2) "cash reserves" (also called "cash" or "reserves"). These cash reserves are further broken down into vault cash (paper bills at the bank available for withdrawal) and cash reserves held in ledger form in an account with the central bank. As described in Chapters Two and Three, cash reserves are simply invented by the central bank, by fiat, whenever it purchases a security.

Counting units in the broad money supply

M2, the Fed's label for the "broad money supply," has a long history in monetary statistics. There are many more "Ms" in the financial lexicon: M0, M1, M2, M3, etc.; but most of these "Ms" have fallen out of use because central bankers decided they had limited analytical value. The Fed's M2 is their preferred measure of the "broad money" supply—that is, the money available for use by the public in everyday economic transactions, including all consumer purchases, business expenditures, investment outlays, and so on.

According to the Fed's "Frequently Asked Questions" page, "The money supply is the total amount of money—cash, coins, and balances in bank accounts—in circulation." [5] As we will see, I believe this description is a good start but is slightly restrictive because of some recently adopted policies of the Treasury and the Fed.

"In circulation" is the key phrase. A commercial bank's cash reserves, whether stored in the bank as paper ("vault cash") or stored as a ledger entry with the Fed, are not counted in the money supply because they are not available for exchange until someone converts a bank deposit to physical cash. A bank's cash reserves are not "in circulation" in the general economy. They circulate only among banks to settle deposit imbalances or when banks borrow reserves from each other to have enough on hand to meet cash withdrawals.

The same condition prevailed from the very beginning of bank credit creation, even under a gold standard. Gold coins, circulating in the economy outside the banking system, were part of the money supply. Circulating banknotes and bank deposits were also counted in the money supply because they were available for exchange. Gold sitting as a cash reserve in the bank vault or on deposit with a central bank was not counted in the money supply because it was not available for exchange.

Today, circulating paper currency (which has replaced gold) and bank deposits, both available for exchange, comprise almost all of what the Fed includes in the broad money supply. However, the Fed's technical description of the broad money supply (M2) has a few inconsistencies. The remainder of this Appendix will describe what the Fed classifies as "broad money" and what I believe are three questionable practices related to their counting methods.

The Fed's three debatable counting techniques are: 1) excluding the Treasury General Account (TGA) from broad money; 2) excluding the Fed's Reverse Repo Program (RRP) balances from broad money; and 3) including "retail money market funds" in broad money.

The Treasury General Account

Before the Great Financial Crash, the Treasury kept much of its money in various private commercial bank accounts. However, as of 2008, all the Treasury's cash is on deposit with the US Federal Reserve in the Treasury General Account (TGA), also known as the government's "checking account." When a person or institution makes a payment to the Treasury, whether it is to pay taxes or lend money to the government by investing in Treasury securities, the payer's bank deposits are reduced, and this money exits the commercial banking system. To balance the commercial bank's books, an equal amount of bank reserves is sent from the payer's bank to the TGA, where it is held on deposit at the Fed. In other words, the US Treasury has its own unique account with the Fed where it parks all US government cash.

This appears to be a simple transfer of money from a private bank account to the government's bank account, similar to what happens when any private party transacts with another private party. However, because the payer's money has left the commercial banking system, the Fed chooses not to count the Treasury's TGA balance as part of the broad money supply. I believe this policy is not justified.[6]

When money is transferred from a private citizen to the Treasury, all that has happened is that purchasing power—money—has passed from the taxpayer or investor to the government. The money is temporarily out of the commercial banking system, but it is still very much available for exchange in the economy because the Treasury will soon spend this money to pay the government's bills. When the Treasury makes a payment to any person or entity, the payee deposits the government's check in a commercial bank. The bank presents the check to the Fed, the Treasury's banker, for payment. The result is the payee gets a commercial bank deposit and the payee's commercial bank gets cash reserves. By the Fed's reckoning, the money supply increases when the government spends money. But this makes little sense because no new money has been created.

Why does this accounting anomaly matter? Because the amount of money held in the TGA can vary significantly. During the COVID pandemic, the TGA balance reached $1.8 trillion (July 2020) due to massive government borrowing, thus understating the money supply by about 10 percent. As the government spent massively, the TGA balance declined to around $50 Billion in June 2023, drastically increasing M2. As of July 10, 2024, the TGA balance was $736 Billion. Left out of the broad money calculation, the changing TGA balance distorts the money supply, in my view. Here is a graph of the overnight Treasury's balance at the Fed as of late July 2024:[7]

Treasury General Account
Treasury Deposits with Federal Reserve Banks - $ billions

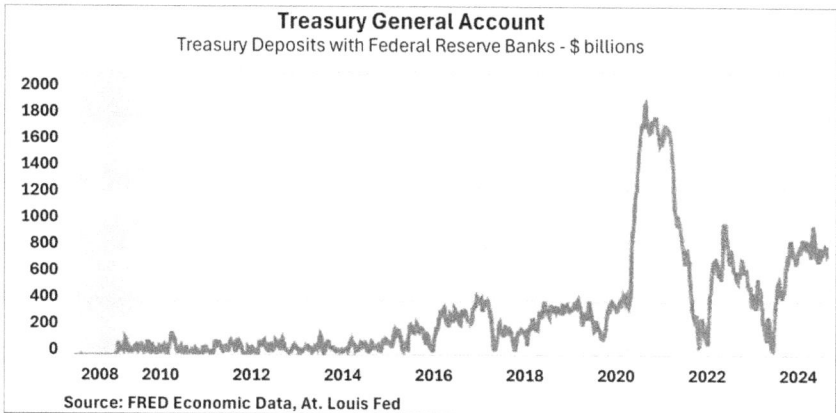

Source: FRED Economic Data, At. Louis Fed

The Fed's Reverse Repo program

The Fed operates an overnight "Reverse Repurchase Program" (ON RRP) that is designed to help control short-term interest rates. Under this program, the Fed borrows money overnight from a list of approved institutional investors, mainly large money market funds, and pays them interest at a rate determined by the Fed. The offer to borrow money at the stated rate is open-ended, which means the Fed will borrow any amount of money offered from its designated customers. This policy sets a floor on short-term interest rates that helps the Fed enforce its official policy rate. As of July 2024, this policy rate was 5.25 to 5.5%. As of July 2024, the overnight "reverse repo rate" was 5.3%, expected to come down when the Fed lowers short-term rates.

The effect of the ON RRP program on money supply is similar to the effect of the TGA account. When an investor lends money to the Fed to invest in an overnight RRP, the investor's bank deposits and the cash reserves of the investor's bank both decline. When bank deposits decline, broad money (M2) also declines. Consequently, by the Fed's accounting method, an investment in RRP reduces M2 by an equal amount.

But does this make sense? To the investor (an overnight lender to the Fed) the RRP program is like a bank deposit that pays high interest. To him, this is definitely money that is available for exchange in the economy. In addition, the Fed's promise to pay out standard money on demand is even more secure than a commercial bank's. After all, the investor's counterparty is the Fed itself! The money is always available the next day if the investor gives notice by the afternoon of the day before. These are funds that could be moved almost instantly back to bank deposits if money market fund investors decide they want to buy stocks or houses or consumer goods. In other words, the money is at least as available to the investor as short-term CDs and savings deposits, which *are* counted in M2. In my view, the mere fact that an investor moves his money from an account at a commercial bank to an account at the Fed does not warrant excluding it from M2. The money is readily available for spending and guaranteed by the ultimate money creator, the US central bank.

We are talking about potentially very large sums in the RRP. In January 2023, the RRP balance reached $2.4 trillion. As of July 2024, it stands at about $400 billion. The RRP facility is a favorite investment of money market funds because it is the most liquid asset they can invest in and is immune to both credit risk and counterparty risk.

In my view, the RRP balance is as "money-like" as any standard bank deposit and, therefore, should be included in M2. A graph of the overnight RRP balance is shown below.[8]

Overnight Reverse Repo Balance at the Fed
($ Billions)

Source: FRED Economic Data, St. Louis Fed

(Chart showing Overnight Reverse Repo Balance at the Fed in $ Billions, with y-axis values 0, 400, 800, 1200, 1600, 2000, 2400, 2800 and x-axis years 2010, 2012, 2014, 2016, 2018, 2020, 2022, 2024)

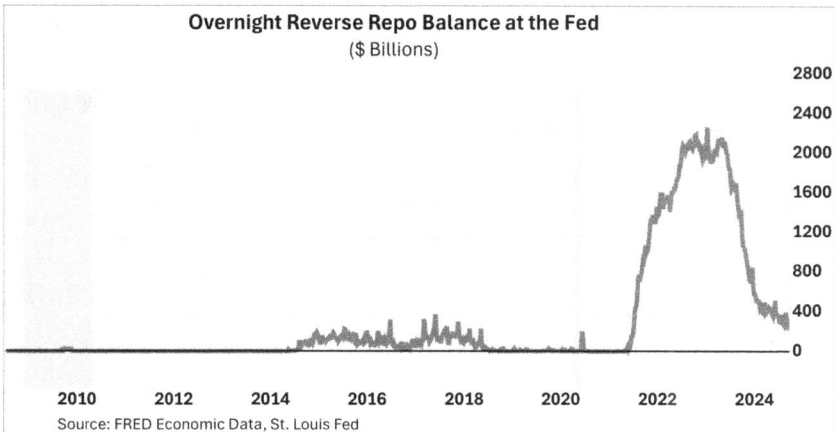

Retail money market funds

As of July 20, 2024, the Fed recorded the broad money supply (M2) at about $21 trillion. The Fed defines M2 as follows:

> M1 plus (1) small-denomination time deposits (time deposits in amounts of less than $100,000) less IRA and Keogh balances at depository institutions; and (2) balances in retail money market funds [MMFs] less IRA and Keogh balances at MMFs.

> M1 consists of (1) currency outside the U.S. Treasury, Federal Reserve Banks, and the vaults of depository institutions; (2) demand deposits at commercial banks (excluding those amounts held by depository institutions, the U.S. government, and foreign banks and official institutions) less cash items in the process of collection and Federal Reserve float; and (3) other liquid deposits, consisting of OCDs ["other checkable deposits"] and savings deposits (including money market deposit accounts).

I have no quarrel with the description of M1. However, I question the inclusion of "retail money market funds" in M2. "Retail" refers to accounts with less than $100,000. Including money market funds seems plausible at first because it is possible to simply write a check against some money market funds, similar to a bank account. However, I think this classification is problematic as it may involve some double-counting.

The relevant question is, does sending money to a money market account create new money or destroy existing money? The correct answer is that it does neither.

When an investor sends money to a money market fund (MMF), the first thing that happens is that the investor's bank deposit becomes the MMF's bank deposit. Next, the MMF will invest these funds into a short-term debt instrument of some kind. In other words, the fund will lend money to a borrower on a very short-term basis. When this loan is made, the MMF's bank deposit becomes the borrower's bank deposit. So far, money in the form of a bank deposit has just changed hands from a lender to a borrower. No new money has been created.

Some of the MMF's investments (loans) will be made with borrowers who have commercial bank accounts. In these cases, the money will be transferred to the borrower's bank account in exchange for some promise to repay the money quickly. This would be the case, for example, if the money market fund invested in the private repurchase agreement (Repo) market, in which money is loaned to various entities who borrow against their own high-quality collateral, such as a portfolio of Treasurys. In these cases, the MMF lends to someone with a commercial bank account. No new money is created, it just changes hands.

The same would be true if the MMF purchased a Treasury Bill from a private owner. Money simply changes hands by moving from one bank account to another. The fund gives up its bank deposit in exchange for a short-term bond.

Another possibility is that the MMF buys Treasurys directly from the Treasury Department. In this case, the official money supply is reduced because the money leaves the commercial banking system and goes to the TGA. But, as discussed above, this is an unwarranted reduction because the money has merely changed hands from the fund to the Treasury. Including the TGA in the money supply, as suggested above, would eliminate the money supply reduction that arises from this money market transaction.

A third possibility is that the MMF loans money to the Fed overnight in the RRP, as described above. In this case, it is just as if the investor transferred his funds to a different commercial bank, except that this "bank" happens to be called the US Federal Reserve. Officially, the Fed removes the RRP balance from M2 because the money is no longer on deposit in the banking system. But I believe this is incorrect because no money is actually destroyed and no purchasing power is lost.

Consequently, if both the Treasury's TGA account and the Fed's overnight RRP accounts were counted in the broad money supply, as I believe they should be, including money market funds in the broad money supply would be double-counting, thus overstating the money supply.

Proposed adjustments to M2

With these three considerations in mind, I believe the following adjustments to the published M2 balance are warranted: First, I would accept the Fed's calculation of M1 and small-time deposits as stated. Second, add the TGA balance. Third, add the Fed's overnight RRP balance. Finally, do *not* count retail money market funds.

These adjustments are summarized in the following table:[9]

	As of July 20, 2024 ($ Billions)	
	Fed's M2	**Modified M2**
M1 as stated by Fed	18063	18063
Small Time Deposits	1119	1119
Adjusted Retail MMF	1829	0
Treasury General Account		767
Fed's Reverse Repo Facility (RRP)		400
Broad Money Supply (M2)	21011	20349

As a concluding point, it is well to remember that the ambiguity surrounding what the Fed counts as "money" does not change the fact that all modern money—whether held as currency in circulation, in the TGA, or as a RRP at the Fed—was originally created as a bank deposit.

APPENDIX 2: THE LEGAL BASIS OF MONEY CREATION IN THE UNITED STATES

Overview; Constitutional authority; Statutory authority

Overview

This Appendix provides a basic description of the legal basis of bank money creation in the United States. Since modern banks in all jurisdictions are permitted to create bank deposits in the same way, it would seem reasonable to believe that the legal basis for this authority is similar across jurisdictions. However, this may not be the case. In at least some jurisdictions, the commercial banks' legal authority to create money is ambiguous. For example, in a 2014 paper, monetary scholar Richard Werner explored the legal basis of bank money creation in the United Kingdom. Werner commented:

> There is also virtually no scholarly literature on the question of which regulations precisely enable banks to create money. These issues are, however, of great interest, especially since the function of banks as the creators and allocators of the money supply is not explicitly stated in any law, statute, regulation, ordinance, directive or court judgment.[1]

In the United States, the legal authority permitting commercial banks to control money creation is widely believed to derive from a combination of Constitutional authority, congressional law, and legal precedent, all supported by decades of customary banking practices. What follows is a discussion of the Constitutional and legislative origins of this authority. My tentative conclusion is that United States banks are legally empowered to create money due to both Constitutional and legislative authority; however, this formal authority depends crucially on both commonly accepted banking practices and judicial precedence. I stress that I am not a legal scholar. I am grateful to Professor Lev Menand, a monetary scholar and professor at Columbia Law School, for pointing me towards the legal citations that follow. Any errors or omissions are entirely my own.

Constitutional authority

The most fundamental legal authority for money creation in the USA comes from the Constitution, which empowered Congress to regulate the value of money. Article 1, Section 8, Clause 5 reads as follows:

> [The Congress shall have Power . . .] To coin Money,
> regulate the Value thereof, and of foreign Coin, and fix
> the Standard of Weights and Measures; . . .

Article 1 Section 10 contains the only mention of gold or silver in the Constitution. This section says that the individual states may not "… coin money, emit bills of credit, [or] make anything but gold and silver Coin a tender payment of debts … ." The text of Article 10 clearly implies that the Founders believed "Money" was only gold and silver, and Congress had the sole power to press it into coins under its power to fix the "Standard of Weights and Measures."

However, over the many decades since the Constitution was ratified, Congressional legislation and numerous court decisions have overruled any alleged Constitutional intent to use only precious metals as standard money. To my knowledge, every effort to restore gold or silver as the only legal standard money has been defeated in the courts.

Statutory authority

The issue we are most concerned with in this Appendix is the legal basis of the creation of "bank money," or what Mises called "fiduciary media." What legal authority gives U.S. government-chartered commercial banks the sole ability to create money in the form of banknotes or deposits? Another way to ask the question is, what legal authority permits banks to make investments (grant loans or purchase securities) without making a payment of prior-existent money?[2]

According to Professor Menand, national banks are explicitly authorized by Congress to create credit money. 12 U.S.C. § 24 (seventh) describes in detail the limits of banks' investment activity. Regarding credit creation, the following language grants federally chartered banks

> … all such incidental powers as shall be necessary to
> carry on the business of banking; by discounting and
> negotiating promissory notes, drafts, bills of exchange,
> and other evidences of debt; by receiving deposits; by
> buying and selling exchange, coin, and bullion; by loan-
> ing money on personal security; and by obtaining, issu-
> ing, and circulating notes according to the provisions of
> this title.[3]

The view among legal scholars seems to be that engaging in these specific actions results in the creation of bank "deposits" that everyone accepts as money. The statute's broad language—"all such incidental powers," "the business of banking," "discounting and negotiating," "receiving deposits," "loaning money," "issuing, and circulating notes"—is said to be the basis of the unique credit-creation authority Congress granted to the banks.[4] Congress also authorized state-chartered banks to exercise these same powers. See 12 U.S.C § 378 (a) (2) .

However, in my view, the statute's plain language, as written, falls short of explicitly granting money-creating authority. If the language cited above specifically empowers federally chartered banks to create credit instruments that must be accepted as money, I fail to see it. If this language does authorize money creation, there must be some common historical understanding or legal precedent that supplies the missing authority.

A search of the legislative history of 12 U.S.C. § 24 (seventh) reveals it is derived from the U.S. Bank Act of 1864. The original legislation has been amended many times over the years. Nowhere do I find any legal definition of the "business of banking" or what it actually means for a bank to "receive deposits."

According to the legal firm *USLegal.com*,

> The business of banking, as *defined by law and custom*, consists in:
>
> a. the issual of notes, payable on demand, *intended to circulate as money*, where the banks are banks of issue;
>
> b. receiving deposits payable on demand;
>
> c. discounting commercial paper;
>
> d. making loans of money on collateral security;
>
> e. buying and selling bills of exchange;
>
> f. negotiating loans and dealing in negotiable securities issued by the government, state and national, and municipal and other corporations. [Italics added.][5]

So, it appears the "business of banking," as understood by legal experts, includes issuing credit instruments intended to be used as money. This makes sense: Since the ancient practice of creating bank money was well-known to American bankers and legislators in the 19th and early 20th centuries, it would seem logical that this assumption was passed down through successive generations of lawyers and judges. Still, it is hard to see how the text of the law conveys explicit money-creation authority.

"Receiving deposits" apparently has a specific legal meaning in banking. Cash deposited in a commercial bank is not there for safekeeping; it becomes the bank's property. What we call a bank "deposit" is really the bank's IOU to the depositor, evidence of the bank's contractual agreement to pay out cash on demand.

A bank "deposit" stands in contrast to a deposit in a nonbank institution, which acts as an intermediary between the depositor and another party. In nonbank institutions, such as brokerage firms, mutual funds, and trust companies, customers' deposits are not listed as either an asset or a liability on the firm's balance sheet. This kind of deposit is segregated from the balance sheet because it is not the institution's property.

So, why is it that only banks can create their own "deposits"? The operation involves what some would say is accounting sleight of hand that is apparently accepted as part of the normal "business of banking." Consider the following scenario of a nonbank called Lending Company that extends a loan. Lending Company agrees, 10 days from now, to purchase Mr. X's promissory note. (Purchasing a promissory note is the same as lending—see Chapter Two.) As soon as the loan contract is signed, but before any money is handed over to Mr. X, both sides of Lending Company's balance sheet would expand: a new asset called a "loan" is recorded, accompanied by a new liability called "accounts payable."

Ten days later, when the loan payment is actually made to Mr. X, cash is deducted from the Lending Company's assets and paid to Mr. X. This payment discharges the "accounts payable" liability. The loan remains an asset on Lending Company's books. The net effect of this two-part transaction is to replace a cash asset with a loan asset. After the payment is made, there is no net change in the size of the lending firm's balance sheet.

But bank loans are different, as they complete only the first step of this two-part process. Suppose an actual bank agrees to loan money to Mr. X. The first step in the loan commitment is identical to the nonbank loan. The loan on the bank's asset side is offset by an "accounts payable" (deposit) entry on the liability side. *However, the bank never "makes a payment" to satisfy the loan commitment.*

Due to its special legal privilege, the bank is allowed to simply re-classify the new accounts payable as a "deposit," even though no money has been deposited into the bank. This, apparently, is the special legal meaning of the bank's ability to "receive deposits," differentiating deposits in banks from deposits in nonbanks.

Richard Werner conceives the "bank account" in this way:

> What banks do is to simply reclassify their accounts payable items arising from the act of lending as 'customer deposits', and the general public, when receiving payment in the form of a transfer of bank deposits, believes that a form of money had been paid into the bank. As a result, the public readily accepts such 'bank deposits' and their 'transfers' to defray payments. They are also the main component of the official 'money supply' as announced by central banks.[6]

We are left with the conclusion that the customary "business of banking" and the widespread (perhaps unwitting) public acceptance of banks as money creators are indispensable supplements to the statutory legal authority to create money.

In any case, the unique accounting that banks engage in is rarely questioned. Bank "credit money," or bank deposits, trade as equivalent to Federal Reserve Notes, but they are not legally equivalent. Bank deposits are redeemable on demand at banks for Federal Reserve notes because banks are legally obligated to make good on their deposit liabilities if the depositor so demands. As we learned in Chapter Two, Federal Reserve notes are not redeemable for anything except other Federal Reserve notes—they do not represent any further actionable legal obligation. Federal Reserve notes are today's gold, the "standard money" of our day. Furthermore, Federal Reserve notes are legal tender for all debts public and private, while bank deposits are not. See 31 U.S.C. § 5103. [7]

Under "free banking," as described in earlier chapters, the banks' credit creation activities relied primarily on the public's trust in the bankers' integrity.[8] Free market banks did not need a government banking license to issue fiduciary media. The public's near-universal confidence in bank fiduciary media was why it traded as equivalent to standard gold specie. The government was hardly involved at all in the banking industry. Under a free-market gold standard, the main legal issue involving bankers was enforcing valid commercial contracts between the bankers and other parties. Of course, parties to a transaction could sue for theft or fraud, but the government did not protect depositors from financial loss due to poor business judgment. It was "caveat emptor," buyer beware.

Today, while public trust still plays a key role in modern banking, this trust is no longer based primarily on the integrity of the bankers. Given the legal differences between Federal Reserve notes (cash) and bank deposits, a lot of regulatory effort goes into ensuring that bank deposits and Federal Reserve notes trade for equivalent value. The FDIC insures deposits. The Fed provides cash reserves to banks through the discount window when they need them to settle interbank transfers. In recent years, it has become increasingly common for the Fed to act as a proactive lender (money creator) to ensure all banks can make good on all withdrawals, as was the case when Silicon Valley Bank failed in March 2023.

In closing, I will quote Richard Werner's concluding remarks in his review of the legal basis of money creation in the United Kingdom:

> Whether the [enabling statutes] were designed for this purpose, and whether it is indeed explicitly lawful for banks to reclassify general 'accounts payable' items as specific liabilities defined as 'customer deposits', without the act of depositing having been undertaken by anyone, is a matter that requires further legal scrutiny, beyond the scope of this paper.[9]

In my view, Werner's call for "further legal scrutiny" in the United Kingdom applies equally to the United States. Why? Because, as this book has pointed out, the way banks create money is not as widely known or as well understood as it was a century ago. This loss of customary or common knowledge should be restored by a firmer, formal legal understanding to safeguard our banking system.

These legal ambiguities also flag the need to educate the public on the facts of modern money creation. As one authoritative writer on the subject concluded:

> Part of the widespread acceptance of bank deposits as payment may be due to the fact that the general public is simply not aware that banks do indeed create the money supply.[10]

Surely, public acceptance and confidence based on ignorance is no way to run a monetary system. A better-educated public would seem to be a solid civic imperative.

APPENDIX 3: PAUL SAMUELSON'S FRACTIONAL FICTION

Overview; Three competing theories;
Fractional reserve banking, Samuelson-style;
Werner's remarkable experiment; Implications

Overview

This Appendix will unveil the falsehoods and half-truths of the late Paul Samuelson's "fractional reserve" banking theory.

To explain Samuelson's view, we will focus on Chapter 14 of his textbook, *Economics*, first published in 1948, and arguably the most famous and most popular textbook on economics ever written. It has been reprinted at least 19 times, most recently in 2010. By 2018, *Economics* had sold over 4,000,000 copies and had been translated into 41 languages.[1]

Right out of the gate, we must explain our terms to avoid confusion. Some economists use the term "fractional reserve banking" to describe any money creation theory that describes how banks end up with cash reserves that are a mere fraction of outstanding bank deposits. However, by that broad classification, even the credit creation theory could be called a "fractional reserve" theory. Throughout this book, we have used the term "fractional reserve banking" to refer to the process of money creation as described in Paul Samuelson's textbook. We focus on Samuelson's explanation because, in universities where fractional reserve banking is still taught, Samuelson's account is still dominant, thus its errors survive. [2]

In this Appendix, I contend that Richard Werner's "credit creation" theory of banking is correct, while Samuelson's "fractional reserve" theory is (at best) only partially true. Either theory will provide a rationale as to why a commercial bank's deposits greatly exceed its cash reserves. The difference between the two theories is that Samuelson invents a false story of banking while Werner accurately describes banking in the real world. Both systems attempt to explain the same bank balance sheet, but the two theories describe money-creation processes that are radically different from each other. Obviously, both explanations cannot be correct.

Three competing theories

According to monetary scholar Richard Werner, three competing banking theories have attempted to explain the banking system and its role in creating money. These are the *credit creation theory*, the *fractional reserve theory*, and the *financial intermediation theory*. Professor Werner has documented these theories and their periods of historical dominance in a 2014 paper, *Can banks individually create money out of nothing? - the theories and the empirical evidence.*[3] In 2016, he updated this research with another frequently cited paper, *A Lost Century in Economics.*[4]

The *credit creation theory* was widely accepted by economists, bankers, and politicians in the 19th and early 20th centuries. This theory holds that banks individually create money by lending or purchasing investment assets. By the mid-20th century, the credit creation theory gave way to the *fractional reserve theory*. This theory agreed with the credit creation theory that money is created in commercial banks; however, it claimed that no single bank could create money and that only a system-wide interaction of many banks could create money through a "deposit multiplier" process. Under this theory, each individual bank is viewed as a pass-through intermediary, not as a money creator.

From the early 1960s, under the influence of John Maynard Keynes, James Tobin, and *The Journal of Money, Credit and Banking*, the *financial intermediation theory* became dominant, according to Werner. This theory does not admit that commercial banks can create money at all; instead, it sees the entire banking system as a pass-through mechanism that borrows depositors' savings to lend out to others. This view is typified by expressions such as the statement, often parroted by contemporary pundits, that "commercial banks lend out other peoples' money."

In the chart below. I have mapped out Werner's scholarly review of economists who typified these three competing theories. (The chart lists some of the more prominent economists; Werner's review is much more thorough.) Reading from left to right, it is apparent that the credit creation theory gave way to the fractional reserve theory during the early 20th century, and that the fractional reserve theory has now been largely (but not entirely) replaced by the financial intermediation theory.

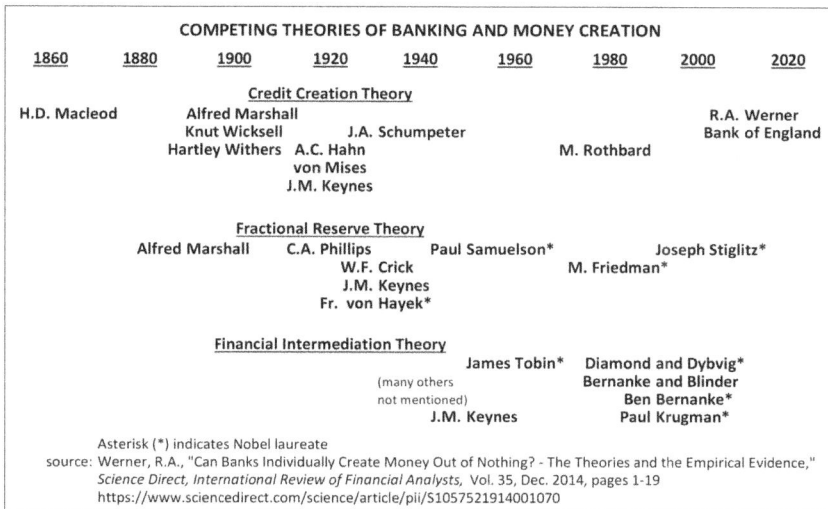

COMPETING THEORIES OF BANKING AND MONEY CREATION

1860	1880	1900	1920	1940	1960	1980	2000	2020

Credit Creation Theory
H.D. Macleod   Alfred Marshall   R.A. Werner
                      Knut Wicksell   J.A. Schumpeter   Bank of England
                      Hartley Withers A.C. Hahn   M. Rothbard
                                    von Mises
                                    J.M. Keynes

Fractional Reserve Theory
          Alfred Marshall   C.A. Phillips   Paul Samuelson*   Joseph Stiglitz*
                            W.F. Crick   M. Friedman*
                            J.M. Keynes
                            Fr. von Hayek*

Financial Intermediation Theory
                                        James Tobin*   Diamond and Dybvig*
                            (many others   Bernanke and Blinder
                            not mentioned)   Ben Bernanke*
                                        J.M. Keynes   Paul Krugman*

Asterisk (*) indicates Nobel laureate
source: Werner, R.A., "Can Banks Individually Create Money Out of Nothing? - The Theories and the Empirical Evidence," *Science Direct, International Review of Financial Analysts*, Vol. 35, Dec. 2014, pages 1-19
https://www.sciencedirect.com/science/article/pii/S1057521914001070

As Werner's research demonstrates, some of the world's most famous economists, including many Nobel laureates, have disagreed on how money is created. John Maynard Keynes, in apparent disagreement with himself, embraced all three views at some point in his career. As Werner points out, very few economists today, including those who write popular textbooks, see bank credit creation as the source of new money. Nearly all undergraduate economics textbooks continue to spread competing and contradictory explanations, year after year, decade after decade.

My own observation is that the credit creation theory has regained some traction in the last ten years, mainly among a vanguard of curious professional investors striving to understand the implications of the government's meddling in the banking system. By contrast, many professional economists and academics still reject or misrepresent the credit creation theory. However, as I will demonstrate in this Appendix, Richard Werner has proved the credit creation theory empirically and inductively by means of an ingenious real-world experiment conducted in 2014.

Fractional reserve banking, Samuelson style

We start by summarizing fractional reserve banking as Samuelson laid it out in Chapter 14 of *Economics*:

Samuelson begins with a historical reference to the English goldsmiths as the originators of modern fractional reserve banking. He then describes modern money creation with a detailed example, which starts when someone deposits $1000 cash into a bank checking account. When the bank receives this cash, it records a deposit—a liability owed to the depositor—and also records the cash as an asset, part of which it can lend out. The bank is subject to legal reserve requirements, which are assumed to be 20%, meaning the bank can only lend out 80% of its total cash reserves. Samuelson assumes the banking system is always "loaned up" to the maximum allowed by its regulators. Therefore, the bank lends out 80% of the new $1000 deposit by writing a check to the borrower for $800 against its $1000 cash balance. This $800 check is then deposited by the borrower into some other bank. This second bank soon lends out 80% of the $800 deposit, or $640, which the second borrower deposits into a third bank. The process continues so that each time the loan proceeds are deposited in another bank, the receiving bank records the deposited check as new money. The mathematical limit on the money created is determined by the regulatory reserve requirement, in this example 20%. Therefore, the maximum amount of deposit money that can be created from the original $1000 cash deposit is $1000 divided by 20%, or $5000.

In describing the first bank's loan, Samuelson emphasizes that this loan does not create money. He writes, "As far as the first bank is concerned, we are through. Having loaned out 80% of its cash, the bank's legal reserves are just enough to match [support] its deposits. There is nothing more it can do [in terms of lending] until the pubic decides to bring in some more money on deposit."

Samuelson assumes cash money had to be deposited before it could be loaned out.

Thus, Samuelson thinks only cash can be loaned. "As every banker knows," writes Samuelson, "he cannot lend money he does not have." So, in Samuelson's world, each individual lending bank is a pass-through intermediary that does not create money by lending. New money is created only when the borrower deposits his loan check into some other bank, and a new deposit is created. Thus, he says, "a system of banks can do what no one bank can do."

But Samuelson's explanation of money creation rests on assertions, not on any reference to the facts of banking, either historic or contemporary. As Samuelson sees it, no money is created by the bank in the process of lending or investing. "A bank cannot eat its cake and have it, too," he claims.

A careful reading of Samuelson's Chapter 14 reveals six significant errors, which I will now discuss in the order he commits them.

Error number one: Samuelson misrepresents the goldsmith bankers, characterizing them as financial intermediaries rather than money creators.

In the first section of Chapter 14 of *Economics*, Samuelson devotes four pages (pages 315 to 319) to describing how modern

A Black Hole in Economics

banking developed from the goldsmith era. He starts with the well-known story of the goldsmiths:

> Modern banks gradually evolved from the old gold-smith establishments in which money and valuables were stored. The practice finally became general of holding far less than 100 percent reserves against deposits, the rest being invested in securities and loans for an interest yield. (page 333)

He then describes a "discovery" made by the goldsmiths: that they could invest most of the depositors' gold because depositors rarely redeem their receipts for real gold, and because regular withdrawals are usually offset by regular deposits. So, he says, 100 percent cash reserves are unnecessary.

However, Samuelson makes no reference to the well-known historical fact that the goldsmiths routinely created more receipts than the gold they held in their vaults. Thus, he omits the goldsmiths' most important "discovery," i.e., the realization that they could single-handedly expand the money supply. This is odd because Samuelson must have been aware of the historians who have documented this practice.

Samuelson thus inaccurately describes the ancient "goldsmith bank" as a pure financial intermediary—an agent who lends or invests deposits on behalf of his customers and takes a fee or a percentage in payment. This assumption is consistent with his assertion, held throughout his entire analysis, that no individual bank can create money. Samuelson also implies that the goldsmith's practice of lending out his customers' property was fraudulent: He imagines that the goldsmith conceals the practice of investing his customer's gold for his own profit, but then gradually, as banking progresses, "the banker no longer feels it necessary to conceal from his depositors what he is doing."

Both these claims are contrary to history. As George Selgin documents in a 2011 paper, *Those Dishonest Goldsmiths*, the goldsmith bankers did, indeed, issue (lend out) "excess certificates." Selgin cites numerous historians who accept that the goldsmiths engaged in credit creation. Furthermore, Selgin demonstrates that there is every reason to believe this practice was an accepted legal practice among the goldsmith's clients.[5]

So right out of the box, in his discussion of the history of banking, Samuelson appears to misunderstand the evolution of early banking, perhaps because of the similarities between money creators and financial intermediaries. For example, a financial intermediary, like a money creator, can still get into trouble with his depositors if he represents that all gold deposits are available all the time. If all depositors want their gold back, but the goldsmith has invested their gold in non-liquid assets that cannot be easily sold, or which have declined in market price, the depositors can lose money in the event of a "run on the bank." This phenomenon is independent of whether the bank has issued excess certificates (created money) or not. A modern-day example would be a money market fund, which does not create money. Under illiquid market conditions, a "run" on a money market fund can "break the buck," which is just a way to say that a holder of shares valued at $1.00 each will receive something less than $1.00 per share when his shares are exchanged for money.

This misunderstanding could have been made by an amateur, but is it likely Samuelson was not aware of how the goldsmith banks operated? After all, he was a Nobel laureate and a brilliant economist, familiar with economic history, and the economists of the 19th and early 20th century knew better. It's hard to see how he could have missed the history of credit creation by the goldsmith bankers. Nevertheless, it appears his flawed view of the goldsmith banks is the fatal first step in his erroneous view of how banks function. This misconception of early banking carries through the rest of his analysis.

Error number two: Samuelson assumes a cash deposit is required to supply the bank with lendable funds.

Based on his incomplete analysis of the Goldsmith banks, Samuelson apparently thinks it is self-evident that an individual bank cannot create money. He, therefore, righteously attempts to discredit the historic credit creation theory, referring to it as a "false explanation" of money creation. An extended quotation is revealing. (My comments are in brackets):

> According to these false explanations, the managers of an ordinary bank are able, by some use of their fountain pens, to lend several dollars for each dollar left on deposit with them. No wonder practical bankers see red when such behavior is attributed to them. [Samuelson implies money creation by an individual bank would be fraudulent.] They only wish they could do so. As every banker well knows, he cannot invest money that he does not have; and any money that he does invest in buying a security or making a loan will soon leave his bank.

Error number three: Samuelson assumes the bank lends out its cash reserves by writing a check to the borrower. ("Like everyone else, he [the banker] writes out a check.")

In Samuelson's world, banks write checks against their cash reserves when they make loans or purchase securities. But in fact, Samuelson is invoking a special case that practically never occurs. Anyone who goes to the bank for a loan knows this. As a first step in a loan application, the bank will always require you to open an account first. The bank benefits from this because account documents help in their due diligence, and because it will encourage the borrower to keep his deposits there. When you get the loan, the bank credits your account with new money, which you are then free to spend, after which the money may or may not leave the bank.

In truth, it is not important if the loaned money "leaves the bank," i.e., whether the borrower deposits the loan check into a competing bank. This is only a problem if the lending bank has lost too many cash reserves. Bank cash reserves typically change very little from day to day because deposit withdrawals are normally offset by nearly equal deposits. And, of course, cash reserves move with deposits from bank to bank (see Chapter Three). Consequently, if the borrower moves his deposit to another bank, it's likely these will be offset by inflows of deposits and reserves from other banks. Samuelson was certainly aware of this fact. Why he thought funds "leaving the bank" was a problem is unclear.

Why did Samuelson rely on a special case in which the bank writes a check on its own cash to the borrower? Perhaps it is because he had already classified individual banks as financial intermediaries whose function is to invest other peoples' money. Therefore, inventing a fictional story in which banks lend out cash supplied by a cash deposit is the only way to make his system appear consistent. The assumption allows him to maintain the fiction that each individual bank is only a pass-through intermediary.

To be fair, under special circumstances, banks occasionally do write checks against their cash reserves. Imagine Bank A wants to buy a company car from a car dealer who keeps his money at Bank B and does not have an account at Bank A. Bank A could write a check against its cash to the car dealer. When the dealer goes to Bank B to deposit this check, Bank B credits him with a new deposit and presents the check back to Bank A for payment. Bank A then sends cash reserves to Bank B. The result is that Bank A receives a new car and loses cash reserves to Bank B, while Bank B creates a new deposit in the car dealer's account. No new money is created in Bank A, but new money *is* created in Bank B when the car dealer deposits the check.

However, these kinds of transactions are rare in the context of the bank's total activity. If it were true that banks make loans by writing out checks against their cash, Samuelson's description might be more believable. But in fact, this is not how banks make loans. As we'll prove shortly, banks fund loans, certainly all large loans, by creating new deposits.

Error number four: Samuelson assumes banks will lend up to the limit of their reserve requirements. Therefore, reserve requirements are the main factor in determining the money supply. Furthermore, since cash reserves are created only by the central bank, the implication is that the central bank neatly controls the money supply by controlling the level of cash reserves. However, as we saw in Chapter Three, the reality is the opposite: commercial banks' lending and investing activities determine cash reserves.

Quoting from the Bank of England:

> In reality, neither are reserves a binding constraint on lending, nor does the central bank fix the amount of reserves that are available. **As with the relationship between deposits and loans, the relationship between reserves and loans typically operates in the reverse way to that described in some economics textbooks**. Banks first decide how much to lend depending on the profitable lending opportunities available to them— which will, crucially, depend on the interest rate set by the Bank of England. It is these lending decisions that determine how many bank deposits are created by the banking system. **The amount of bank deposits in turn influences how much central bank money [*i.e., cash reserves*] banks want to hold in reserve** (to meet withdrawals by the public, make payments to other banks, or meet regulatory liquidity requirements), **which is then, in normal times, supplied on demand by the Bank of England** [Italics and bold added.]
>
> —*Money Creation In The Modern Economy*, Bank of England, Quarterly Bulletin, Q1 2014

Samuelson's assumption that cash reserves are a constraint on lending leads to some silly conclusions. For example, he claims that if a widow withdraws $1000 cash from her bank account, then bank deposits will shrink by five times that amount because the money supply is a neat multiple of the cash reserves in the banking system. But in fact, because deposits are not a neat multiple of cash reserves, cash withdrawals do not shrink the money supply, they merely change the form of the money from a deposit to currency-in-circulation. (See Chapter Two.)

Central bankers have long believed that cash reserves should not be a constraint on lending. Consistent with this premise, the Bank of Canada, the Bank of England, and the US Fed have zero reserve requirements. Other central banks, such as the European Central Bank and the Bank of Japan, have reserve requirements so small that they are insignificant.

The fact is that in the post-gold era, central banks have always created enough cash reserves to keep their commercial banks well-supplied to meet withdrawals and interbank payments. If many people withdraw cash, this will indeed reduce cash reserves in commercial banks; however, it's a simple matter for central banks to replace cash reserves by purchasing assets via open market operations.

Samuelson's attempt to make a direct connection between the level of cash reserves in the banking system and the money supply is thus highly misleading.

Error number five: Samuelson says no single bank can create money, but the case of a monopoly bank contradicts this assertion.

Samuelson says many competing banks can create money while no single bank can. But this completely ignores many real-world banking jurisdictions in which one monopoly bank, or a very small number of banks, can easily create all the money the economy needs. For example, Soviet Russia had a single "mono-bank." Banks in other authoritarian jurisdictions, which often exist in inflationary countries like Argentina, normally have only a few banks. Canada has only five banks of any importance. The UK is similar. None of these jurisdictions are lacking a sufficient money supply because of a shortage of competing banks.

Samuelson partially acknowledges this monopoly bank problem but attempts to deal with it by imagining a monopoly bank with many branches. This would presumably allow rapid money creation because borrowers would be redepositing their cash loans right back into a separate branch of the same bank. So, says Samuelson, a single monopoly bank would be able to do what each small bank could not do as long as the monopoly bank had many branches.

But this admission then raises the question: why would a monopoly bank write out checks against its cash reserves, only to have those checks deposited right back into the same bank? With a monopoly bank, everyone has an account with the same bank. Samuelson obviously knows that people transact primarily by moving account entries from one bank account to another. So why wouldn't the monopoly bank simply credit the borrower's account—i.e., create a new deposit—when making the loan? Writing a check to be deposited to "another bank" would be pointless, as there are no other banks available to receive the deposit.

If you grant this is the only logical way for a monopoly bank to make a loan, then the next question would be: why wouldn't a network of independent banks also do the same? In a dynamic banking system, where deposits are leaving and entering all banks in nearly equal amounts, there is little risk of *net* deposits "soon leaving the bank." In cases where banks feel the need to increase their reserves to meet redemptions, they take measures to attract deposits, and reserves follow. Consequently, a network of banks has the same incentive as a monopoly bank to lend by creating deposits. And, as Appendix 2 explains, we know individual banks have the legal authority to do so.

In light of these inconsistencies, Samuelson's model of money creation by multiplying the deposits of many banks simply makes no sense.

Despite the many holes in Samuelson's theory, we have still not definitively proved him wrong. So far, the three competing theories of money creation are mostly assertions by their proponents. Samuelson says the bank does not create money when lending, while others like H.A Macleod and Richard Werner claim they do. Since both versions do account for money creation, but each in a different way, we seem to have a stand-off, a "state of muddlement" as one economic historian put it.

But Richard Werner has a solution:

One reason for this "state of muddlement" is likely to be the methodology dominant in 20th century economics, namely the hypothetico-deductive method. Unproven 'axioms' are 'posed' and unrealistic assumptions added, to build a theoretical model. This can be done for all three theories, and we would be none the wiser about which of them actually applied. How can the issue be settled? *The only way the facts can be established is to leave the world of deductive theoretical models and consider empirical reality as the arbiter of truth*, in line with the inductive methodology. In other words, it is to empirical evidence we must turn to settle the issue." [Italics added.]

This leads us to Werner's reality-based assessment of Samuelson's theory.

Error Number Six: Samuelson gets the loan accounting wrong, which Richard Werner proves with an empirical test of the accounting for a real-world loan.

If Samuelson is correct that each individual bank is a financial intermediary, the accounting for the creation of a loan on any individual bank's balance sheet must look like this:[6]

Bank Balance Sheet Changes Under Samuelson's Fractional Reserve Theory

Under Samuelson's FRB, an initial cash deposit is required to fund a loan

Assets		Liabilities	
Excess Reserves	+200	Deposits	+200

These cash reserves are then loaned out and replaced with a loan asset

Excess Reserves	-200		
Loans or investments	+200		
Changes to balance sheet due to loan	0	0	

No new money (bank deposit) results from this loan

Under Samuelson's explanation, there will be no net increase in the balance sheet, either in assets or liabilities, when the loan is made.

Instead, cash ("excess") reserves will be replaced by a loan asset. (Of course, the accounting would be exactly the same if banks were solely financial intermediaries, which also do not create money when lending.)

On the other hand, if the credit creation theory is correct, the bank's balance sheet will increase equally on both sides when the loan is made. The increase in loan assets will be exactly matched by an increase in deposits, like this:

Bank Balance Sheet Changes Under the Credit Creation Theory			
Under the Credit Creation Theory, no prior deposit is required to create money			
Assets		Liabilities	
Loans or investments +200		Deposits +200	(in borrower's account)
Changes to balance sheet due to loan +200		+200	
The bank creates new money (a new bank deposit) to fund the loan			

Now, to prove or disprove the credit creation theory, all we must do is observe the changes in an actual bank balance sheet to see what happens when a real loan is made.

Werner's remarkable experiment

What a simple idea! Just examine a bank balance sheet before and after a loan and see if the transaction created new money! If the new loan asset and new deposit liability are both present in equal amounts, only the credit creation theory can be correct. On the other hand, if there is no net increase in the balance sheet, we know the bank is acting as an intermediary, which would imply that either the credit intermediation theory or Samuelson's fractional reserve theory could be correct.

One wonders why this experiment was not done years ago because, without it, we are stuck with one assertion against another. Surprisingly, Werner found that no such empirical test had ever been reported in peer-reviewed journals. Why was this never done before?

One possible reason is that the debate was confined to the academic world of economics, which does not value empirical observation. Under current conditions, these theories seem plausible to the "experts" who inhabit their respective theoretical worlds; therefore, these inhabitants see no reason to test their views against reality. In my view, this explanation is consistent with the rationalism that dominates modern economics and finance theory.

Another more practical reason is that a forensic examination of a bank's computer ledger is not easy to accomplish. The problem lies in the fact that all modern banks are highly automated, operating nearly 24/7; their records are sensitive and private; and their software is proprietary. The day-to-day changes in a bank balance sheet consist of many entries, large and small, recording a constant inflow and outflow of deposits, expenses, loans, and loan payoffs. In a large bank, these transactions number in the thousands or millions daily. So, isolating the balance sheet effects of a single loan while not exposing the records to privacy and intellectual property violations would be difficult. Werner found that banks were not eager to cooperate when he started looking for volunteer banks to help him conduct the experiment.

Eventually, a manager of a small bank (Raiffeisenbank Wildenberg e.G., located in a small town in the district of Lower Bavaria) agreed to help. The bank was operationally comparable to all banks, large and small: it used the same software, accounting standards, auditors, and statement-generating practices. Thus, Werner could be sure his conclusion was universal to all banks. In other words, all he needed was one test to make a valid inductive leap that applied to the general bank population.

Werner devised a test whereby he would take out a large loan from this very small bank. In this way, the size of his transaction would be visible against the remainder of the bank's daily activity. He would examine the bank's balance sheet before and after the loan was made, then attempt to isolate the loan transaction to see if it was accompanied by an equal increase on both sides of the balance sheet.

Werner arranged to take out a loan of E 200,000, which would be paid back immediately after the observation period. He would then examine the accounting record before and after the loan transaction to see whether it matched the credit creation theory.

To summarize this experimental setup: Either new money for the loan is created by the act of making the loan, or the loaned money comes out of another account from within the bank. These are the only two possibilities. Therefore, when a loan is made, the balance sheet can change in only one of two mutually exclusive ways. Either it will expand under the credit creation theory, or it will remain the same under either the fractional reserve or financial intermediation theory, both of which see individual banks as intermediaries.

What were the results of the experiment?

A forensic examination of the accounting changes in the balance sheet, before and after the loan was made. The results are summarized below. (I encourage readers to refer to Werner's paper for "full color."[7])

1. New funds in the amount of E 200k appeared in Werner's bank account, in his name, as a "current account" or what American bankers would call a checking account.
2. After accounting for all other known uses of cash, the bank's cash reserves did not change during the observation period, proving the loan could not have been sourced from the bank's cash reserves.
3. The bank's staff confirmed they did not need to check reserve amounts before extending the loan, even though the loan (E 200k) was a significant proportion of the bank's reserves.
4. No other banks were involved in the transaction.
5. No prior deposit was required to extend the loan.
6. An accounting analysis that accounted for and eliminated all other transactions showed that assets (loans) and liabilities (customer deposits) both increased by exactly the amount of the loan: E 200k.

These results match only the credit creation theory, and do not match either the fractional reserve theory or the intermediation theory. Therefore, we can conclude from this unique experiment that only the credit creation theory of banking explains the increase in the money supply that took place when this loan was made. As this loan conformed to all the procedures, supervision, and auditing standards of every bank under the jurisdiction of the European Central Bank, we can induce the universal principal that money is created in exactly the manner revealed by the experiment.

Werner commented on these results:

> Henceforth, economists need not rely on assertions concerning banks. We now know, based on empirical evidence, why banks are different ... from both non-bank financial institutions and corporations: it is because they can individually create money out of nothing.

> Thus it can now be said with confidence for the first time—possibly in the 5000 years' history of banking—that it has been empirically demonstrated that each individual bank creates credit and money out of nothing, when it extends what is called a 'bank loan.' The bank does not loan any existing money, but instead creates new money .... The implications are far-reaching.

Why was it important that Richard Werner disproved Samuelson's explanation, once and for all? After all, both the credit creation theory and the fractional reserve theory wind up in the same place, in the sense that both theories agree that money is created in the banking system.

I'll first provide my own answer, then finish with some observations from Professor Werner.

Implications

Werner's definitive proof raises several important inferences, including implications for voters, investors, knowledge systems, and the evolution of economic theory. I'll touch on each of these briefly and strongly encourage readers to consult Werner's papers for a fuller discussion. In forthcoming Substack articles, I'll address these repercussions in more detail.

Implications for the voting public

As I mentioned in Chapter One, trying to understand money creation without the credit creation theory is like trying to hit a fastball while wearing beer goggles. You might hit the ball occasionally, but you will be lucky to do so. Samuelson's theory is a special impediment to understanding because it is not only wrong, but also mind-numbingly complex. Purging his fictional banking machinery frees the mind to grasp the simple truths of banking.

By understanding how money creation is abused by the government, voters can see why current government spending policies are both unsustainable and inflationary; and why, conversely, money creation in an industry of privately owned banks is both productive and non-inflationary.

When the time comes to reform our monetary system, knowing how the present system works will help voters find the most knowledgeable political representatives to entrust with the task.

Implications for investors

First, understanding the direct role of individual banks in money creation allows one to see that commercial bank lending and economic growth are connected at the exact point where the new money is applied to productive investment. In other words, because each loan is new money, we can directly see how new purchasing power affects the prices of the specific goods on which it is spent. On the other hand, if one did not see a bank loan as new money, but only as a pass-through transaction, one might not be alert to the direct effect on prices when the loan is made.

Understanding money creation at the individual bank level allows one to see that credit extended for different types of investments affects the economy differently. For example, loans for investment in the stock market will immediately affect the price of stocks, while loans to purchase cars will immediately impact the price of cars, and so on.

The credit creation theory tells us that all modern money is created *in* commercial banks; however, all money is not created *by* commercial bankers. When the government intervenes in bank lending or investing, the discipline of the market is lost. Instead of new money going to its most important uses, as determined by the free market, the new money is less productive.

Understanding this, investors can better anticipate the effect of government policy on investment outcomes. For example, understanding the inflationary role of new money in financing excessive government debt allows one to see the adverse effect of inflation on interest rates. This, in turn, would alert one to the heightened risk of owning long-term government bonds in an inflationary period.

Implications for broken knowledge systems

The confusion and controversy over how money is created—an issue that should be standard knowledge among economists and their students—is evidence of a defective knowledge system. The situation resembles other broken knowledge systems, such as some biased (but popular) accounts of history, the counterfeit "scientific consensus" regarding climate science, and the "common knowledge" prevailing in some fields of medicine, to name a few.

Why does this broken system endure? First, consider the fact that false information about money and banking has persisted for a century in academia. In part, this persistence is due to uncorrected thinking errors, which persist because economics and finance in Academia are dominated by fanciful theories that are not held to the empirical and inductive standards required to explain the real world. Werner's breakthrough experiment should be a beacon of clear thinking to the cloistered academic economists who maintain these theories.

Deliberate obfuscation by central bankers may be another reason money creation is so misunderstood. Central bankers have a well-deserved reputation as mystical soothsayers rather than hard-nosed economists. Alan Greenspan, while clearly a brilliant economist, was the original master of "Fedspeak," a contrived and deliberately ambiguous dialect. He was also the first activist Fed governor who routinely intervened in the financial markets. Ben Bernanke followed in his footsteps. During the Great Financial Crisis, Bernanke first publicly affirmed, then later denied, that the Fed "prints money." (Which was it, Ben?) Bernanke sometimes spoke of banks as "redirecting savings," yet his 2002 speech, quoted in Chapter Five, advocating the monetization of private assets, showed he clearly understands how central banks use commercial banks to create money. Janet Yellen and Jerome Powel have continued the tradition. Today, there is an entire sub-industry of pundits whose only job is to "interpret" central bank communications. Many observers have remarked how much more transparent and open central bankers become after they retire from active service and become spokesmen for the investment industry. These facts suggest central bankers' obfuscation is intentional.

(Thomas Jordan, the recently retired chair of the Swiss National Bank, is an honest exception to this apparent policy of obfuscation. His plain-language speech on how banks create money is included in the reference section and is well worth reading.)[8]

The broken knowledge system will likely be fixed, not by ivory tower academics, but by investors who require theories that explain the real world. This probably explains why the credit creation theory has garnered more interest from the investment community in recent years than from the academic world.

Implications for economic theory

A better understanding of the credit creation theory of banking has important implications for the evolution of economic theory. Two great theorists, the UK economist Richard Werner and the late

Austrian economist Joseph Schumpeter, should have the last word on this issue.[9]

Here are excerpts from Werner's closing words in his 2014 paper, *Can Banks Individually Create Money Out of Nothing?*

> ... the empirical evidence presented in this paper has revealed that the many supporters of the *financial intermediation theory* and also the adherents of the *fractional reserve theory* are flat-earthers that believe in what is empirically proven to be wrong and which should have been recognizable as being impossible upon deeper consideration of the accounting requirements.
>
> ...
>
> That such important insights as bank credit creation could be made to disappear from the agenda and even knowledge of the majority of economists over the course of a century delivers a devastating verdict on the state of economics and finance today. As a result, the public understanding of money has deteriorated as well. Today, the vast majority of the public is not aware that the money supply is created by banks, that banks do not "lend" money [quotation marks added] and that each bank creates new money when it extends a loan.
>
> ...
>
> Progress in economics and finance research would require researchers to build on the correct insights derived by economists at least since the 19th century (such as Macleod, 1856). The overview of the literature on how banks function, in this paper and in Werner (2014b), has revealed that economics and finance as research disciplines have on this topic failed to progress in the 20th century. The movement from the accurate *credit creation theory* to the misleading, inconsistent and incorrect *fractional reserve theory* to today's

dominant, yet wholly implausible and blatantly wrong *financial intermediation theory* indicates that economists and finance researchers have not progressed, but instead regressed throughout the past century. That was already Schumpeter's assessment, and things have since further moved away from the *credit creation theory*.

Finally, here is Joseph Schumpeter on the credit creation theory, from his 1954 book, *History of Economic Analysis* (quoted by Werner):

> … this alters the analytic situation profoundly and makes it highly inadvisable to construe bank credit on the model of existing funds being withdrawn from previous uses by an entirely imaginary act of saving and then lent out by their owners. It is much more realistic to say that the banks 'create credit,' that is, that they create deposits in their act of lending, than to say that they lend the deposits that have been entrusted to them. And the reason for insisting on this is that depositors should not be invested with the insignia of a role which they do not play. The theory to which economists clung so tenaciously makes them out to be savers when they neither save nor intend to do so; it attributes to them an influence on the 'supply of credit' which they do not have. The theory of 'credit creation' not only recognizes patent facts without obscuring them by artificial constructions; it also brings out the peculiar mechanism of saving and investment that is characteristic of fully fledged capitalist society and the true role of banks in capitalist evolution (p. 1114).

We close with a sage observation by today's pre-eminent financial writer, Jim Grant:

> In science and engineering, progress is cumulative; we stand on the shoulders of giants. In money and markets,

progress is rather cyclical; we keep making the same mistakes.

—Jim Grant, Grant's Interest Rate Observer, Nov 10, 2023

NOTES

Introduction

[1] I receive no compensation from these or any other investment services. As far as I know, they are blissfully unaware of my recommendations.

Chapter 1

[1] Matt Levine, "SVB Couldn't Ignore Its Losses, But the Fed Can,"*Bloomberg*, March 13, 2023, https://www.bloomberg.com/opinion/articles/2023-03-13/svb-couldn-t-ignore-its-losses-but-the-fed-can.

[2] Hat tip to Ben Hunt of epsilontheory.com for this helpful expression.

[3] Andrew Hook, "Examining Modern Money Creation," *The Journal of Economic Education*, June 12, 2023, 1, https://sussex.figshare.com/articles/journal_contribution/Examining_modern_money_creation_an_institution-centered_explanation_and_visualization_of_the_credit_theory_of_money_and_some_reflections_on_its_significance/23489696.

[4] Richard Werner, "Can banks individually create money out of nothing," *International Review of Financial Analysis*, December 2014 https://www.sciencedirect.com/science/article/pii/S1057521914001070.

[5] Richard Werner, "A Lost Century in Economics: Three theories of banking and the conclusive evidence," *International Review of Financial Analysis*, July 2016, https://www.sciencedirect.com/science/article/pii/S1057521915001477

[6] Werner, Richard, "A Lost Century In Economics," 376.

[7] J.K Galbraith, *Money: Whence it Came, Where it Went*, (Boston, Houghton-Mifflin, 1975), 21, https://www.amazon.com/Money-Whence-Came-Where-Went/dp/0691171661/

[8] Paul A. Samuelson, *Economics, An Introductory Analysis* (McGraw-Hill, 1948), 324.

Chapter 2

[1] The oldest surviving goldsmith's receipt dates from 1633. Historically, goldsmiths acting as bankers became widespread in England in the 17th and 18th Centuries. Before this period, the practice of issuing gold certificates existed all over Europe, but England and Scotland were where banking really flourished. See Henry Dunning Macleod, *The Theory and Practice of Banking Volume 2* (Hardpress, 2017). See also: Junchul Kim, "How modern banking originated: The London goldsmith-bankers' institutionalization of trust," *Business History*, July 7, 2011, https://www.tandfonline.com/doi/abs/10.1080/00076791.2011.578132.

[2] Louis Even, *Michael Journal*, October 16, 2015, https://www.michaeljournal.org/articles/social-credit/item/the-birth-and-death-of-money.

[3] See Appendix 1 for a fuller discussion of the definition of money.

[4] Ludwig von Mises, *Human Action* (Henry Regnery Company, 1966), Kindle Edition, location 8659 and following.

[5] According to economist George Selgin, credit-money creation in the banks "has prevailed under every sort of bank regulatory regime, from the earliest beginnings of banking, not excepting regimes that involved very little regulation, like those of Scotland, Canada, and Sweden, and that lacked even a trace of government guarantees or other sorts of artificial support." Quoted in ed. Kevin Dowd, *The Experience of Free Banking* (London Publishing Partnership, 2023). Kindle Edition, locations 334-337.

[6] Murray Rothbard, *The Mystery Of Banking* (Ludwig von Mises Institute, [1983] 2008), 80.

[7] For a complete discussion of this issue, see George Reisman, *Capitalism: A Treatise on Economics*, (TJS Books, 2020), Kindle Edition, 514-515. Reisman

does not take sides in this discussion, although in his public lectures, he has expressed misgivings about banks issuing fiduciary media.

[8] Ludwig von Mises, *Human Action*, Kindle Edition. Location 8908.

[9] Kevin Dowd, *The Experience of Free Banking*, 7.

[10] Kevin Dowd, "Bank of England Not Necessary, Says Landmark IEA 'Free Banking' Book," *Cobden Centre*, January 10, 2024 https://www.cobdencentre.org/2024/01/bank-of-england-not-necessary-says-landmark-iea-free-banking-book/

[11] "Executive Order 6102," *Wikipedia* https://en.wikipedia.org/wiki/Executive Scott _Order_6102.

[12] Scott Hein, "Deficits and Inflation," Federal Reserve Bank of St. Louis, March 1981, 3, https://files.stlouisfed.org/files/htdocs/publications/review/81/03/Deficits_Mar1981.pdf.

[13] US Federal Reserve, *The Fed Explained: What the Central Bank Does*, 2021 edition, 37, https://www.federalreserve.gov/aboutthefed/files/the-fed-explained.pdf.

Chapter 3

[1] "What is the money supply? Is it important?" *U.S. Federal Reserve FAQs*, updated July 19, 2024, https://www.federalreserve.gov/faqs/money_12845.htm. The Fed makes a few exceptions to this general rule, which we discuss in Appendix 1.

[2] U.S Federal Reserve Money Stock Measures H.6 Release https://www.federalreserve.gov/releases/h6/20240723/.

[3] Paul Sheard, "Repeat After Me: Banks Cannot and Do Not 'Lend Out' Reserves," *RatingsDirect*, August 13, 2013, 13: "All banknotes (other than new ones received in exchange for old ones) start life as a bank deposit." https://www.hks.harvard.edu/sites/default/files/centers/mrcbg/programs/senior.fellows/2019-20%20fellows/BanksCannotLendOutReservesAug2013_%20(002).pdf.

[4] See Appendix 1, "Defining Money," for a full discussion of this issue.

[5] Samuelson, *Economics*, Chapter 14, 323-332.

[6] Stephen Cecchetti, "The Deposit Expansion Multiplier," *Money, Banking and Financial Markets* (McGraw-Hill Higher Education, 2017), Kindle Edition, 1062.

[7] Joshua Feinman. "Reserve Requirements: History, Current Practice, and Potential Reform" *U.S Federal Reserve Bulletin*, 1993, https://www.federalreserve.gov/monetarypolicy/0693lead.pdf.

[8] Bank of England, "Money Creation in the Modern Economy," *Quarterly Bulletin*, Q1 2014, 15, https://www.bankofengland.co.uk/-/media/boe/files/quarterly-bulletin/2014/money-creation-in-the-modern-economy.

[9] The label "quantitative easing" was originally coined by Richard Werner when he was advising the Bank of Japan in 1993. The Bernanke version turned out to be much different from what Werner had proposed. See Richard Werner, *Quantitative Easing and the Quantity Theory of Credit*, Royal Economic Society, https://res.org.uk/newsletter/july-2013-newsletter-quantitative-easing-and-the-quantity-theory-of-credit/.

[10] Bank of England, "Money Creation in the Modern Economy," *Quarterly Bulletin*, Q1 2014, 14, https://www.bankofengland.co.uk/-/media/boe/files/quarterly-bulletin/2014/money-creation-in-the-modern-economy.

[11] Marshall Gittler, "Why Quantitative Easing Isn't Printing Money," CNBC online, May 23, 2013, https://www.cnbc.com/id/100760150.

[12] See Appendix 3, "Paul Samuelson's Fractional Fiction," for a detailed critique.

[13] See "Banking and the expansion of the money supply," *Khan Academy*, https://www.khanacademy.org/economics-finance-domain/ap-

macroeconomics/ap-financial-sector/banking-and-the-expansion-of-the-money-supply-ap/a/banking-and-the-expansion-of-the-money-supply.

[14] Russel Napier, *The Solid Ground Newsletter,* September 4, 2023, 3 (subscription required).

Chapter 4

[1] Henry D. MacLeod, *Theory of Credit*, Vol 2 Part 1 (Princeton Library, 1894), 594.

[2] Dowd, et al., *The Experience Of Free Banking,*.

[3] Lev Menand, *The Fed Unbound* (Columbia Global Reports, 2022), Kindle Edition, 68. https://www.amazon.com/Fed-Unbound-Central-Banking-Crisis/dp/1735913707/.

[4] Menand, *The Fed Unbound*, 70–73.

[5] Ayn Rand, "America's Persecuted Minority: Big Business," *Capitalism: The Unknown Ideal* (Penguin Publishing Group, 1967), Chapter 3, Kindle Edition, 44.

[6] "Richard Cantillon," *Wikipedia*, https://en.wikipedia.org/wiki/Richard_Cantillon.

[7] "Quantity Theory of Money" *Wikipedia*, https://en.wikipedia.org/wiki/Quantity_theory_of_money

[8] James Buchan, *John Law: A Scottish Adventurer of the Eighteenth Century,"* quoted in *Grant's Interest Rate Observer*, August 2, 2024 (subscription required). *Essai sur la Nature du Commerce en General* was published posthumously in 1755. https://www.adamsmith.org/blog/the-cantillion-effect.

[9] Cantillon's *Essai sur la Nature du Commerce en General* was published posthumously in 1755. https://www.adamsmith.org/blog/the-cantillion-effect.

[10] "McDonald's Statistics 2024," enterpriseAppsToday.com, https://www.enterpriseappstoday.com/stats/mcdonalds-statistics.html.

[11] J.A. Schumpeter, *Die Theorie der wirtschaftlichen Entwicklung* (Translation: *Theory of Economic Development*), (Harvard University Press, 1912), 197. Quoted in Werner, "Can banks individually create money out of nothing?" https://www.sciencedirect.com/science/article/pii/S1057521914001070#bb0450).

[12] Richard A. Werner, "Success Development Policy: Harnessing Money and Institutional Design, *Shifting from Central Planning to a Decentralized Economy*, January 15, 2917. https://professorwerner.org/category/articles-essays/.

[13] Reisman, *Capitalism: A Treatise on Economics,* Kindle Edition, 517-518. "Demand for money" is usually measured by the "velocity" of money, or the number of times the average dollar is spent in a period. The lower the velocity, the higher the demand for money, i.e., the stronger the desire to hold money, and vice versa.

[14] "Panic of 1907," *Wikipedia*, https://en.wikipedia.org/wiki/Panic_of_1907.

[15] James Grant, *The Forgotten Depression: 1921: The Crash That Cured Itself* (Simon & Schuster, 2014), Kindle edition, 254.

[16] For a thorough discussion of the economic costs of "renewable" energy, see Alex Epstein, *Fossil Future: Why Global Human Flourishing Requires More Oil, Coal, and Natural Gas – Not Less* (Portfolio, 2022), Kindle edition.

Chapter 5

[1] Ayn Rand, *Introduction to Objectivist Epistemology* (Penguin, 1990), quoted in the Ayn Rand Lexicon. http://aynrandlexicon.com/lexicon/definitions.html.

[2] Seth Carpenter, Global Chief Economist at Morgan Stanley, "A Headwind for Policy Normalization: Morgan Stanley adds El Nino to List of Inflation Risks," *Zerohedge*, September 10, 2023,

https://www.zerohedge.com/markets/headwind-policy-normalization-mor-gan-stanley-adds-el-nino-list-inflation-risks.

[3] Mises Institute, *Transcript of remarks before the Conference on the Economics of Mobilization, held at White Sulphur Springs, West Virginia, April 6-8, 1951, under the sponsorship of the University of Chicago Law School.* https://mises.org/library/economic-freedom-and-intervention-ism/html/p/123.

[4] Reisman, *Capitalism*, Kindle Edition, 219. As I cannot do full justice to the topic of inflation in this chapter, I recommend reading Chapter 7, which includes a thorough discussion of inflation, shortages, and price controls.

[5] R. A. Werner, *Princes of the Yen*, (Quantum Publishers, 2018). *Princes of the Yen*, video version: https://www.youtube.com/watch?v=p5Ac7ap_MAY.

6 "M2 for Japan." *FRED Economic data*, https://fred.stlouisfed.org/se-ries/MYAGM2JPM189S.

[7] Despite its overvalued economy, Japan was able to invest overseas because the currency market (currency traders) did not devalue the Yen. According to Werner, they didn't devalue because they did not see or understand the excess money creation. The same thing happened in the USA during the 1950s and 60s when US banks created excess dollars. US corporations used this plentiful, overvalued ("hot") money to buy up European corporations.

[8] Ben Bernanke, "Deflation: Making Sure 'It' Doesn't Happen Here," *Remarks by Governor Ben S. Bernbanke Before the National Econimists Club, Washington D.C., November 21, 2002*, https://www.federalre-serve.gov/boarddocs/speeches/2002/20021121/default.htm.

[9] Ben Bernanke, "Aiding the Economy: What the Fed did and why," *Washington Post*, Nov 10, 2010, https://www.federalre-serve.gov/newsevents/other/o_bernanke20101105a.htm.

[10] Jim Brown, "Central Banks Move Beyond the Fascist Frontier," *The Objective Standard*, December 12, 2015, https://theobjectivestandard.com/author/jbrowntheobjectivestandard-com/.

[11] Tepper's remarks at Ira Sohn investment conference, quoted in *Barron's*, May 4, 2015: https://www.barrons.com/articles/live-from-sohn-dont-fight-four-feds-david-tepper-says-1430773991.

[12] CPI during the QE years grew at only 1.83% per year on average. See *FRED Economic Data*, https://fred.stlouisfed.org/series/CPIAUCSL.

[13] "Consumer Price Index," *FRED Economic Data*, https://fred.stlouisfed.org/series/CPIAUCSL. To see the relationship between money supply and CPI, see "Money Supply and Inflation Over 150 Years," *Advisor Channel*, https://advisor.visualcapitalist.com/chart-money-supply-and-inflation-over-150-years/.

[14] This period is similar to the late 19th Centuryan—other period of high productivity, high real growth, and low consumer price increases.

[15] "Median Sales Price of Houses," *FRED Economic Data*, https://fred.stlouisfed.org/series/MSPUS.

[16] "Unmasking Inflation," *HardmoneyJim*, August 8, 2021, https://jim3c5.substack.com/p/unmasking-inflation.

[17] "On the systematic mispricing of debt," *Grant's Interest Rate Observer*, May 15, 2015, Vol. 33, No. 10 (subscription required).

[18] Sydney Homer and Richard Scylla, *A History of Interest Rates* (John Wiley, 2005).

[19] Jim Bianco, "The Fed's Cure Risks Being Worse Than the Disease," *Bloomberg*, March 27, 2020, https://www.bloomberg.com/view/articles/2020-03-27/federal-reserve-s-financial-cure-risks-being-worse-than-disease?embedded-checkout=true.

[20] "Consumer Price Index," *FRED Economic Data*, https://fred.stlouisfed.org/series/CPIAUCSL. "Personal Consumption Expenditures (PCE) Index" contains the main data used to calculate gross domestic product, or GDP. https://fred.stlouisfed.org/series/DPCCRV1Q225SBEA.

[21] Ben Bernanke, "Deflation: Making Sure 'It' Doesn't Happen Here," *The Federal Reserve Board, Remarks by Governor Ben S. Bernanke Before the National Economists Club, Washington, D.C., November 21, 2002.* https://www.federalreserve.gov/boarddocs/speeches/2002/20021121/default.htm.

[22] Henry Hazlitt, *Economics in One Lesson* (Currency Books, 1979), Chapter 23, 176.

Chapter 6

[1] "10-Year Real Interest Rate," *FRED Economic Data*, https://fred.stlouisfed.org/series/REAINTRATREARAT10Y.

[2] USDebtclock.org: https://www.usdebtclock.org. The U.S. median household income estimate is from Motio Research as of January 2024. https://seekingalpha.com/article/4675233-median-household-income-january-2024.

[3] "Federal Surplus or Deficit," *FRED Economic Data*, https://fred.stlouisfed.org/series/MTSDS133FMS. The deficit for FY 2023, which ended on September 30, clocked in at $2.0 trillion. The Congressional Budget Office estimates future deficits: The recently updated numbers project the annual deficit to grow to $2.7 trillion by 2033, raising the funded debt held by the public to nearly $47 trillion. https://www.cbo.gov/publication/59159.

[4] "The Budget and Economic Outlook: 2023 to 2033," *Congressional Budget Office*, https://www.cbo.gov/publication/58848.

[5] "Consumer Price Index," *FRED Economic Data*, https://fred.stlouisfed.org/series/CPIAUCSL.

[6] Enquiring minds who wish to dissect this formula can start at: https://en.wikipedia.org/wiki/Dividend_discount_modeld.

[7] Chris Edwards, "Federal Debt and Unfunded Entitlement Promises," *Cato Institute*, January 21, 2022, https://www.cato.org/blog/federal-debt-unfunded-entitlement-promises.

See also Romina Boccia, "Medicare and Social Security Are Responsible for 95 Percent of U.S. Unfunded Obligations," Marc 28, 2023, https://www.cato.org/blog/medicare-social-security-are-responsible-95-percent-us-unfunded-obligations.

"The $175.3 trillion Doomsday Clock Is Ticking – That Is The Estimated Unfunded Social Security And Medicare Liability," *Open The Books*, March 4, 2024, https://www.openthebooks.com/substack-the-1753-trillion-doomsday-clock-is-ticking--that-is-the-estimated-unfunded-social-security-and-medicare-liability/.

[8] Gross Domestic Product," *FRED Economic Data*, https://fred.stlouisfed.org/series/GDP. "M2," *FRED Economic Data*, https://fred.stlouisfed.org/series/WM2NS.

[9] "Global gross domestic product (GDP) at current prices from 1985 to 2029," *Statista*, https://www.statista.com/statistics/268750/global-gross-domestic-product-gdp/. Occam Investing, "How much money is in the world?" *Occam Investing*, https://occaminvesting.co.uk/how-much-money-is-in-the-world/.

[10] "Legendary investor Paul Tudor Jones says a "debt bomb" is about to go off in in the US," *Fortune*, Feb 2024, https://fortune.com/2024/02/07/paul-tudor-jones-debt-bomb-u-s-deficit/.

See also Tom Coburn, *The Debt Bomb*, 2013, 2021, https://www.amazon.com.

[11] Stockman, David, "Thanks, Fed! The Road to Fiscal Armageddon," *Contra Corner*, September 22, 2023 (subscription only), https://www.davidstockmanscontracorner.com/thanks-fed-the-road-to-fiscal-armageddon/.

[12] Historical tax rates from Bianco Research online (subscription required): https://www.biancoresearch.com/a-history-of-the-highest-lowest-tax-brackets-in-the-u-s-2/.

Government sources of income: https://www.biancoresearch.com/the-u-s-governments-sources-of-income-3/.

[13] Tax regimes in some other countries report higher tax revenue/GDP ratios. The US percentage is more comparable to these if you include total tax from federal, state, county, and city tax authorities.

[14] Art Laffer does not take personal credit for this idea, which has been known for centuries. However, he made the concept famous at a 1974 meeting with Donald Rumsfeld and Dick Cheney. Laffer drew the diagram on a napkin to make a point. An attending economist named Jude Wanniski named it the Laffer Curve. https://en.wikipedia.org/wiki/Laffer_curve.

[15] "Market Yield on US Treasury Securities at 10-Year Constant Maturity," *FRED Economic Data*, https://fred.stlouisfed.org/series/DGS10.

"Federal Debt" Total Public Debt," *FRED Economic Data*, https://fred.stlouisfed.org/series/GFDEBTN.

"Federal Outlays: Interest as a Percent of Gross Domestic Product," *FRED Economic Data*, https://fred.stlouisfed.org/series/FYOIGDA188S.

[16] "Oneill Says Cheney Told Him: Deficits Don't Matter," *Chicago Tribune*, Jan 12, 2004, https://www.chicagotribune.com/2004/01/12/oneill-says-cheney-told-him-deficits-dont-matter/.

[17] "Gold is back, and it has a message for us," *Financial Times*, April 15, 2024, https://www.ft.com/content/bdcb7d8a-e958-4910-9d1b-a6a519812503.

[18] "Federal Government Current Expenditures: Interest Payments," *FRED Economic Data*, https://fred.stlouisfed.org/series/A091RC1Q027SBEA.

[19] The Committee for a Responsible Federal Budget is a nonpartisan, non-profit organization committed to educating the public on issues with significant fiscal policy impact. https://www.crfb.org/about-us.

https://www.crfb.org/papers/interest-payments-federal-budget.

Chapter 7

[1] Russell Napier, quoted from his May 2024 financial history course, which I attended in Edinburgh, UK. https://www.libraryofmistakes.com.

[2] "Who Regulates Whom? An Overview of the U.S. Financial Regulatory Framework," *Congressional Research Service*, October 13, 2023, https://sgp.fas.org/crs/misc/R44918.pdf.

[3] *Chapwood Index*, https://chapwoodindex.com/the-solution/.

[4] *John Williams' Shadow Government Statistics*, http://www.shadowstats.com.

[5] "Inflation for the Long Run, *Grant's Interest Rate Observer*, January 27, 2023 (Subscription only).

[6] "Tobacco Master Settlement Agreement," *Wikipedia*, https://en.wikipedia.org/wiki/Tobacco_Master_Settlement_Agreement.

[7] As this chapter is being written, California is planning to enact a new "clean air" tax that will raise the cost of gasoline in the Golden State (already the nation's highest) by about $1.00 per gallon by the end of 2025. Although there are currently no direct U.S. taxes on carbon dioxide emissions, these do exist in Europe, and it's possible the US government will try to adopt similar measures.

[8] "What Is A Dynasty Trust?" *Investopedia*, https://www.investopedia.com/terms/d/dynasty-trust.asp.

[9] "How To Defeat Financial Repression," *HardmoneyJim*, February 18, 2023, https://jim3c5.substack.com/p/how-to-defeat-financial-repression.

[10] For an explanation of GDP spending categories, see "Gross Domestic Product," *Bureau of Economic Analysis*, https://www.bea.gov/data/gdp/gross-domestic-product.

[11] Douglas Holtz-Eakin, "The Freddie Mac Second Mortgage Proposal," *American Action Forum*, May 16, 2024, https://www.americanaction-forum.org/insight/the-freddie-mac-second-mortgage-proposal/.

[12] "Bank Term Funding Program," *Board of Governors of the Federal Reserve System*, https://www.federalreserve.gov/financial-stability/bank-term-funding-program.htm.

[13] "California Enacts Bill Allowing Local Governments to Charter Banks," *ABA Banking Journal*, October 3, 2019, https://bankingjournal.aba.com/2019/10/california-enacts-bill-allowing-local-governments-to-charter-banks/.

[14] "Time to relook at the SLR," *ISDA*, March 6, 2024, https://www.isda.org/2024/03/06/time-to-relook-at-the-slr/.

See also "Supplementary Leverage Ratio (SLR)," *Risk.net*, https://www.risk.net/definition/supplementary-leverage-ratio-slr.

[15] See *TreasuryDirect.gov*, https://treasurydirect.gov/about/.

[16] As of this writing (July 2024) the Treasury yield curve is "inverted," which means very short-term bonds (T-bills) are yielding more than longer-term bonds. This occurs when the Federal Reserve forcibly raises short-term rates to slow the economy in an attempt to control CPI inflation.

[17] Charles Peabody, "Yield Curve Control Starts In the U.S." *Portales Partners*, May 2, 2024 (subscription only). Portales Partners is a research group serving professional investors. https://www.bloomberg.com/profile/company/2920947Z:US.

[18] Russell Napier, lecture notes from May 2024 course on financial history, Edinburgh, UK.

Chapter 8

[1] David Foster Wallace, *Wikipedia,* https://en.wikipedia.org/wiki/David_Foster_Wallace.

[2] "'Consumer Price Index for All Urban Consumers," *FRED Economic Data,* https://fred.stlouisfed.org/series/CPIAUCSL. During the 53-year period, January 1971 through January 2024, CPI increased at an average annual compound rate of 3.95%.

[3] "Home Ownership Affordability Monitor," *Federal Reserve Bank of Atlanta,* https://www.atlantafed.org/center-for-housing-and-policy/data-and-tools/home-ownership-affordability-monitor.

[4] *Charlie Bilello Blog,* https://bilello.blog/2024/the-state-of-the-markets-june-2024.

[5] It's worth noting that the cost of owning a home is the greatest single monthly expense for millions of Americans, yet these costs are not reflected in the consumer price index, and have not been since 1983. This is one of many good reasons not to rely solely on the official CPI numbers to gauge inflation's effect on your personal life.

[6] For analysis of US financial sanctions against Russia, see Brown, Jim, "Monetary Cancel Culture," *HardmoneyJim,* March 22, 2022, https://jim3c5.substack.com/p/13-monetary-cancel-culture.

[7] Kiley, Michael T. (2018). "Quantitative Easing and the 'New Normal' in Monetary Policy," *Finance and Economics Discussion Series 2018-004. Washington: Board of Governors of the Federal Reserve System,* https://doi.org/10.17016/FEDS.2018.004. https://www.federalreserve.gov/econres/feds/files/2018004pap.pdf.

[8] Jason Cumming, "The End of the New Normal," *Financial Times,* November 2, 2023, https://www.ft.com/content/255623ed-ef7e-4874-820c-02763d2c055e.

[9] *TreasuryDirect.gov*, https://www.treasurydirect.gov/marketable-securities/tips/.

[10] "Zombie" companies are firms that barely generate enough pre-tax income to pay their interest costs. When interest rates are very low, Zombies can limp along for years, devouring scarce labor and capital.

[11] Ali Dibadj and Matt Peron, "Higher-for-Longer Rates Are an Opportunity for Active Investors," *Barron's,* June 18, 2024, https://www.barrons.com/articles/higher-for-longer-rates-opportunity-active-investors-returns-860bad4c.

[12] Mohammed El-Erian, "Why passive investing makes less sense in the current environment," *Financial Times*, January 24, 2023, https://www.ft.com/content/3003cae0-fb3d-43fd-8938-86b87daba7e7.

[13] State Homestead Laws, *Findlaw*, https://www.findlaw.com/state/property-and-real-estate-laws/homestead.html.

[14] Greg Ip, "You Might Be Buying Your House at the Top of the Market," *Wall Street Journal*, June 27, 2024, https://www.wsj.com/finance/investing/home-prices-overvalued-housing-market-4f8be55b.

[15] Kamol Alimukhamedov, *Gold Investing Handbook for Asset Managers*, (The World Bank Treasury, 2024), https://documents1.worldbank.org/curated/en/099610302282427760/pdf/IDU136aee178198b114722197d515b4a9f9ef84a.pdf.

[16] Monetary Metals & Co, of Scottsdale, AZ, is a company that enables investors to earn interest on gold, paid in gold. The author is a director and investor in the company. See https://monetary-metals.com.

[17] "2024 Central Bank Gold Reserves Survey," *World Gold Council*, June 18, 2024, https://www.gold.org/goldhub/data/2024-central-bank-gold-reserves-survey.

[18] Jim Brown, "Why Everyone Should Own Gold," *HardmoneyJim*, March 4, 2023, https://jim3c5.substack.com/p/why-everyone-should-own-gold.

[19] Aitken Advisors Homepage: https://www.aitkenadvisors.com.

[20] Note: These are recommendations, not "endorsements." With the exception of Monetary Metals & Co., where I sit on the Board of Directors, I receive no compensation from any of these investment services. As far as I know, they are unaware of my existence.

Appendix 1

[1] William Stanley Jevons, *Money and the Mechanism of Exchange* (Online Library of Liberty), https://oll.libertyfund.org/titles/jevons-money-and-the-mechanism-of-exchange#lf0191_label_006.

[2] "Definitions," *The Ayn Rand Lexicon,* http://aynrandlexicon.com/lexicon/definitions.html.

[3] Von Mises, *Human Action*, 194.

[4] Galbraith, *Money: Whence it Came, Where It Went,* 6.

[5] "What is the money supply? Is it important?" FAQs, *Board of Governors of the Federal Reserve System,* https://www.federalreserve.gov/faqs/money_12845.htm.

[6] See Joseph T. Salerno, "The True Money Supply: A measure of the supply of the medium of exchange in the U.S. Economy," *Mises Institute*, February 6, 2023, https://mises.org/library/true-money-supply-measure-supply-medium-exchange-us-economy-0#:~:text=The%20%22True%22%20Money%20Supply%20(,of%20exchange%20in%20society.2.

[7] "Liabilities and Capital: Liabilities: Deposits with F.R. Banks, Other Than Reserve Balances: U.S. Treasury, General Account," *FRED Economic Data,* https://fred.stlouisfed.org/series/WTREGEN.

[8] "Liabilities and Capital: Liabilities: Reverse Repurchase Agreements," *FRED Economic Data*, https://fred.stlouisfed.org/series/WREPODEL.

[9] "M1," FRED Economic Data. https://fred.stlouisfed.org/series/WM1NS and "M2," https://fred.stlouisfed.org/series/WM2NS.

Appendix 2

[1] R.A. Werner, "How do banks create money, and why can other firms not do the same? An explanation for the coexistence of lending and deposit-taking," *International Review of Financial Analysis,* Volume 36, December 2014, 71-77, https://www.sciencedirect.com/science/article/pii/S1057521914001434.

[2] Both the fractional reserve theory of banking (Samuelson version) and the financial intermediary theory incorrectly assume that *existing* money is paid from the banker to the borrower. See Appendix 3.

[3] "12 U.S.C. § 24 - U.S. Code - Unannotated Title 12. Banks and Banking § 24. Corporate powers of associations," *Findlaw*, https://codes.findlaw.com/us/title-12-banks-and-banking/12-usc-sect-24/. See also Title 62 of the Revised Statutes. Derived from National Bank Act of 1864, https://www.govregs.com/uscode/title12_chapter2_subchapterI_section24_notes.

[4] "12 U.S.C. § 24 - U.S. Code - Unannotated Title 12. Banks and Banking § 24. Corporate powers of associations," *Findlaw*, https://codes.findlaw.com/us/title-12-banks-and-banking/12-usc-sect-24/.

[5] "Business of Banking Law and Legal Definition," *USLegal.com*, https://definitions.uslegal.com/b/business-of-banking/.

[6] Werner, *How do banks create money, and why can other firms not do the same? An explanation for the coexistence of lending and deposit-taking*, 71-77.

[7] "31 U.S.C. § 5103. Legal tender," *Title 31 – Money and Finance*: "United States coins and currency (including Federal reserve notes and notes of Federal reserve banks and national banks) are legal tender for all debts, public

charges, taxes, and dues. Foreign gold or silver coins are not legal tender for debts." https://www.govinfo.gov/content/pkg/USCODE-2022-title31/pdf/USCODE-2022-title31-subtitleIV-chap51-subchapI-sec5103.pdf.

[8] Dowd, Kevin, *The Experience of Free Banking*, 3-5.

[9] Werner, "How do banks create money, and why can other firms not do the same? An explanation for the coexistence of lending and deposit-taking," 71-77.

[10] Josh Ryan-Collins et al, *Where Does Money Come From? A Guide to the UK Monetary and Banking System* (New Economics Foundation, 2012), 140.

Appendix 3

[1] Paul Samuelson (1915–2009) was the first American to win the Nobel Memorial Prize in Economic Science (1970) for contributions that ranged over many different fields. He attended the University of Chicago as an undergraduate, earned a PhD from Harvard, and spent his entire career as a professor at MIT. He popularized the ideas of John Maynard Keynes and wrote a famous textbook, *Economics*, that attempted to explain Keynesian principles to undergraduates. Over a long career, he wrote many other papers, books, and treatises. He was a champion of mathematics in economic analysis. He served as an economic advisor to John Kennedy, Lyndon Johnson, the U.S. Treasury, and on the President's Council of Economic Advisors. He wrote a column in *Newsweek* for many years. He was a "mixed" economist, in the sense that he favored a combination of market forces and government action to achieve economic goals. See *Wikipedia*, https://en.wikipedia.org/wiki/Paul_Samuelson. See also Maggie Koerth, "The Economics Nobel Isn't Really a Nobel," *FiveThirtyEight*, October 7, 2016, https://fivethirtyeight.com/features/the-economics-nobel-isnt-really-a-nobel/.

[2] Paul Samuelson, *Economics*, 1948. In Chapter 14, "Fundamentals of the Banking System and Deposit Creation," Samuelson lays out this theory in detail, 310-336.

[3] Richard Werner, "Can banks individually create money out of nothing? – The theories and the empirical evidence," *International Review of Financial Analysis*, December 2014, 1-19, https://www.sciencedirect.com/science/article/pii/S1057521914001070.

[4] Richard Werner, "A Lost Century in Economics: Three theories of banking and the conclusive evidence," *International Review of Financial Analysis*, Volume 46, July 2016, 361-379, https://www.sciencedirect.com/science/article/pii/S1057521915001477.

[5] George Selgin, "Those Dishonest Goldsmiths," *SSRN,* April 14 2020, https://papers.ssrn.com/sol3/papers.cfm?abstract_id=1589709.

[6] These illustrations are adapted from Werner, "Can banks individually create money out of nothing? – the Theories and the Empirical Evidence."

[7] Richard Werner, "A Lost Century in Economics, etc.," *International Review of Financial Analysis*, July 2016, https://www.sciencedirect.com/science/article/pii/S1057521915001477.

[8] Thomas J. Jordan, "How money is created by the central bank and the banking system," *Swiss National Bank Zurich,* January 16, 2018, https://www.snb.ch/en/publications/communication/speeches/2018/ref_20180116_tjn.

[9] Werner, "Can banks individually create money out of nothing? — The theories and the empirical evidence."

Recommended Reading

Most of the ideas in this book are not original to me. I learned most of what I know from the great economists of history and other thought leaders. George Reisman, now retired, remains the greatest living economist, in my view. Among active contemporary economists, Richard Werner, more than any other writer, has clarified my understanding of money creation in the modern economy. Other vital thinkers are listed below or cited elsewhere in this book.

Recommended Books

MacLeod, Henry D., *The Theory of Credit, Volume 1*, Legare Street Press, 2022, originally published in 1889. Macleod's understanding of money creation is resurrected in this scholarly reprint.

Withers, Hartley, *The Meaning Of Money*, Nabu Press, 2010. This book was originally published in 1909.

Ryan-Collins, Josh et al., *Where Does Money Come From? A Guide To The U.K. Monetary and Banking System*, New Economics Foundation, London, 2017. This anthology includes chapters by Richard Werner and an introduction by the estimable Charles A.E. Goodhart, Professor Emeritus of the London School of Economics. This is the only book on money creation I can recommend as a textbook. It is written from the perspective of the United Kingdom's money and banking system, which in all essential respects parallels the U.S. system.

Menand, Lev, *The Fed Unbound*, Columbia Global Reports, 2022. Menand is Associate Professor of Law at Columbia Law School and an expert on the legal basis of money creation and the history of American banking. His insight into the increasing activism of the Fed is enlightening. Professor Menand's generous personal correspondence helped me kick-start the writing of this book.

Yang, Joseph, *Central Banking 101*, Joseph Yang, 2021. Yang is a former Fed bond trader who has seen the financial plumbing from the inside. This book's great virtue is its accuracy in explaining money creation mechanics, at the level of both commercial banks and central banks.

Werner, Richard A., *Princes of the Yen: Japan's Central Bankers and the Transformation of the Economy*, Quantum Publishers, 2018. *Princes* analyzes Japan's great asset inflation of 1970–1989, one of the most significant investment bubbles of all time. Werner demonstrates that Japan's policy of "directed bank credit" (money creation directed by regulators to the real estate sector) caused the real estate price bubble that eventually spilled over into the stock market before its historic crash in 1989. *Princes* was a best-seller in Japan, selling over 100,000 copies, outselling even *Harry Potter* for a short time.

Leonard, Christopher, *The Lords of Easy Money: How the Federal Reserve Broke the American Economy*, Simon and Schuster, 2022. Leonard, a financial journalist, analyzes the Fed's increasing influence on money creation following the Great Financial Crisis of 2008–9. Leonard's narrative is seen mostly through the eyes of Kansas City Fed Chairman Thomas Hoenig, the lone dissenter to the Fed's policy of Quantitative Easing. Readable, journalistic style, and informative.

Samuelson, Paul, *Economics: An Introductory Analysis*, McGraw Hill, New York, 1948. I mention this traditional textbook mainly to point out its errors in describing "fractional reserve banking." These errors are important because, 75 years after its first printing, they are still being taught today in college-level courses as the standard description of money creation.

Galbraith, J.K., *Money, Whence It Came, Where It Went.* Despite his neo-Keynesian views, which I do not agree with, Galbraith demonstrates a solid grasp of the mechanics of money creation., illustrating that the facts of money creation in commercial banks are independent of ideological preference.

Reisman, George, *Capitalism: A Treatise on Economics*, TJS Books, 2020. *Capitalism* is a tour-de-force covering every aspect of economic science. It is a must-have reference. I recommend owning it in both hardback and Kindle version so you can easily search words or topics.

Von Mises, Ludwig, *Human Action*, Henry Regnery Company, 1966. Mises was George Reisman's teacher. Human Action has been called the largest and most scientific defense of freedom ever published.

Von Mises, Ludwig, *The Theory Of Money And Credit*, Skyhorse, 2013. Originally published in 1912, Ludwig von Mises's *The Theory of Money and Credit* remains today one of economic theory's most influential and controversial treatises.

Menger, Carl, *The Origins of Money, 2016,* originally published in 1892. Menger explains that Individuals, not the government, decide what the most marketable good is for use as a medium of exchange.

Dowd, Kevin, et al., *The Experience Of Free Banking*, The Institute of Economic Affairs, 2023. This book presents a history of free banking, including assessments of free banking in Australia, the United States, Canada, China, Colombia, France, Scotland, Switzerland, and a world overview. The main finding is that free, unregulated banking is stable, productive, and non-inflationary.

Recommended Journal Articles

McLeay, Michael, et al., *Money Creation In The Modern Economy*, The Bank Of England Monetary Analysis Directorate, Quarterly Bulletin 2014 Q1. This article may have sparked a revolution of new understanding among investors. Credit the Bank of England authors with a clear, accurate description of money creation. The article also clarifies several misconceptions about bank reserves and the so-called "money multiplier."

Werner, Richard A., "Can Banks individually create money out of nothing? The theories and the empirical evidence," *International Review of Financial Analysis*, Volume 36, December 2014, 1–19. This article presents the first empirical evidence in the history of banking on the question of whether banks can create money out of nothing. A ground-breaking empirical test is conducted, whereby money is borrowed from a cooperating bank while its internal records are monitored to establish whether, in the process of making the loan available to the borrower, the bank transfers these funds from other accounts within or outside the bank, or whether they are newly created. This study establishes for the first time, inductively, that banks individually create money "out of nothing."

Werner, Richard A., "How do banks create money, and why can other firms not do the same? An explanation for the coexistence of lending and deposit-taking," *International Review of Financial Analysis*, vol. 36, December 2014, 71-77.

Werner, Richard A., "A lost century in economics: three theories of banking and the conclusive evidence," *International Review of*

Financial Analysis, Vol. 46, July 2016, 361-379. This paper amplifies previous work by Werner, cited above, providing additional empirical evidence of money creation in an individual bank.

Werner's website is also well worth perusing: https://professorwerner.org/.

Jordan, Thomas J., "How money is created by the central bank and the banking system," transcript of speech by Thomas J. Jordan, Chairman of the Governing Board, Swiss National Bank Zurich, January 16, 2018. Jordan is a rarity—a candid central banker who accurately describes the money-creating power of banks. The speech includes a good discussion of the issues surrounding "sovereign money" (aka "standard money"), including digital currencies.

Hook, Andrew, "Examining Modern Money Creation," *The Journal of Economic Education*, Volume 53, 2022, Issue 3, 210-231. Professor Hook offers insight into the structure of the monetary system and provides data confirming the widespread ignorance of money creation.

Sommer, Joseph A. "Where is a bank account?" *Maryland Law Review*, Volume 57, Issue 1, Article 4, 1998. This lengthy article examines the elemental legal nature of a bank deposit.

Sheard, Paul, "Repeat After Me: Banks Cannot And Do Not 'Lend Out' Their Reserves," *Standard and Poors Rating Direct*. Sheard was formerly Chief Global Economist and Head of Global Economics and Research at Standard and Poors. In mathematical terms, Sheard explains the mechanics of money creation.

Wang, Joseph, "Primer: A Deposit's Life," *Traders Summit*, April 10, 2023. A good step-by-step analysis of money creation emphasizing the accounting involved.

INDEX OF NAMES

ABOUT THE AUTHOR

Jim Brown holds a Bachelor of Science degree from the U.S. Air Force Academy, an MBA from Harvard Business School, and is a Chartered Financial Analyst. His career progression includes being an Air Force pilot, airline pilot, financial analyst, investment group director, and CEO. He has 40 years of experience as a securities analyst and portfolio manager. Formerly, he was the President and CEO of the Ayn Rand Institute and served on its board of directors for six years, retiring in 2023. He currently serves on the Board of Directors for Monetary Metals & Co and the Board of Advisors for the Brandes Institute. Jim and his wife, Kathy, operate their family office from their home in Jackson Hole, Wyoming.

Jim writes on Substack as HardmoneyJim.

Twitter: @hardmoneyjim
LinkedIn: Jim Brown, CFA

www.ingramcontent.com/pod-product-compliance
Lightning Source LLC
Chambersburg PA
CBHW060542200326
41521CB00007B/456